Re-Engineering Legacy Software

T0350952

Re-Engineering Legacy Software

CHRIS BIRCHALL

MANNING
SHELTER ISLAND

Manning Publications Co.
20 Baldwin Road
PO Box 761
Shelter Island, NY 11964

Development editor: Karen Miller
Technical development editor: Robert Wenner
Copyeditor: Andy Carroll
Proofreader: Elizabeth Martin
Technical proofreader: René van den Berg
Typesetter: Dottie Marsico
Cover designer: Marija Tudor

ISBN 9781617292507
Printed in the United States of America
1 2 3 4 5 6 7 8 9 10 – EBM – 21 20 19 18 17 16

brief contents

contents

preface

The motivation to write this book has been growing gradually throughout my career as a software developer. Like many other developers, I spent the majority of my time working with code written by other people and dealing with the various problems that entails. I wanted to learn and share knowledge about how to maintain software, but I couldn't find many people who were willing to discuss it. Legacy almost seemed to be a taboo subject.

I found this quite surprising, because most of us spend the majority of our time working with existing software rather than writing entirely new applications. And yet, when you look at tech blogs or books, most people are writing about using new technologies to build new software. This is understandable, because we developers are magpies, always looking for the next shiny new toy to entertain us. All the same, I felt that people should be talking more about legacy software, so one motivation for this book is to start a discussion. If you can improve on any of the advice in this book, please write a blog about it and let the world know.

At the same time, I noticed that a lot of developers had given up on any attempt to improve their legacy software and make it more maintainable. Many people seemed to be afraid of the code that they maintained. So I also wanted the book to be a call to arms, inspiring developers to take charge of their legacy codebases.

After a decade or so as a developer, I had a lot of ideas rolling around in my head plus a few scattered notes that I hoped to turn into a book someday. Then, out of the blue, Manning contacted me to ask if I wanted to contribute to a different book. I pitched them my idea, they were keen, and the next thing I knew I was signing a contract, and this book was a reality.

Of course, that was only the start of a long journey. I'd like to thank everybody who helped take this project from a nebulous idea to a completed book. I couldn't have done it on my own!

acknowledgments

This book would not have been possible without the support of many people. I've been lucky enough to work with a lot of highly skilled developers over the years who have indirectly contributed countless ideas to this book.

Thanks to everybody at Infoscience, particularly the managers and senior developers who gave me the freedom to experiment with new technologies and development methodologies. I like to think I made a positive contribution to the product, but I also learned a lot along the way. Special mention goes to Rodion Moiseev, Guillaume Nargeot, and Martin Amirault for some great technical discussions.

I'd also like to thank everybody at M3, where I had my first taste of release cycles measured in days rather than months. I learned a lot, especially from the "tigers" Lloyd Chan and Vincent Péricart. It was also at M3 that Yoshinori Teraoka introduced me to Ansible.

Right now I'm at the *Guardian*, where I'm incredibly lucky to work with so many talented and passionate developers. More than anything else, they have taught me what it means to really work in an agile way, rather than merely going through the motions.

I'd also like to thank the reviewers who took the time to read the book in manuscript form: Bruno Sonnino, Saleem Shafi, Ferdinando Santacroce, Jean-François Morin, Dave Corun, Brian Hanafee, Francesco Basile, Hamori Zoltan, Andy Kirsch, Lorrie MacKinnon, Christopher Noyes, William E. Wheeler, Gregor Zurowski, and Sergio Romero.

This book also owes a great deal to the entire Manning editorial team. Mike Stephens, the acquisitions editor, helped me get the book out of my head and onto paper. Karen Miller, my editor, worked tirelessly to review the manuscript. Robert Wenner, my technical development editor, and René van den Berg, technical proofreader, both made invaluable contributions. Kevin Sullivan, Andy Carroll, and Mary Piergies helped take the finished manuscript through to production. And countless other people reviewed the manuscript or supported me in myriad other ways, some of which I probably didn't even know about!

Finally I would like to thank my wife, Yoshiko, my family, my friends Ewan and Tomomi, Nigel and Kumiko, Andy and Aya, Taka and Beni, and everybody else who kept me sane while I was writing. Especially Nigel, because he is awesome.

about this book

This book is ambitious in scope, setting itself the aim of teaching you everything you need to do in order to transform a neglected legacy codebase into a maintainable, well-functioning piece of software that can provide value to your organization. Covering absolutely everything in a single book is, of course, an unachievable goal, but I've attempted to do so by approaching the problem of legacy software from a number of different angles.

Code becomes legacy (by which I mean, roughly, *difficult to maintain*) for a number of reasons, but most of the causes relate to humans rather than technology. If people don't communicate enough with each other, information about the code can be lost when people leave the organization. Similarly, if developers, managers, and the organization as a whole don't prioritize their work correctly, technical debt can accrue to an unsustainable level and the pace of development can drop to almost zero. Because of this, the book will touch on organizational aspects time and again, especially focusing on the problem of information being lost over time. Simply being aware of the problem is an important first step toward solving it.

That's not to say that the book has no technical content—far from it. We'll cover a wide range of technologies and tools, including Jenkins, FindBugs, PMD, Kibana, Gradle, Vagrant, Ansible, and Fabric. We'll look in detail at a number of refactoring patterns, discuss the relative methods of various architectures, from monoliths to microservices, and look at strategies for dealing with databases during a rewrite.

Roadmap

Chapter 1 is a gentle introduction, explaining what I mean when I talk about legacy software. Everybody has their own definitions of words like "legacy," so it's good to make sure we understand each other from the start. I also talk about some of the factors that contribute to code becoming legacy.

In chapter 2 we'll set up the infrastructure to inspect the quality of the codebase, using tools such as Jenkins, FindBugs, PMD, Checkstyle, and shell scripting. This will give you solid, numerical data to describe the code's quality, which is useful for a number of reasons. First, it lets you define clear, measurable goals for improving quality, which provides structure to your refactoring efforts. Second, it helps you to decide where in the code you should focus your efforts.

Chapter 3 discusses how to get everybody in your organization on board before starting a major refactoring project, as well as providing some tips on how to tackle that most difficult of decisions: rewrite or refactor?

Chapter 4 dives into the details of refactoring, introducing a number of refactoring patterns that I've often seen used successfully against legacy code.

In chapter 5 we'll look at what I call *re-architecting*. This is refactoring in the large, at the level of whole modules or components rather than individual classes or methods. We'll look at a case study of re-architecting a monolithic codebase into a number of isolated components, and compare various application architectures including monolithic, SOA, and microservices.

Chapter 6 is dedicated to completely rewriting a legacy application. The chapter covers the precautions needed to prevent feature creep, the amount of influence the existing implementation should have on its replacement, and how to smoothly migrate if the application has a database.

The next three chapters move away from the code and look at infrastructure. In chapter 7 we'll look at how a little automation can vastly improve the onboarding process for new developers, which will encourage developers from outside the team to make more contributions. This chapter introduces tools such as Vagrant and Ansible.

In chapter 8 we'll continue the automation work with Ansible, this time extending its use to staging and production environments.

Chapter 9 completes the discussion of infrastructure automation by showing how you can automate the deployment of your software using tools like Fabric and Jenkins. This chapter also provides an example of updating a project's toolchain, in this case migrating the build from Ant to Gradle.

In chapter 10, the final chapter, I'll offer a few simple rules that you can follow to hopefully prevent your code from becoming legacy.

Source code

All source code in the book is in a `fixed-width font like this`, which sets it off from the surrounding text. In many listings, the code is annotated to point out key concepts. In some listings comments are set within the code, indicating what the developer would see in the "real world."

We have tried to format the code so that it fits within the available page space in the book by adding line breaks and using indentation carefully.

All the code used in the book is available for download from www.manning.com/books/re-engineering-legacy-software. It is also available on GitHub at https://github.com/cb372/ReengLegacySoft.

Author Online

Purchase of *Re-Engineering Legacy Software* includes free access to a private web forum run by Manning Publications where you can make comments about the book, ask technical questions, and receive help from the author and from other users. To access the forum and subscribe to it, point your web browser to www.manning.com/re-engineering-legacy-software. This page provides information on how to get on the forum once you are registered, what kind of help is available, and the rules of conduct on the forum. It also provides links to the source code for the examples in the book, errata, and other downloads.

Manning's commitment to our readers is to provide a venue where a meaningful dialog between individual readers and between readers and the author can take place. It is not a commitment to any specific amount of participation on the part of the author, whose contribution to the forum remains voluntary (and unpaid). We suggest you try asking the author challenging questions lest his interest strays!

The Author Online forum and the archives of previous discussions will be accessible from the publisher's website as long as the book is in print.

About the author

Chris Birchall is a senior developer at the *Guardian* in London, working on the back-end services that power the website. Previously he has worked on a wide range of projects including Japan's largest medical portal site, high-performance log management software, natural language analysis tools, and numerous mobile sites. He earned a degree in Computer Science from the University of Cambridge.

About the cover

The figure on the cover of *Re-Engineering Legacy Software* is captioned "Le commisaire de police," or "The police commissioner." The illustration is taken from a nineteenth-century collection of works by many artists, edited by Louis Curmer and published in Paris in 1841. The title of the collection is *Les Français peints par eux-mêmes*, which translates as *The French people painted by themselves*. Each illustration is finely drawn and colored by hand and the rich variety of drawings in the collection reminds us vividly of how culturally apart the world's regions, towns, villages, and neighborhoods were just 200 years ago. Isolated from each other, people spoke different dialects and languages. In the streets or in the countryside, it was easy to identify where they lived and what their trade or station in life was just by their dress.

Dress codes have changed since then and the diversity by region, so rich at the time, has faded away. It is now hard to tell apart the inhabitants of different continents, let alone different towns or regions. Perhaps we have traded cultural diversity for a more varied personal life—certainly for a more varied and fast-paced technological life.

At a time when it is hard to tell one computer book from another, Manning celebrates the inventiveness and initiative of the computer business with book covers based on the rich diversity of regional life of two centuries ago, brought back to life by pictures from collections such as this one.

Part 1

Getting started

If you're planning to re-engineer a legacy codebase of any reasonable size, it pays to take your time, do your homework, and make sure you're going about things the right way. In the first part of this book we'll do a lot of preparatory work, which will pay off later.

In the first chapter we'll investigate what *legacy* means and what factors contibute to the creation of unmaintainable software. In chapter 2 we'll set up an inspection infrastructure that will allow us to quantitatively measure the current state of the software and provide structure and guidance around refactoring.

What tools you use to measure the quality of your software is up to you, and it will depend on factors such as your implementation language and what tools you already have experience with. In chapter 2 I'll be using three popular software-quality tools for Java called FindBugs, PMD, and Checkstyle. I'll also show you how to set up Jenkins as a continuous integration server. I'll refer to Jenkins again at various points in the book.

Understanding the challenges of legacy projects

1

This chapter covers

- What a legacy project is
- Examples of legacy code and legacy infrastructure
- Organizational factors that contribute to legacy projects
- A plan for improvement

Hands up if this scene sounds familiar: You arrive at work, grab a coffee, and decide to catch up on the latest tech blogs. You start to read about how the hippest young startup in Silicon Valley is combining fashionable programming language X with exciting NoSQL datastore Y and big data tool Z to change the world, and your heart sinks as you realize that you'll never find the time to even try any of these technologies in your own job, let alone use them to improve your product.

Why not? Because you're tasked with maintaining a few zillion lines of untested, undocumented, incomprehensible legacy code. This code has been in production since before you wrote your first Hello World and has seen dozens of developers come and go. You spend half of your working day reviewing commits to make sure that they don't cause any regressions, and the other half fighting fires when a bug inevitably slips through the cracks. And the most depressing part of it is that as time goes by, and more code is added to the increasingly fragile codebase, the problem gets worse.

But don't despair! First of all, remember that you're not alone. The average developer spends much more time working with existing code than writing new code, and the vast majority of developers have to deal with legacy projects in some shape or form. Secondly, remember that there's always hope for revitalizing a legacy project, no matter how far gone it may first appear. The aim of this book is to do exactly that.

In this introductory chapter we'll look at examples of the types of problems we're trying to solve, and start to put together a plan for revitalization.

1.1   *Definition of a legacy project*

First of all, I want to make sure we're on the same page concerning what a legacy project is. I tend to use a very broad definition, labeling as *legacy* any existing project that's difficult to maintain or extend.

Note that we're talking about a project here, not just a codebase. As developers, we tend to focus on the code, but a project encompasses many other aspects, including

- Build tools and scripts
- Dependencies on other systems
- The infrastructure on which the software runs
- Project documentation
- Methods of communication, such as between developers, or between developers and stakeholders

Of course, the code itself is important, but all of these factors can contribute to the quality and maintainability of a project.

1.1.1   *Characteristics of legacy projects*

It's neither easy nor particularly useful to lay down a rule about what counts as a legacy project, but there are a few features that many legacy projects have in common.

OLD

Usually a project needs to exist for a few years before it gains enough entropy to become really difficult to maintain. In that time, it will also go through a number of generations of maintainers. With each of these handoffs, knowledge about the original design of the system and the intentions of the previous maintainer is also lost.

LARGE

It goes without saying that the larger the project is, the more difficult it is to maintain. There is more code to understand, a larger number of existing bugs (if we assume a constant defect rate in software, more code = more bugs), and a higher probability of a new change causing a regression, because there is more existing code that it can potentially affect. The size of a project also affects decisions about how the project is maintained. Large projects are difficult and risky to replace, so they are more likely to live on and become legacy.

INHERITED

As is implied by the common meaning of the word legacy, these projects are usually inherited from a previous developer or team. In other words, the people who originally wrote the code and those who now maintain it are not the same individuals, and they may even be separated by several intermediate generations of developers. This means that the current maintainers have no way of knowing why the code works the way it does, and they're often forced to guess the intentions and tacit design assumptions of the people who wrote it.

POORLY DOCUMENTED

Given that the project spans multiple generations of developers, it would seem that keeping accurate and thorough documentation is essential to its long-term survival. Unfortunately, if there's one thing that developers enjoy less than writing documentation, it's keeping that documentation up to date. So any technical documents that do exist must invariably be taken with a pinch of salt.

I once worked on the software for a forum in which users could post messages in threads. The system had an API that allowed you to retrieve a list of the most popular threads, along with a few of the most recently posted messages in each of those threads. The API looked something like the following listing.

```
/**
 * Retrieve a list of summaries of the most popular threads.
 *
 * @param numThreads
 *      how many threads to retrieve
 * @param recentMessagesPerThread
 *      how many recent messages to include in thread summary
 *      (set this to 0 if you don't need recent messages)
 * @return thread summaries in decreasing order of popularity
 */
public List<ThreadSummary> getPopularThreads(
        int numThreads, int recentMessagesPerThread);
```

According to the documentation, if you only wanted a list of threads and you didn't need any messages, you should set `recentMessagesPerThread` to 0. But at some point the behavior of the system changed, so that 0 now meant "include every single message in the thread." Given that this was a list of the most popular threads in the application, most of them contained many thousands of messages, so any API call that passed a 0 now resulted in a monster SQL query and an API response many MB in size!

1.1.2 Exceptions to the rule

Just because a project fulfills some of the preceding criteria doesn't necessarily mean it should be treated as a legacy project.

A perfect example of this is the Linux kernel. It's been in development since 1991, so it's definitely old, and it's also large. (The exact number of lines of code is difficult to determine, as it depends on how you count them, but it's said to be around 15 million at the time of writing.) Despite this, the Linux kernel has managed to maintain a very high level of quality. As evidence of this, in 2012 Coverity ran a static analysis scan on the kernel and found it to have a defect density of 0.66 defects/kloc, which is lower than many commercial projects of a comparable size. Coverity's report concluded that "Linux continues to be a 'model citizen' open source project for good software quality." (The Coverity report is available at http://wpcme.coverity.com/wp-content/uploads/2012-Coverity-Scan-Report.pdf.)

I think the primary reason for Linux's continued success as a software project is its culture of open and frank communication. All incoming changes are thoroughly reviewed, which increases information-sharing between developers, and Linus Torvalds' uniquely "dictatorial" communication style makes his intentions clear to everybody involved with the project.

The following quote from Andrew Morton, a Linux kernel maintainer, demonstrates the value that the Linux development community places on code review.

> Well, it finds bugs. It improves the quality of the code. Sometimes it prevents really really bad things from getting into the product. Such as rootholes in the core kernel. I've spotted a decent number of these at review time.
>
> It also increases the number of people who have an understanding of the new code—both the reviewer(s) and those who closely followed the review are now better able to support that code.
>
> Also, I expect that the prospect of receiving a close review will keep the originators on their toes—make them take more care over their work.
>
> —Andrew Morton,
> kernel maintainer, discussing the value of
> code review in an interview with LWN in 2008
> (https://lwn.net/Articles/285088/)

1.2 Legacy code

The most important part of any software project, especially for an engineer, is the code itself. In this section we'll look at a few common characteristics usually seen in legacy code. In chapter 4 we'll look at refactoring techniques that you can use to alleviate these problems, but for now I'll whet your appetite with a few examples and leave you to think about possible solutions.

1.2.1 Untested, untestable code

Given that technical documentation for software projects is usually either nonexistent or unreliable, tests are often the best place to look for clues about the system's behavior and design assumptions. A good test suite can function as the de facto documentation for a project. In fact, tests can even be more useful than documentation, because they're more likely to be kept in sync with the actual behavior of the system. A socially responsible developer will take care to fix any tests that were broken by their changes to production code. (Any developer in my team who breaks this social contract is sent straight to the firing squad!)

Unfortunately, many legacy projects have almost no tests. Not only this, but the projects are usually written without testing in mind, so retroactively adding tests is extremely difficult. A code sample is worth a thousand words, so let's look at an example that illustrates this.

Listing 1.1 Some untestable code

```java
public class ImageResizer {
    /* Where to store resized images */
    public static final String CACHE_DIR = "/var/data";

    /* Maximum width of resized images */
    private final int maxWidth =
            Integer.parseInt(System.getProperty("Resizer.maxWidth", "1000"));

    /* Helper to download an image from a URL */
    private final Downloader downloader = new HttpDownloader();

    /* Cache in which to store resized images */
    private final ImageCache cache = new FileImageCache(CACHE_DIR);

    /**
     * Retrieve the image at the given URL
     * and resize it to the given dimensions.
     */
    public Image getImage(String url, int width, int height) {
        String cacheKey = url + "_" + width + "_" + height;

        // First look in the cache
        Image cached = cache.get(cacheKey);
        if (cached != null) {
            // Cache hit
            return cached;
        } else {
            // Cache miss. Download the image, resize it and cache the result.
            byte[] original = downloader.get(url);
            Image resized = resize(original, width, height);
            cache.put(cacheKey, resized);
            return resized;
        }
    }

    private Image resize(byte[] original, int width, int height) {
        ...
    }
}
```

The ImageResizer's job is to retrieve an image from a given URL and resize it to a given height and width. It has a helper class to do the downloading and a cache to save the resized images. You'd like to write a unit test for ImageResizer so that you can verify your assumptions about how the image resizing logic works.

Unfortunately, this class is difficult to test because the implementations of its dependencies (the downloader and the cache) are hardcoded. Ideally you'd like to mock these in your tests, so that you can avoid actually downloading files from the internet or storing them on the filesystem. You could provide a mock downloader that simply returns some predefined data when asked to retrieve an image from http://example.com/foo.jpg. But the implementations are fixed and you have no way of overriding them for your tests.

You're stuck with using the file-based cache implementation, but can you at least set the cache's data directory so that tests use a different directory from production code? Nope, that's hardcoded as well. You'll have to use /var/data (or C:\\var\\data if you're on Windows).

At least the `maxWidth` field is set via system property rather than being hardcoded, so you can change the value of this field and test that the image-resizing logic correctly limits the width of images. But setting system properties for a test is extremely cumbersome. You have to

1 Save any existing value of the system property.
2 Set the system property to the value you want.
3 Run the test.
4 Restore the system property to the value that you saved. You must make sure to do this even if the test fails or throws an exception.

You also need to be careful when running tests in parallel, as changing a system property may affect the result of another test running simultaneously.

1.2.2   *Inflexible code*

A common problem with legacy code is that implementing new features or changes to existing behavior is inordinately difficult. What seems like a minor change can involve editing code in a lot of places. To make matters worse, each one of those edits also needs to be tested, often manually.

Imagine your application defines two types of users: Admins and Normal users. Admins are allowed to do anything, whereas the actions of Normal users are restricted. The authorization checks are implemented simply as `if` statements, spread throughout the codebase. It's a large and complex application, so there are a few hundred of these checks in total, each one looking like the following.

```
public void deleteWibble(Wibble wibble)
                 throws NotAuthorizedException {
    if (!loggedInUser.isAdmin()) {
       throw new NotAuthorizedException(
          "Only Admins are allowed to delete wibbles");
    }
       ...
}
```

One day you're asked to add a new user type called Power User. These users can do more than Normal users but are not as powerful as Admins. So for every action that Power Users are allowed to perform, you'll have to search through the codebase, find the corresponding `if` statement, and update it to look like this.

```
public void deleteWibble(Wibble wibble)
                throws NotAuthorizedException {
    if (!(loggedInUser.isAdmin() || loggedInUser.isPowerUser()) {
        throw new NotAuthorizedException(
            "Only Admins and Power Users are allowed to delete wibbles");
    }
        ...
}
```

We'll come back to this example in chapter 4 and look at how you could refactor the application to be more amenable to change.

1.2.3 *Code encumbered by technical debt*

Every developer is occasionally guilty of writing code that they know isn't perfect, but is good enough for now. In fact, this is often the correct approach. As Voltaire wrote, *le mieux est l'ennemi du bien* (perfect is the enemy of good).

In other words, it's often more useful and appropriate to ship something that works than to spend excessive amounts of time striving for a paragon of algorithmic excellence.

But every time you add one of these good enough solutions to your project, you should plan to revisit the code and clean it up when you have more time to spend on it. Every temporary or hacky solution reduces the overall quality of the project and makes future work more difficult. If you let too many of them accumulate, eventually progress on the project will grind to a halt.

Debt is often used as a metaphor for this accumulation of quality issues. Implementing a quick-fix solution is analogous to taking out a loan, at some point this loan must be paid back. Until you repay the loan by refactoring and cleaning up the code, you'll be burdened with interest payments, meaning a codebase that's more difficult to work with. If you take out too many loans without paying them back, eventually the interest payments will catch up with you, and useful work will grind to a halt.

For example, imagine your company runs InstaHedgehog.com, a social network in which users can upload pictures of their pet hedgehogs and send messages to each other about hedgehog maintenance. The original developers didn't have scalability in mind when they wrote the software, as they only expected to support a few thousand users. Specifically, the database in which users' messages are stored was designed to be easy to write queries against, rather than to achieve optimal performance.

At first, everything ran smoothly, but one day a celebrity hedgehog owner joined the site, and InstaHedgehog.com's popularity exploded! Within a few months, the site's userbase had grown from a few thousand users to almost a million. The DB, which wasn't designed for this kind of load, started to struggle and the site's performance suffered. The developers knew that they needed to work on improving scalability, but achieving a truly scalable system would involve major architectural changes, including sharding the DB and perhaps even switching from the traditional relational DB to a NoSQL datastore.

In the meantime, all these new users brought with them new feature requests. The team decided to focus initially on adding new features, while also implementing a few stop-gap measures to improve performance. This included adding a couple of DB indexes, introducing ad hoc caching measures wherever possible, and throwing hardware at the problem by upgrading the DB server. Unfortunately, the new features vastly increased the complexity of the system, partially because their implementation involved working around the fundamental architectural problems with the DB. The caching systems also increased complexity, as anybody implementing a new feature now had to consider the effect on the various caches. This led to a variety of obscure bugs and memory leaks.

Fast forward a few years to the present day, and you're charged with maintaining this behemoth. The system is now so complex that it's pretty much impossible to add new features, and the caching systems are still regularly leaking memory. You've given up on trying to fix that, opting instead to restart the servers once a day. And it goes without saying that the re-architecting of the DB was never done, as the system became complex enough to render it impossible.

The moral of the story is, of course, that if the original developers had tackled their technical debt earlier, you wouldn't be in this mess. It's also interesting to note that debt begets debt. Because the original technical debt (the inadequate DB architecture) was not paid off, the implementation of new features became excessively complex. This extra complexity is itself technical debt, as it makes the maintenance of those features more difficult. Finally, as an ironic twist, the presence of this new debt makes it more difficult to pay off the original debt.

1.3   *Legacy infrastructure*

Although the quality of the code is a major factor in the maintainability of any legacy project, just looking at the code doesn't show you the whole picture. Most software depends on an assortment of tools and infrastructure in order to run, and the quality of these tools can also have a dramatic effect on a team's productivity. In part 3 we'll look at ways to make improvements in this area.

1.3.1   *Development environment*

Think about the last time you took an existing project and set it up on your development machine. Approximately how long did it take, from first checking the code out of version control to reaching a state where you could do the following?

- View and edit the code in your IDE
- Run the unit and integration tests
- Run the application on your local machine

If you were lucky, the project was using a modern, popular build tool and was structured in accordance with that build tool's conventions, so the setup process was complete in a matter of minutes. Or perhaps there were a few dependencies to set up, such as a database and a message queue, so it took a couple of hours of following the instructions in the README file before you could get everything working. When it comes to legacy projects, however, the time taken to set up the development environment can often be measured in days!

Setting up a legacy project often involves a combination of

- Downloading, installing, and learning how to run whatever arcane build tool the project uses
- Running the mysterious and unmaintained scripts you found in the project's /bin folder
- Taking a large number of manual steps, listed on an invariably out-of-date wiki page

You only have to run this gauntlet once, when you first join the project, so working to make the process easier and faster may not seem worth the effort. But there are good reasons to make the project setup procedure as smooth as possible. First, it's not just you who has to perform this setup. Every single developer on your team, now and in the future, will have to do it as well, and the cost of all those wasted days adds up.

Second, the easier it is to set up the development environment, the more people you can persuade to contribute to the project. When it comes to software quality, the more eyes you have on code the better. You want to avoid a situation where the only developers able to work on a project are those who have already bothered to set it up on their machines. Instead you should strive to create an environment in which any developer in the organization can make contributions to the project as easily as possible.

1.3.2 Outdated dependencies

Nearly any software project has some dependencies on third-party software. For example, if it's a Java servlet web application, it will depend on Java. It also needs to run inside a servlet container such as Tomcat, and may also use a web server such as Apache. Most likely, it will also use various Java libraries such as Apache Commons.

The rate at which these external dependencies change is outside of your control. Keeping up with the latest versions of all dependencies is a constant effort, but it's usually worthwhile. Upgrades often provide performance improvements and bug fixes, and sometimes critical security patches. While you shouldn't upgrade dependencies just for the sake of it, upgrading is usually a Good Thing.

Dependency upgrades are a bit like household chores. If you wash the dishes, vacuum the carpets, and give the house a quick once-over every few days, it's no big deal, but if you fall behind on your chores, it turns into a major mission when you finally get around to it. Keeping a project's dependencies up to date is just the same. Regularly upgrading to keep up with the latest minor version is a matter of a few minutes' work per month, but if you get lazy and fall behind, before you know it you're one or more major versions out of date, and you're looking at a major investment of development and testing resources and a lot of risk when you finally get around to upgrading.

I once witnessed a development team spending months trying to upgrade their application from Java 6 to Java 7. For years they'd resisted upgrading any of their dependencies, mostly because they were afraid of breaking some obscure part of the application. It was a large, sprawling legacy application with few automated tests and no specifications, so nobody had a clear idea of how the application was currently behaving or how it was supposed to behave. But when Java 6's end of service life rolled around, the team decided it was time to bite the bullet. Unfortunately, upgrading to Java 7 meant that they also had to upgrade a whole host of other dependencies. This resulted in a slew of breaking API changes, as well as subtle and undocumented changes in behavior. This particular story doesn't have a happy ending—after a few weeks battling to work around an obscure change in the behavior of XML serialization, they gave up on the upgrade and rolled back their changes.

1.3.3 *Heterogeneous environments*

Most software will be run in a number of environments during its lifetime. The number and names of the environments are not set in stone, but the process usually goes something like this:

1 Developers run the software on their local machines.
2 They deploy it to a test environment for automatic and manual testing.
3 It is deployed to a staging environment that mimics production as closely as possible.
4 It is released and deployed to the production environment (or, in the case of packaged software, it's shipped to the customer).

The point of this multistage process is to verify that the software works correctly before releasing it to production, but the value of this verification is directly affected by the degree of parity you can achieve between the environments. Unless the staging environment is an exact replica (within reason) of the production environment, its value in showing you how the software will behave in production is severely diminished. Similarly for the development and test environments, the more faithfully they replicate production, the more useful they'll be, allowing you to spot environment-related issues with the software quickly, without having to deploy it to the staging environment. For example, using the same version of MySQL across all environments obviates any risk of a tiny change in behavior between MySQL versions causing the software to work correctly in one environment and fail in another.

However, keeping these multiple environments perfectly aligned is easier said than done, especially without the aid of automation. If they're being managed manually, they are pretty much guaranteed to diverge. This divergence can happen in a few different ways.

- *Upgrades trickle down from production*—Say the ops team upgrades Tomcat in production in response to a zero-day exploit. A few weeks later, somebody notices that the upgrade hasn't been applied to the staging environment, so it's done there as well. A few months after that, somebody finally gets around to upgrading the test environment. The Tomcat on the developers' machines works fine, so they never bother upgrading.
- *Different tools in different environments*—You might use a lightweight database such as SQLite or H2 on developers' machines but a "proper" database in other environments.
- *Ad hoc changes*—Say you're prototyping an experimental new feature that depends on Redis, so you install Redis in the test environment. In the end, you decide not to go ahead with the new feature, so Redis is no longer needed, but you don't bother uninstalling it. A couple of years later, there's still a Redis instance running in the test environment, but nobody can remember why.

As this inter-environment divergence accumulates over time, eventually it's likely to lead to that most dreaded of software phenomena, the *production-only bug*. This is a bug caused by an interaction between the software and its surrounding environment that occurs only in production. No amount of testing in the other environments will help you to catch this bug because it never occurs in those environments, so they've become basically pointless.

In part 3 we'll look at how you can use automation to keep all your environments in sync and up to date, helping to make development and testing run more smoothly and avoid problems like this.

1.4 Legacy culture

The term *legacy culture* is perhaps a little contentious—nobody wants to think of themselves and their culture as legacy—but I've noticed that many software teams who spend too much time maintaining legacy projects share certain characteristics with respect to how they develop software and communicate among themselves.

1.4.1 Fear of change

Many legacy projects are so complex and poorly documented that even the teams charged with maintaining them don't understand everything about them. For example,

- Which features are no longer in use and are thus safe to delete?
- Which *bugs* are safe to fix? (Some users of the software may be depending on the bug and treating it as a feature.)
- Which users need to be consulted before making changes to behavior?

Because of this lack of information, many teams come to respect the status quo as the safest option, and become fearful of making any unnecessary changes to the software. Any change is seen purely as a risk, and the potential benefits of changes are ignored. Thus the project enters a kind of stasis, whereby the developers expend most of their energy on maintaining the status quo and trying to protect the software from all externalities, like a mosquito trapped in a blob of amber.

The irony is that by being so risk-averse that they don't allow the software to evolve, they often leave their organization exposed to a very major risk, that of being left behind by its competitors. If your competitors can add new features faster than you can, which is quite likely if your project has entered stasis mode, then it's only a matter of time before they steal your customers and push you out of the market. This is, of course, a much larger risk than those the development team was worried about.

But it doesn't have to be this way. Although a gung-ho approach, whereby all risks are ignored and changes are rolled out willy-nilly, is certainly a recipe for disaster, a more balanced approach is feasible. If the team can maintain a sense of perspective, weighing each change's risks against its benefits, as well as actively seeking out the missing information that will help them to make such decisions, the software will be able to evolve and adapt to change.

A few examples of possible changes for a legacy project, with their associated risks and benefits, are shown in table 1.1. There's also a column suggesting how you could gather more information about the risks.

Table 1.1   Changes, benefits and risks for a legacy project

Changes	Benefits	Risks	Actions required
Removing an old feature	• Easier development • Better performance	• Somebody is still using the feature	• Check access logs • Ask users
Refactoring	• Easier development	• Accidental regression	• Code review • Testing
Upgrading a library	• Bug fixes • Performance improvements	• Regression due to a change in the library's behavior	• Read the changelog • Review library code • Manually test major features

1.4.2   Knowledge silos

The biggest problem encountered by developers when writing and maintaining software is often a lack of knowledge. This may include

- Domain information about the users' requirements and the functional specifications of the software
- Project-specific technical information about the software's design, architecture, and internals
- General technical knowledge such as efficient algorithms, advanced language features, handy coding tricks, and useful libraries

A benefit of working on a team is that if you're missing a particular piece of knowledge, a fellow team member might be able to provide it. For this to happen, either you need to ask them for the information, or, even better, they need to give it to you of their own accord.

This sounds obvious, but unfortunately on many teams this giving and receiving of knowledge doesn't happen. Unless you work hard to foster an environment of communication and information sharing, each individual developer becomes a metaphorical silo of information, with all their valuable knowledge sitting untapped inside their heads instead of being shared for the benefit of the whole team.

Factors contributing to a paucity of communication within a team can include

- *Lack of face-to-face communication*—I often see developers chatting on Skype or IRC even though they're sitting right next to each other. These tools have their uses, especially if your team includes remote workers or you want to send somebody a message without disturbing them, but if you want to talk in real time to somebody sitting three feet away from you, using IRC to do so just isn't healthy!
- *Code ego*—"If I let anybody figure out how my code works, they might criticize it." This is a common mindset among developers, and it can be a serious barrier to communication.
- *Busy-face*—Projecting an air of busyness is a common defense strategy used by developers to avoid being piled with unwelcome work. (I'm guilty of this, making sure to slip on my headphones and a stressed-looking expression whenever I see anybody in a suit approaching my desk.) But this can also make these people less approachable to other developers who want to ask them for advice.

There are a number of things you can try in order to increase communication within your team, including code review, pair programming, and hackathons. We'll discuss this further in the final chapter of the book.

1.5 Summary

After a whole chapter of moaning about the state of software development, it looks like we have our work cut out for us if we want to tackle all of these problems. But don't worry, we don't have to fix everything at once. In the rest of the book, we'll attempt to revitalize legacy projects one step at a time.

Here are some takeaway points from this chapter:

- Legacy software is often large, old, inherited from somebody else, and poorly documented. But there are exceptions to the rule: the Linux kernel largely fulfills all of those criteria, but its quality is high.
- Legacy software often lacks tests and is difficult to test. Low testability implies few tests, but the converse is also true. If a codebase currently has few tests, it probably has an untestable design and writing new tests for it is thus difficult.
- Legacy code is often inflexible, meaning that it takes a lot of work to make a simple change. Refactoring can improve the situation.
- Legacy software is encumbered by years' worth of accumulated technical debt.
- The infrastructure on which the code runs, all the way from the developer's machine through to production, deserves attention.
- The culture of the team that maintains the software can be an impediment to improvement.

Finding your starting point

This chapter covers
- Deciding where to focus your refactoring efforts
- Thinking more positively about your legacy software
- Measuring the quality of software
- Inspecting your codebase using FindBugs, PMD, and Checkstyle
- Using Jenkins for continuous inspection

After reading chapter 1, you should have a clear idea of what legacy software is and why you'd want to improve it. In this chapter we'll look at how to formulate a plan for improvement and how to measure your progress once the plan is in place.

2.1 Overcoming feelings of fear and frustration

Let's start with a small thought experiment. I want you to choose one piece of legacy software that you have experience maintaining. Think hard about this software and try to remember everything you can about it. Every bug you fixed, every new feature you added, every release you made. What kind of problems did you encounter? Was it a nightmare just getting the thing to run on your local machine, or working out how to deploy it to production? Are there any classes in particular that you grew to hate? Any memories of whole days wasted on failed refactoring missions? How about edit-and-pray fixes that led to horrific bugs in production?

I hope that little therapy session wasn't too traumatic. Now that you have the details of your chosen software fresh in your mind, I want you to ask yourself one question: "How does this software make me *feel*?" If you're anything like me, your emotional response to legacy code will not be entirely positive.

Although it's natural to harbor some negative feelings toward legacy software, those feelings can be very damaging because they cloud our judgment and prevent us from working effectively to make improvements. In this chapter we're going to look at ways to overcome some of these negative emotions and develop a more positive attitude. We'll also look at some tools and techniques for approaching refactoring in an objective scientific way, unencumbered by emotional baggage.

In particular, I want to look at two emotions that are often provoked by legacy code: fear and frustration.

2.1.1 Fear

I have worked on code in the past that has caused me to think like this:

- Every time I touch a line of code, I break something completely unrelated. It's just too fragile to work with.
- I should get in and get out without touching anything I don't absolutely have to handle.

Even if your reaction to working on legacy software is less dramatic than mine, you'll probably have developed a certain sense of fear toward at least some of the codebase. This will cause you, often subconsciously, to program more defensively and become more resistant to large changes. You probably have a clear idea of which classes or packages are most dangerous, and you'll avoid touching them if possible. This is counterproductive, because this "dangerous" code is exactly what should be receiving the most attention from developers, and it's probably a good candidate for refactoring.

Fear of code is often fear of the unknown. In a large codebase, there are likely large swaths of code that you don't understand well. It's this unexplored territory that scares you the most, because you don't know what the code is doing, how it's doing it, and how it's linked to the parts you're more familiar with.

Let's say you're tasked with maintaining your company's employee time-tracking system, codenamed TimeTrack. It's a legacy Java application that was developed in-house years ago, mostly by just one developer who has now left the company. Unfortunately he left little in the way of tests or documentation, and the only useful document you could find was the architecture diagram in figure 2.1.

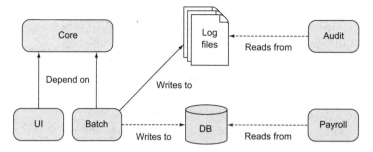

Figure 2.1   Architecture of TimeTrack, the employee time-tracking system

The application has a number of components:

- *Core* implements the complex business logic and includes a number of utility classes.
- *UI* provides a web interface for employees to fill in their hours worked. It also provides functionality for managers to construct and download reports about how employees are spending their time. It's built using a legacy homegrown web framework based on Struts.
- *Batch* contains a number of nightly batches that insert data into the Payroll system's database.
- *Audit* collects and processes the logs output by the nightly batches in order to generate compliance reports for the annual tax audit.

So far your only maintenance has been to add a few small features to the web UI, so you're reasonably familiar with the UI component, but you've hardly touched the other components. You'd like to clean up some of the spaghetti code you found in the Core component, but you know that the nightly payroll batches also depend on Core, and you're scared that you might break those. (If the whole company's payroll ended up being incorrect or delayed, you wouldn't be popular!) In other words, you're scared of the parts of the system that you know least about.

The best way to overcome this fear of the unknown is simply to dive into the code and start playing around with it. Open up the Core project in your IDE and try renaming methods, moving methods between classes, introducing new interfaces, adding comments—basically anything you can think of that makes the code cleaner and more readable. This process is known as *exploratory refactoring*. It has a couple of benefits.

BENEFITS OF EXPLORATORY REFACTORING
Most importantly, exploratory refactoring increases your understanding of the code. The more you explore, the more you understand. The more you understand, the less there is to fear. Before you know it, you'll be a master of the codebase, with at least a cursory knowledge of most of the moving parts and the dependencies between them. This will make it a lot easier to make changes in the future, whether they're bug fixes, new features, or more refactorings, without any fear of unexpected side effects.

Increased understanding of the codebase is the primary purpose of exploratory refactoring, and it can be even more effective if you get more developers involved. Try exploratory refactoring with another developer, or even getting the whole team in a room and going through the code together on a big screen. Each developer will be slightly more familiar with different parts of the code, and this is a great chance to share that knowledge.

As a secondary benefit, exploratory refactoring improves the readability of the code. Note that the point of exploratory refactoring is not to achieve deep, revolutionary changes at the architectural level. But it should at least provide noticeable improvements to the readability of the code at the level of individual classes and methods. These improvements are cumulative, so if you and your team get into the habit of performing exploratory refactoring regularly, you'll notice the code becomes gradually easier to work with.

HELP IS AT HAND

When performing exploratory refactoring, always remember that you have strong allies you can rely on to protect you.

The version control system

If your refactoring gets out of hand and you don't feel confident that the code still works correctly, all it takes is one command to revert your changes and put the code back into a known, safe state. This is an excellent safety net, allowing you to experiment with all kinds of ambitious changes to the code, safe in the knowledge that you can always back out if you get into trouble.

The IDE

Modern IDEs such as Eclipse and IntelliJ offer powerful refactoring functionality. They are capable of performing a wide range of standard refactorings, and they can do in milliseconds what would take a human minutes or hours of tedious editing to achieve. What's more, they can perform these refactorings much more safely than a human—an IDE never makes a typo!

If you're serious about refactoring, learn how to use your IDE effectively. Make sure you go through every single item in the Refactor menu and check exactly what it does.

The compiler

Assuming you're working with a statically compiled language such as Java, the compiler can help you discover the effects of your changes quickly. After each refactoring step, run the compiler and check that you haven't introduced any compilation errors. Using the compiler to obtain quick feedback like this is often called *leaning on the compiler.*

If you're using a dynamic language such as Python or Ruby, there's no compiler to lean on, so you'll have to be more careful. This is one reason why many Ruby developers are so passionate about automated testing. They use tests to provide the support that they can't get from the compiler.

Other developers

Everybody makes mistakes, so it's always a good idea to have a coworker review the changes you've made. Alternatively, you may want to try working in a pair when you refactor. One developer (the "navigator") can check for mistakes and provide advice while the other developer (the "driver") focuses on performing the refactoring.

CHARACTERIZATION TESTS

As a complement to explanatory refactoring, you could also try adding characterization tests (a coin termed by Michael Feathers). These are tests that demonstrate how a given part of the system currently behaves. Note that the goal is to describe how the system *actually* behaves, which may not necessarily be the same as what's written in the spec. When it comes to legacy code, preserving the existing behavior is usually the most important goal. Writing these characterization tests can help to solidify your understanding of the code's behavior, and they give you the freedom to make changes to the code in the future, safe in the knowledge that you've protected yourself against unintended regressions.

Say the TimeTrack application's Core component includes a number of similar, but subtly different, utility methods for manipulating and formatting dates and timestamps. They're unhelpfully named things like `convertDate`, `convertDate2`, `convertDate_new`, and so on. You might want to write some characterization tests to work out exactly what each of these methods does and how they differ from each other.

2.1.2 *Frustration*

Here are some more negative and unhelpful thoughts that legacy software has provoked in me in the past:

- I wouldn't even know where to begin fixing this big ball of mud.
- Every class is as bad as the previous (or next) one. Let's pick classes at random and start refactoring.
- I've had it with this `WidgetManagerFactoryImpl`! I'm not doing anything else until I've rewritten it.

Working with legacy code can sometimes be very frustrating. Even the simplest fix can involve touching 20 different instances of the same copy-pasted code, adding a new feature can take days when it should really take minutes, and trying to follow the logic of excessively complex code can be a real mental strain. This frustration can often lead to one of two outcomes: loss of motivation or desperate measures.

LOSS OF MOTIVATION

You give up your refactoring efforts as hopeless, and resign yourself to a future of legacy drudgery. The software seems to be doomed, and there's no way to save it.

DESPERATE MEASURES

You start randomly stabbing at the codebase with a refactoring tool. You'll probably start with your least favorite class, the one you've had your eye on for a few months now, and after that you'll move on to a few more randomly chosen classes until your cathartic urges have been sated. At this point, you go back to doing "real" work, until a few weeks later when enough frustration builds up and forces you to go through the same cycle again.

These maverick refactoring sessions provide a satisfying endorphin rush, and assuming that your refactoring crusades are successful, you're making a positive difference to the quality of the software. But the important question is, how much of a difference? Certainly you've improved the classes that you've refactored, but are these classes valuable in the context of the codebase as a whole? Are they on the critical path of many code changes, meaning that developers often have to read and update them, or are they relatively minor nooks and crannies of the codebase that just happened to irritate you? And quantitatively, how much of a difference have you made? What percentage of the codebase have you managed to cover? Without solid data, it's hard to answer these questions.

SOLUTIONS

Marking the software as doomed and giving up on it obviously doesn't help anybody, so we need a way to maintain motivation and remind ourselves that our refactoring efforts are making a difference. We can do this by choosing one or more metrics that indicate the quality of the code. If we measure these metrics regularly, we can look at how they change over time, giving us a simple indicator of how the code's quality is improving. Visualizing this trend on a graph and making it visible to the team can be a really good motivator. If we find that the numbers aren't improving, that will give us a specific goal to aim for. This can be more motivating than a vague feeling of "must improve quality."

As for the desperate refactoring raids, it seems like we need a more systematic approach if we're going to make a real impact on improving the quality of the code. We need a way to decide, with justification, exactly what the first target for refactoring should be. And after we finish working on our chosen target, we should be able to use the same decision-making process to choose the next target, and the one after that, as we proceed in our refactoring. Refactoring is a never-ending process, so we need data that can help us make decisions based on a given snapshot of the software, both now and in the future.

To summarize, we want to gather data about our software for two reasons:

- To show the quality of the software and how that quality is changing over time.
- To decide what our next refactoring target should be. This may be a part of the code that is quantitatively worse than others (according to some measure of goodness), or it may be code whose refactoring provides a lot of value to the team, perhaps because it's a class that's often touched by developers when they implement bug fixes or new features.

In the rest of this chapter, we'll discuss techniques and tools that you can use to gather this data and make it visible to your team. By the end of the chapter, you'll have a system in place to automatically and continuously measure quality using a variety of metrics, collect the results, and visualize them using graphs and dashboards.

2.2   Gathering useful data about your software

We want to gather metrics about legacy software in order to help us answer the following questions:

- What state is the code in to start with? Is it really in as bad shape as you think?
- What should be your next target for refactoring at any given time?
- How much progress are you making with your refactoring? Are you improving the quality fast enough to keep up with the entropy introduced by new changes?

First we need to decide what to measure. This depends largely on the particular software, but the simple answer is measure everything you can. You want as much raw data as you can get your hands on, to help guide you in your decision-making. This may include some of the following metrics, as well as many others that are not on the list.

2.2.1   Bugs and coding standard violations

Static analysis tools can analyze a codebase and detect possible bugs or poorly written code. Static analysis involves looking through the code (either the human-readable source code or the machine-readable compiled code) and flagging any pieces of code that match a predefined set of patterns or rules.

A bug-finding tool such as FindBugs may flag any code that fails to close an Input-Stream that it has opened, because this may result in a resource leak and should thus be considered a bug. A style-checking tool such as Checkstyle searches for code that violates a given set of style rules. It may flag any code that's incorrectly indented or is missing a Javadoc comment.

Of course the tools aren't perfect, and they produce both false positives (flagging code as a bug even though it's not) and false negatives (failing to detect a serious bug). But they provide a good indication of the overall state of the codebase and can be very useful when choosing your next refactoring target, as they can pinpoint hotspots of poor quality code.

For Java code, the big three tools are FindBugs, PMD, and Checkstyle. I'll show you how to apply them to a project in section 2.3.

> **OTHER LANGUAGES**   This book only discusses tools for Java code, but most mainstream programming languages have their associated analysis tools. If you're working in Ruby, you'll probably want to look at tools such as Rubocop, Code Climate, and Cane.

2.2.2   Performance

One goal of your refactoring may be to improve the performance of a legacy system. If that's the case, you'll need to measure that performance.

PERFORMANCE TESTS

If you already have performance tests, great! If not, you'll need to write some. You can start with very simple tests. For example, remember the TimeTrack system whose architecture we looked at in figure 2.1? The Audit component is in charge of processing the logs output by the nightly batches and generating reports from them. Say the batches output tens of thousands of logs every night, and the Audit component needs to handle a year's worth of logs. That adds up to a lot of data, so we're interested in maximizing the performance of the system.

If you wanted to test the performance of the Audit component, you could start with the following test:

1 Start the system in a known state.
2 Feed it 1 million lines of dummy log data.
3 Time how long it takes to process the data and generate an audit report.
4 Shut down the system and clean up.

Over time, you could extend the test to provide more fine-grained performance data. This might involve making changes to the system under test, such as adding performance logging or timing APIs to measure the performance of various parts of the system.

If starting up the whole system before the test (and tearing it down afterward) is slow and cumbersome, you may instead want to write more fine-grained tests that measure the performance of individual subsystems rather than the system as a whole. These tests are often easier to set up and quicker to run, but they depend on being able to run individual parts of the software in isolation. With a legacy application, this is often easier said than done, so you may need to put in some refactoring effort before you're able to write tests like these.

Say the Audit component has three stages in its processing pipeline, as shown in figure 2.2: parsing the incoming log data, calculating the report's content, and rendering the report and writing it to a file. You may want to write separate performance tests for each stage, so that you can find the bottlenecks in the system. But if the code for each processing stage is highly coupled, it's difficult to test any one stage in isolation. You'll need to refactor the code into three separate classes before you can write your performance tests. We'll talk more about techniques for refactoring in chapter 4.

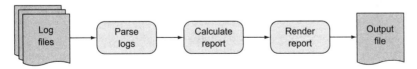

Figure 2.2　The Audit component's processing pipeline

MONITORING PERFORMANCE IN PRODUCTION

If your software is a web application, it's easy to collect performance data from the production system. Any decent web server will be able to output the processing time of every request to a log file. You could write a simple script to aggregate this data to calculate percentile response times per hour, per day, and so on.

For example, assuming your web server outputs one access log file per day and the request processing time is the final column of the tab-separated file, the following shell snippet would output the 99th percentile response time for a given day's accesses. You could run this script every night and email the results to the development team.

**Selects only the final
column of the log file**

```
awk '{print $NF}' apache_access_$(date +%Y%m%d).log | \
  sort -n | \
    awk '{sorted[c]=$1; c++;} END{print sorted[int(NR*0.99-0.5)]}'
```

**Sorts the requests in order of
increasing processing time**

**Prints the row that's 99%
of the way down the file**

This script is very primitive, but it provides you with one simple, understandable piece of data per day that you can use to track the quality of your software. Using this as a starting point, you could write a more powerful program in your favorite scripting language. You may wish to consider

- Filtering out noise, such as images, CSS, JavaScript, and other static files
- Calculating per-URL performance metrics so that you can flag performance hotspots
- Outputting the results as a graph to make it easier to visualize performance
- Building an online app to allow team members to view performance trends, once you have a few months' worth of data

But before you get too carried away, be aware that there already are plenty of tools available to help you with this kind of analysis. It's better to use existing open source tools wherever possible, rather than hacking together a bunch of scripts that merely reinvent the wheel. One excellent tool that I use to measure and visualize the performance of production systems is Kibana.

Kibana makes it easy to build dashboards for visualizing log data. It relies on a search engine called Elasticsearch, so before you can use Kibana you need to get your log data into an Elasticsearch index. I usually do this using a system called Fluentd. The great thing about this setup is that log data is fed directly from the production servers to Elasticsearch, making it visible on the Kibana dashboard within seconds. So you can use it not only for visualizing long-term performance trends of your system, but also for monitoring the performance of the production system in real time, allowing you to spot issues and react to them quickly.

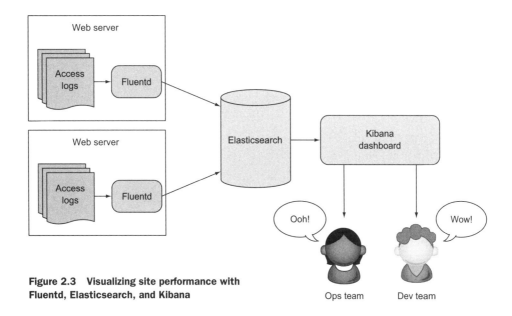

Figure 2.3 Visualizing site performance with Fluentd, Elasticsearch, and Kibana

Figure 2.3 shows a typical setup. Application logs are collected by Fluentd and forwarded in real time to Elasticsearch, where they're indexed and made available for viewing on Kibana dashboards.

Figure 2.4 shows a detail from a Kibana dashboard. Kibana lets you visualize your log data in a number of different ways, including line and bar graphs.

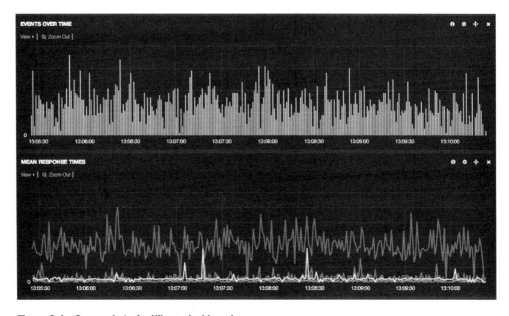

Figure 2.4 Screenshot of a Kibana dashboard

With Kibana it's easy to build dashboards that are understandable to all members of your organization, not just developers. This can be useful when trying to communicate the benefits of your refactoring project or to demonstrate your team's progress to nontechnical stakeholders. Permanently displaying the dashboard in a highly visible position in the office can also be a great motivator.

2.2.3 *Error counts*

Measuring performance is all well and good, but it doesn't matter how fast your code runs if it's not doing its job correctly (giving users the results they expect and not throwing any errors).

A count of the number of errors happening in production is a simple but useful indicator of the quality of your software, as seen from the end-user's perspective. If your software is a website, you could count the number of `500 Internal Server Error` responses that your server generates per day. This information should be available in your web server's access logs, so you could write a script to count the error responses every day and email this number to your developers. The system based on Fluentd and Kibana introduced in the previous section could also be used to visualize the frequency of errors. If you want more detailed error information, such as stack traces, and you want to view errors in real time, I recommend a system called Sentry.

If your software runs in customers' environments rather than your own data center, you don't have the luxury of access to all production log data, but it's still possible to estimate the number of errors occurring. For example, you could introduce an automatic error-reporting feature into your product that contacts your server whenever an exception occurs. A more low-tech solution would be to simply count the support requests you receive from angry customers.

2.2.4 *Timing common tasks*

Remembering that we're planning to improve the software and its development process as a whole, and not just the code, metrics such as the following may be useful.

TIME TO SET UP THE DEVELOPMENT ENVIRONMENT FROM SCRATCH

Every time a new member joins your team, ask them to time how long it takes to get a fully functional version of the software and all relevant development tools running on their local machine. In chapter 7 we'll look at how to use automation to reduce this time, thus lowering the barrier to entry for new developers and allowing them to start being productive as soon as possible.

TIME TAKEN TO RELEASE OR DEPLOY THE PROJECT

If creating a new release is taking a long time, it may be a sign that the process has too many manual steps. The process of releasing software is inherently amenable to automation, and automating the process will both speed it up and reduce the probability of human error. Making the release process easier and faster will encourage more frequent releases, which in turn leads to more stable software. We'll discuss automation of release and deployment in chapter 9.

This metric can be a good indicator of communication between team members. Often a developer will spend days tracking down a bug, only to find out later that another team member had seen a similar problem before and could have fixed the issue within minutes. If bugs are getting fixed more quickly, it's likely that the members of your team are communicating well and sharing valuable information.

2.2.5 Commonly used files

Knowing which files in your project are edited most often can be very useful when choosing your next refactoring target. If one particular class is edited by developers very often, it's an ideal target for refactoring.

Note that this is slightly different from the other metrics because it's not a measure of project quality, but it's still useful data.

You can use your version control system to calculate this data automatically. If you're using Git, here's a one-liner that will list the 10 files that were edited most often during the last 90 days.

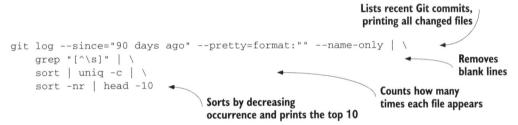

```
git log --since="90 days ago" --pretty=format:"" --name-only | \
    grep "[^\s]" | \
    sort | uniq -c | \
    sort -nr | head -10
```

Lists recent Git commits, printing all changed files

Removes blank lines

Counts how many times each file appears

Sorts by decreasing occurrence and prints the top 10

Here's the result of running the previous command against a randomly chosen project, Apache Spark:

```
59 project/SparkBuild.scala
  52 pom.xml
  46 core/src/main/scala/org/apache/spark/SparkContext.scala
  33 core/src/main/scala/org/apache/spark/util/Utils.scala
  28 core/pom.xml
  27 core/src/main/scala/org/apache/spark/rdd/RDD.scala
  21 python/pyspark/rdd.py
  21 docs/configuration.md
  17 make-distribution.sh
  17 core/src/main/scala/org/apache/spark/rdd/PairRDDFunctions.scala
```

This shows that, excluding build files, the most commonly edited file was SparkContext.scala. If this were a legacy codebase that you were looking to refactor, it would probably be wise to focus your attention on this file.

In applications that have been in production for a long time, many areas of the applications become fairly static, while development tends to cluster around just a few hotspots of functionality. In the case of our TimeTrack application, for example, you might find that the UI for registering hours worked hasn't changed for years, whereas managers are regularly coming up with feature requests for new and obscure ways to generate reports. In this case, it would obviously make sense to focus any refactoring efforts on the report generation module.

2.2.6 *Measure everything you can*

I've given you a few examples of data that you can collect, but this list is by no means exhaustive. When it comes to defining and measuring metrics, the possibilities are endless. A quick brainstorming session with your team will no doubt provide you with plenty of other ideas for metrics to measure.

Of course, just because you can measure something, it doesn't mean it's necessarily useful data. You could measure the number of Zs in your codebase, the average number of fingers on a developer's hand, or the distance between the production server and the moon, but it's hard to see how these relate to quality!

Silly examples aside, it's always better to have too much information than not enough. A good rule of thumb is, if in doubt, measure it. As you and your team work with the data, you'll gradually discover which metrics are most suitable for your particular needs. If a given metric isn't working for you, feel free to drop it.

2.3 *Inspecting your codebase using FindBugs, PMD, and Checkstyle*

When preparing to refactor a legacy codebase, using static analysis tools to search for bugs, design issues, and style violations is a great place to start.

Three of the most popular static analysis tools for Java code are FindBugs, PMD, and Checkstyle. Although these tools all work by analyzing Java code and reporting issues, they have slightly different purposes.

FindBugs, as the name implies, attempts to find potential bugs in Java code. By potential, I mean that running the code may result in a bug, depending on the way it's used and the data that's passed to it. It's impossible for any automated tool to decide with 100% confidence that a particular piece of code is a bug, not least because the definition of bug is highly subjective. One man's bug may be another man's feature! Having said that, FindBugs is very good at detecting code that's either suspicious or downright wrong.

PMD is also a tool for finding problem code, and its rulesets have some overlap with those of FindBugs. But whereas FindBugs looks for code that's buggy, PMD is useful for finding code that, while technically correct, doesn't follow best practices and is in need of refactoring. For example, although FindBugs will point out code that may dereference a null pointer (leading to a dreaded `NullPointerException`), PMD can tell you if there's an excessively high degree of coupling between objects.

Finally, there's Checkstyle, which you can use to ensure that all source code follows your team's coding standards. Ensuring consistency of little things like formatting and naming across the whole codebase can make a big difference to readability. You spend a lot more of your time reading code than writing it, and this is especially true for legacy code. It makes sense to try to make the code as readable as possible.

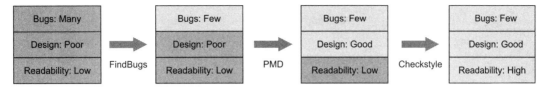

Figure 2.5 Improving code using static analysis tools

I recommend applying the tools in this order: FindBugs, PMD, and Checkstyle as illustrated in figure 2.5. This will help you fix problems in order of importance:

1 Fix critical bugs such as `NullPointerExceptions`
2 Fix design issues by refactoring
3 Fix code formatting to improve readability

There's little point in having beautifully formatted code if the overall design is spaghetti, and it's equally pointless to refactor code that doesn't even work correctly.

2.3.1 Running FindBugs in your IDE

The first thing we want to do with our legacy codebase is to search for and remove any obviously incorrect code. We'll use FindBugs to help us.

FindBugs is a free, open source tool developed by the University of Maryland. It works by analyzing the bytecode generated by the Java compiler and searching for suspicious patterns. For each instance it finds, it assigns a confidence rating, indicating how likely it believes the code to be buggy. Each pattern in the FindBugs database is also assigned a scariness ranking, indicating how bad it would be if that kind of bug existed in your code. For example, a `NullPointerException` usually has a much more serious effect on the running of your program than forgetting to add a `serialVersionUID` to a `Serializable` class.

FindBugs can be run in a number of ways, but the easiest way is to use an IDE plugin. That way you can click on a bug and jump straight to the offending code. The IDE plugins also allow you to filter by package, bug severity, bug category, and so on, so you can cut down on noise and focus on important bugs. Plugins are available for Eclipse, IntelliJ IDEA, NetBeans, and probably many other IDEs. Consult your IDE documentation for instructions on how to install the plugin.

> **DON'T FORGET TO COMPILE** FindBugs runs on compiled bytecode, whereas what you see in your IDE is the source code. If the source code and bytecode aren't in sync, the result of a FindBugs analysis can be quite confusing. Make sure you've compiled the code before running FindBugs.

The screenshot in figure 2.6 shows the result of running the FindBugs IDE plugin in IntelliJ IDEA. In this case, the codebase was quite small and FindBugs found only one bug in the whole project. (If you want to try it for yourself, the project I used is available on GitHub: https://github.com/cb372/externalized. Note that you'll need to

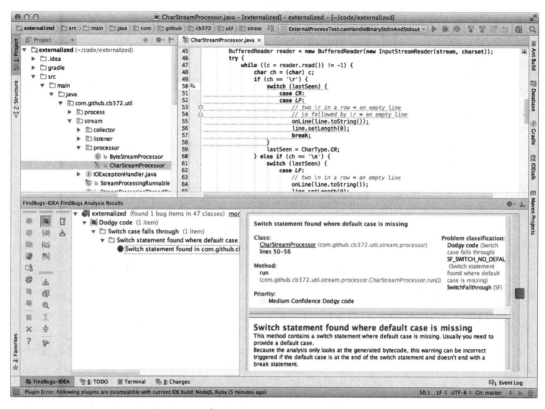

Figure 2.6   An example FindBugs analysis result

check out the `0.3.0` tag because the bug is fixed in later versions.) The plugin shows information about the location and severity of the bug, along with a plain English description of the FindBugs rule that was violated. Double-clicking on the bug will open the offending source file in an editor so you can inspect and fix it.

The issue that FindBugs found is a valid one. This is code that I wrote, and it looks like I forgot to add a `default` case to a `switch` statement—a common mistake committed by lazy programmers like myself! In this example, the missing case doesn't actually lead to incorrect behavior, but it's still good practice to always include a `default` case to make it easier for readers to understand the code.

Usually the explanation provided by FindBugs makes it quite obvious how to fix the code in order to resolve the warning. An appropriate fix in this case is shown in the following listing.

> **Listing 2.1   A fix for the FindBugs warning**

```
switch (lastSeen) {
    case CR:
    case LF:
        // two \r in a row = an empty line
```

```
        // \n followed by \r = an empty line
        onLine(line.toString());
        line.setLength(0);
        break;
    default:
        // not a line-break - do nothing
        break;
}
```

Adding this default case makes my intentions clearer to anybody reading the code

By the way, this example also demonstrates the fallibility of FindBugs. In the file where FindBugs found the missing `default` statement, there are actually two more examples of exactly the same problem, but for some reason FindBugs failed to find them. It goes to show that sometimes automated tools are no match for good old-fashioned code review!

Figure 2.7 shows the result of running FindBugs on a much larger Java codebase, the `camel-core` module of the Apache Camel project. This result is rather more interesting, as FindBugs found many more bugs. You can see that the tool has helpfully arranged them by category, allowing you to focus on fixing certain categories of bugs first. You can also group them by scariness rank, ranging from Of Concern to Scariest.

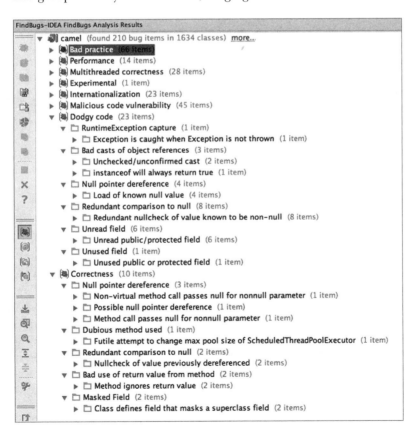

Figure 2.7 Running FindBugs on a larger codebase

2.3.2 *Handling false positives*

FindBugs is a powerful tool, but there are limits to the capabilities of static analysis. Occasionally FindBugs may produce a false positive, flagging a piece of code as a bug even though you, a human, can see that it's not.

USING ANNOTATIONS

Luckily, the FindBugs developers prepared for this eventuality and provided us with a way to mark a specific piece of code as "not a bug." You can use an annotation to tell FindBugs not to check a certain field or method against one or more rules. Let's look at an example to see how this works.

The class in the next listing has one private field, name. For whatever reason, the class always uses Java reflection to get and set this field, so to a static analysis tool such as FindBugs, it looks like the field is never accessed.

> **Listing 2.2 A FindBugs false positive caused by Java reflection**

```
public class FindbugsFalsePositiveReflection {          The setter uses reflection,
    private String name;                                so it accesses the field by
                                                          specifying its name.
    public void setName(String value) {
        try {
            getClass().getDeclaredField("name").set(this, value);
        } catch (NoSuchFieldException | IllegalAccessException e) {
            e.printStackTrace();
        }                                                 The getter is the same:
    }                                                       it doesn't directly
                                                          reference the field.
    public String getName() {
        try {
            return (String) getClass().getDeclaredField("name")
                .get(this);
        } catch (NoSuchFieldException | IllegalAccessException e) {
            e.printStackTrace();
            return null;
        }
    }
}
```

Sure enough, if you run FindBugs on this code, it will give you a warning saying that the name field is unused and should be removed from the class. But you can see that the field is obviously used, so you want to tell FindBugs that, with all due respect, in this particular case it's completely wrong. Let's add an annotation to do exactly that.

To use the FindBugs annotations, you need to add them as a dependency. They're packaged as a JAR and are available on Maven Central. At the time of writing, the latest version is 3.0.1u2. If you're using Maven, add the following dependency to your pom.xml file.

```
<dependency>
    <groupId>com.google.code.findbugs</groupId>
    <artifactId>annotations</artifactId>
    <version>3.0.1u2</version>
</dependency>
```

Once you have a dependency on the annotations library, you can add an annotation to the name field. This listing shows the field with the annotation added.

Listing 2.3 A field with a FindBugs @SuppressWarning annotation

```
@SuppressFBWarnings(
        value = "UUF_UNUSED_FIELD",
        justification = "This field is accessed using reflection")
private String name;
```

The annotation has two fields: value and justification. You use the value field to tell FindBugs which bug patterns you want to suppress. The justification field is a comment to remind yourself and other developers why you've suppressed the warning.

USING AN EXCLUSION FILE

Annotations are useful when you have only a few false positives, but sometimes Find-Bugs can produce a large number of false positives, making the results difficult to work with. In these cases, going through every class and adding annotations is very laborious, so you might want an easy way to suppress whole categories of warnings at the package or project level. You can achieve this using an exclusions file. Let's look at another example.

A data analyst has recently joined your company, charged with studying how employees are spending their time, in the hope of finding ways to improve efficiency and cut costs. They have asked you to add an API to the TimeTrack application so they can easily retrieve information in XML format about hours worked. You decide to add the API to the application's existing UI component, which is built on a homegrown web framework based on Struts.

When generating API responses, you need to serialize your model classes into XML. Luckily the homegrown web framework takes care of this for you, but it imposes a couple of arbitrary restrictions on your code:

- All dates must be instances of java.util.Date (so you can't use immutable date types such as those found in the Joda Time library).
- You have to use arrays to store lists of values, because the framework doesn't know how to serialize collection types such as java.util.ArrayList.

With these restrictions in mind, your model class for an employee's recorded work on a given day might look like the following.

Listing 2.4 WorkDay bean

```
package com.mycorp.timetrack.ui.beans;

public class WorkDay {
    private int employeeId;
    private Date date;
    // work record = tuple of (projectId, hours worked)
    private WorkRecord[] workRecords;
```

```
    public int getEmployeeId() {
        return employeeId;
    }

    public void setEmployeeId(int employeeId) {
        this.employeeId = employeeId;
    }

    public Date getDate() {                          ◄───  Returns a java.util.Date,
        return date;                                       which is mutable
    }

    public void setDate(Date date) {
        this.date = date;
    }

    public WorkRecord[] getWorkRecords() {           ◄───  Returns an array, which
        return workRecords;                                is also mutable
    }

    public void setWorkRecords(WorkRecord[] workRecords) {
        this.workRecords = workRecords;
    }
}
```

If you run FindBugs on this code, you'll find that it produces four warnings. Two of them are telling you that you shouldn't store a reference to a mutable object (such as WorkRecord[] or java.util.Date) that you were passed as an argument to a public method. This is because the class that passed you the object could unexpectedly alter its internal state later, which might lead to confusing bugs.

The other two warnings are similar. They tell you not to return a mutable object as the result of a public method, because the caller might update the mutable object after it receives it.

These are reasonable recommendations, but you can't sensibly comply with them because your hands are tied by the limitations of the web framework. In theory you could fix the warnings by making copies of all mutable objects returned from getters or passed into setters. But in this particular case, it would be unnecessary boilerplate, because you know that these getters and setters will only be called by the web framework's XML serialization code.

Because you don't plan to address these warnings, you want to simply suppress them, reducing unnecessary noise in your FindBugs analysis reports. You can do this with an exclusion filter, which you define in an XML file and pass to FindBugs. The following listing shows an appropriate exclusion file for the XML API.

Listing 2.5 An exclusion filter definition for FindBugs

```
<FindBugsFilter>
  <Match>
    <Bug pattern="EI_EXPOSE_REP,EI_EXPOSE_REP2" />
    <Package name="com.mycorp.timetrack.ui.beans" />
  </Match>
</FindBugsFilter>
```

USE VERSION CONTROL   Check this file into your version control system, along with the code, so that all developers can be sure that they're using the same exclusion filters.

You can use exclusion filters like this to eliminate a lot of noise from your FindBugs reports. It's good to set a baseline with as few warnings as possible, so you can easily spot new bugs that are introduced by changes to the code.

2.3.3   *PMD and Checkstyle*

Another popular static analysis tool for Java is PMD. Unlike FindBugs, PMD works by analyzing Java source code rather than the compiled bytecode. This means it can search for some categories of problems that FindBugs can't. For example, PMD can check for readability issues, such as inconsistent use of braces, or code cleanliness issues such as duplicate import statements.

   Some of PMD's most useful rules relate to code design and complexity. For example, it has rules for detecting excessive coupling between objects, or classes with high cyclomatic complexity. This kind of analysis can be very useful when looking for your next refactoring target.

CYCLOMATIC COMPLEXITY   *Cyclomatic complexity* is a count of the number of different paths your program can take inside a given method. Usually it's defined as the sum of the number of `if` statements, loops, `case` statements, and `catch` statements in the method, plus 1 for the method itself. In general, the higher the cyclomatic complexity, the more difficult a method is to read and maintain.

Just like FindBugs, the easiest way to run PMD is to use a plugin for your favorite IDE. Figure 2.8 shows an example result from running PMD via the IntelliJ IDEA QA-Plug plugin. Note that for the same project for which FindBugs produced only one warning a few pages ago, PMD found a whopping 260 violations!

PMD IS NOISY BY DEFAULT   When run with the default settings, PMD can be very noisy. For example, PMD wants you to add a `final` modifier to method arguments whenever possible, which can result in thousands of warnings for a typical codebase. If PMD spits out myriad warnings the first time you run it, don't despair. It probably means you need to tune your PMD ruleset to disable some of the more noisy rules.

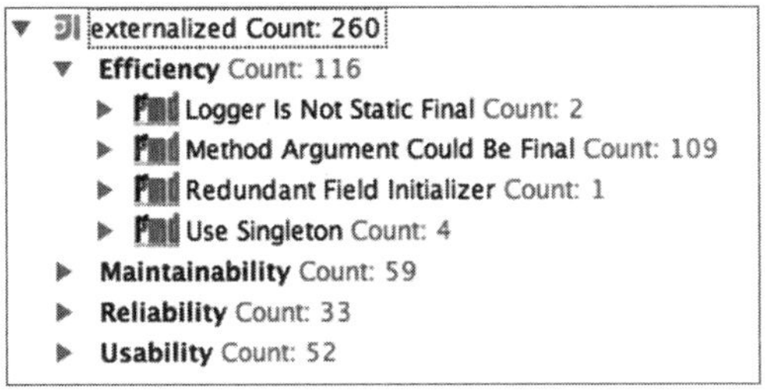

▼ ▤ externalized Count: 260
   ▼ **Efficiency** Count: 116
      ▶ ▦ Logger Is Not Static Final Count: 2
      ▶ ▦ Method Argument Could Be Final Count: 109
      ▶ ▦ Redundant Field Initializer Count: 1
      ▶ ▦ Use Singleton Count: 4
   ▶ **Maintainability** Count: 59
   ▶ **Reliability** Count: 33
   ▶ **Usability** Count: 52

Figure 2.8   An example PMD analysis result

CUSTOMIZING YOUR RULESET

You'll probably need to tune PMD's ruleset until you find the rules that are right for your code and your team's coding style. The PMD website includes excellent documentation on the ruleset, with examples for most rules, so take some time to read through the docs and decide which rules you want to apply.

SUPPRESSING WARNINGS

Just like FindBugs, PMD allows you to suppress warnings at the level of individual fields or methods using Java annotations. PMD uses the standard `@java.lang.Suppress-Warnings` annotation, so there's no need to add any dependencies to your project. You can also disable PMD for a specific line of code by adding a NOPMD comment. The following listing shows the various ways of suppressing PMD warnings.

```
@SuppressWarnings("PMD")                                  Suppresses all PMD warnings
public void suppressWarningsInThisMethod() {              for the method
    ...
}

@SuppressWarnings("PMD.InefficientStringBuffering")       Suppresses a specific
public void suppressASpecificWarningInThisMethod() {      PMD warning
    ...
}

public void suppressWarningsOnOneLine() {                 Suppresses all PMD warnings
    int x = 1;                                            related to a specific line
    int y = x + 1; //NOPMD
    ...
}
```

CHECKSTYLE

Checkstyle is another tool that works by analyzing your Java source code. It has a wide-ranging ruleset, ranging from details such as whitespace and formatting up to higher-level issues relating to class design and complexity metrics. Most of Checkstyle's rules have options and parameters that can be tuned to match your team's coding standards. If your team has a strong opinion about the maximum acceptable number of lines in a method, you can tell Checkstyle what this value should be.

Some of Checkstyle's rules (such as `CyclomaticComplexity`) are also provided by PMD, so if you're planning to use both tools, it's best to tune your rulesets to avoid overlap. It's also worth noting that, just like PMD, Checkstyle can be quite noisy if you enable all the rules. It's a good idea to disable rules that aren't relevant to your codebase or coding style. This can be done with an XML file and/or annotations, just like PMD.

After looking at both FindBugs and PMD, you should get the idea, so I won't say any more about Checkstyle. Suffice it to say that FindBugs, PMD, and Checkstyle each have their individual strengths. When all three are used in concert, they can provide some very useful insights into the quality of your codebase.

To recap the use cases for these tools:

- FindBugs is useful for finding subtle bugs related to thread-safety, correctness, and so on, that are easy to miss in code review.
- PMD has a lot of overlap with FindBugs, but it works against the source code instead of the compiled bytecode, so it can catch a different class of bugs.
- Checkstyle has some overlap with PMD, but it's more useful for validating code style against a coding standard rather than finding bugs.

2.4 Continuous inspection using Jenkins

In the previous section you learned how to use static analysis tools to generate reports on code quality. But so far we've only looked at running the tools from inside a developer's IDE. This is a really useful way to inspect a project, but it has a couple of drawbacks:

- Results are only visible to that developer. It's difficult to share this information with the rest of the team.
- The process is dependent on developers remembering to run the tools regularly.

In this section, we're going to look at how to solve these problems by using a build server to automate the inspection process and make its results visible to the whole team.

2.4.1 Continuous integration and continuous inspection

Ideally we want a system that will automatically monitor the quality of the code, without any effort on the developer's part, and make this information available to all members of the team. We can do this by setting up a workflow like the one shown in figure 2.9, whereby a build server automatically runs the inspection tools every time a developer checks in some new code, and makes the results available on a dashboard for team members to view at their leisure.

Whenever a developer checks a new change into version control, a build is automatically triggered on the build server. The build server checks that the software builds, and it performs other tasks such as running static analysis tools or automated tests.

If there's a problem with the build, such as if the change caused the code to stop compiling or introduced a new FindBugs warning, the build server will notify the developer who made the commit. With this quick feedback, the developer should be able to remedy their mistake easily.

The build server also provides an online dashboard that team members can use to check the state of the software at any given time. This way, information about the software's quality is available to everybody, and nobody is left out of the loop.

Using a build server in this way is sometimes called *continuous inspection*. It's an offshoot of *continuous integration* (CI), a practice that evolved in the late 1990s as part of the extreme programming (XP) movement. Because of the close relationship with CI, build servers are often known as CI servers. I'll use the two terms interchangeably.

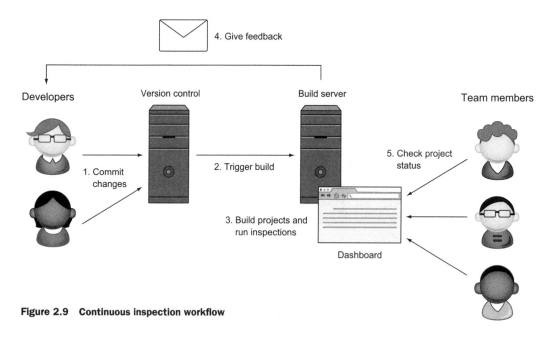

Developers   Version control   Build server   Team members

1. Commit
changes   2. Trigger build

5. Check project
status

3. Build projects and
run inspections

Dashboard

4. Give feedback

Figure 2.9   Continuous inspection workflow

In this book I'll be using Jenkins as the CI server. There are plenty of other CI servers
available, so if you're not already using Jenkins, you may wish to try a few others
before making your choice. Popular CI servers include TeamCity from JetBrains, Atlas-
sian's Bamboo, and hosted solutions such as Travis.

Without further ado, let's get Jenkins installed and ready to build and inspect our
code.

2.4.2   Installing and setting up Jenkins

First things first, Jenkins needs a machine to run on. When you set Jenkins up for production use, it will need to be on a server that's accessible to your whole team, but for
now it's probably easiest to install it on your local machine so you can play around
with it. Jenkins is very easy to install, with native packages available for Windows, OS X,
and various flavors of UNIX. It comes with an embedded web server, and it can automatically install most of the tools it needs, so the only thing you need to prepare in
advance is a JDK.

Once you've installed and started Jenkins, the UI should be available at
http://localhost:8080/. If all has gone well, it should look something like figure 2.10.
Post-install setup mostly consists of

- Telling Jenkins where to find tools such as Maven. It can automatically download and install most tools if you tell it to.
- Installing plugins. Jenkins is highly modular, with a huge number of plugins
  available. For example, plugins are needed for such operations as cloning a Git
  repository and integrating with FindBugs.

Figure 2.10   A brand new Jenkins install

2.4.3   *Using Jenkins to build and inspect code*

We're going to ask Jenkins to inspect code using FindBugs, PMD, and Checkstyle. So far we've only used these tools from within the IDE, but we can't very well expect Jenkins to fire up an IDE like a developer would. Let's integrate the tools with Maven, which Jenkins knows how to run. Each tool has a corresponding Maven plugin, so integration is very simple. You just need to add three `plugin` blocks to your pom.xml. Take a look at the respective Maven plugins' online documentation for more details. If you want a sample project to try with Jenkins, there's a simple example project inside the book's accompanying source code archive, and it's also available on GitHub at https://github.com/cb372/ReengLegacySoft/tree/master/02/NumberGuessingGame.

When you create a new Jenkins job, there are a lot of settings, but you can use the default values for almost everything. Here's what I did to create and configure a new job:

1   Create the job, giving it a name and choosing the Build A Maven2/3 Project option.
2   Fill in the details of my Git repository.
3   Tell Jenkins which Maven tasks to run: `clean compile findbugs:findbugs pmd:pmd checkstyle:checkstyle`.
4   Enable integration with FindBugs, PMD, and Checkstyle in order to publish their respective reports on the dashboard.
5   Save the changes to settings, and run the build.

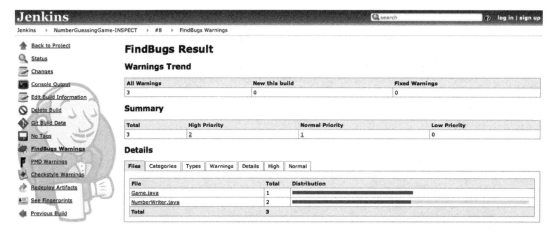

Figure 2.11   Browsing FindBugs results in the Jenkins UI

Once the build completes, you should be able to browse the warnings that were output by the various tools. For example, the FindBugs warnings report may look something like figure 2.11.

Try fixing a few warnings and running the build again. This time around, now that you have more than one build, Jenkins will automatically display a trend graph showing how the number of warnings is changing over time. If you can make sure that this graph slopes downwards, meaning your bug count is decreasing, it can be a great motivator for your team! Figure 2.12 shows some example trend graphs.

2.4.4   *What else can we use Jenkins for?*

You've had a taste of what Jenkins can do for you, but we've really only scratched the surface. With its enormous range of plugins, the ability to run arbitrary shell scripts as well as every build tool you've ever heard of, and features for linking builds together into complex workflows, the possibilities really are infinite.

Here are just some of the things I've successfully automated with Jenkins:

- Running unit tests
- Executing end-to-end UI tests using Selenium
- Generating documentation
- Deploying software to staging environments
- Publishing packages to a Maven repository
- Running complex multistage performance tests
- Building and publishing auto-generated API clients

As you can see, the sky's the limit. In many successful development teams that I've been a part of, Jenkins has been a core member of the team. Not only does the automation of repetitive tasks improve the team's productivity, Jenkins can also act as a

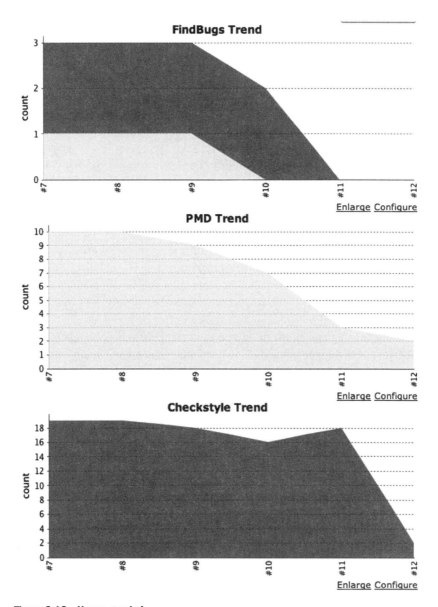

Figure 2.12 Happy graphs!

communications hub. It's the place where all useful, up-to-date information about the software is stored, and all of the team's workflows are codified. If you want to know the correct way to run the unit tests or deploy the system, just open up the appropriate Jenkins job and take a peek at the configuration.

Jenkins can also help to bridge gaps in communication between developers and less technical members of the team. I once worked on a site that displayed various ranking data. Every hour, a bunch of scripts would run to recalculate this ranking data and update the DB. A tester asked me how he could manually kick this update process in the staging environment, so that he didn't have to wait an hour before he could do his manual testing. Within a couple of minutes, I had whipped up a Jenkins job to SSH into the staging server and run the scripts for him, so he was able to update the ranking data whenever he liked, just by pressing a button.

Finally, I have a couple of tips to help you make the most of Jenkins in your team.

VERSION CONTROL HOOKS

One of the most important features of Jenkins is its integration with your version control system (VCS). Every time you check in some code, Jenkins should automatically start building the code to check that there were no unexpected side effects to your change. If it finds something wrong, Jenkins can provide feedback by failing the build and perhaps sending you an angry email.

The faster this feedback, the more useful it is. If the lag between checking in the code and receiving a notification of a failed build is 10 or 20 minutes, you'll likely have moved on to a different task by the time you receive the notification. You'll have to stop what you're doing, context-switch back to what you were doing 20 minutes ago, and fix the problem.

Reducing this lag can be done in two ways. Make the build itself faster (or at least make it fail faster when something is wrong), or reduce the time it takes for the build to start. If you've set up Jenkins to poll your VCS for changes once every 5 minutes, it could take 4 minutes 59 seconds for your checked-in code to even get noticed, which is wasted time.

There's a simple solution to this. Instead of configuring Jenkins to poll, set up the VCS to tell Jenkins about changes as soon as they occur. This can be done by configuring a hook in your VCS system. The details depend on the particular VCS implementation that you're using, but most modern VCS solutions have support for Webhooks or something similar.

BACKUPS

For many teams, once they start using Jenkins, it quickly becomes a pillar of their development infrastructure. Just like any other piece of infrastructure, it's important to plan for failure and take regular backups. The Jenkins instance that I use at work has hundreds of important jobs configured, so I shudder to think what chaos would ensue if one day the hard disk failed and we didn't have that data backed up.

Luckily, all of Jenkins' data is stored in XML files, so it's amenable to backing up. The only folder you need to back up is JENKINS_HOME. (The System Information screen in the Jenkins UI will tell you where this is.) Make sure to exclude the workspace folder, as this contains the workspaces for all jobs. It might be several GB in size, depending on the number and scale of Jenkins jobs you're running.

REST API

Jenkins comes with a powerful REST API built in, which can be very useful. I once had to make a very similar change to the configurations of a large number of jobs. This would have been tedious to do using the UI, so I wrote a script to do all the grunt work, making use of the REST API to update the job configurations.

There's also a Jenkins command-line interface that makes automation of common administration tasks a breeze.

2.4.5 *SonarQube*

If you're interested in taking continuous inspection beyond Jenkins, it's worth taking a look at the SonarQube tool (www.sonarqube.org). SonarQube is a standalone server dedicated to tracking and visualizing code quality. It has an excellent dashboard-based UI (there's a demo available online at http://nemo.sonarqube.org/), and it does a really good job of gathering and displaying all code-quality data in one place.

SonarQube provides so much data in so many interesting combinations that if you're not careful you can waste hours wandering through it all, so I try to avoid checking it too often. I tend to use a CI server such as Jenkins to get quick feedback on the effects of code changes (such as whether the change has introduced a new Find-Bugs warning), and look at SonarQube less regularly, to keep track of the general trend of the code quality or when searching for the next hotspot to refactor.

2.5 *Summary*

- It's worth being aware of the psychological barriers that can prevent you from tackling a legacy codebase rationally.
- Before you start refactoring, you should have a measurement infrastructure in place to guide you. Let the data show you where to focus your efforts and help you measure your progress.
- There are plenty of free tools available to help you. In this chapter we looked at FindBugs, PMD, Checkstyle, and Jenkins.
- A CI server such as Jenkins can act as a communications hub for your team.

Part 2

Refactoring to improve the codebase

We set up the inspection infrastructure in chapter 2, and we're now ready to start work on re-engineering our legacy software.

Chapter 3 will focus on a very important decision, namely whether to refactor a codebase or to throw it away and rewrite from scratch. This decision is often risky, because it's made at the start of the project when you don't yet have much information to guide you, so we'll also look at how to reduce that risk by taking a more incremental approach.

Chapters 4, 5, and 6 look in detail at three options for re-engineering software: refactoring, re-architecting, and the Big Rewrite. In a sense, they're all variants of each other, just working at different scales. Refactoring is restructuring of code at the level of methods and classes, re-architecting is refactoring at the level of modules and components, and the Big Rewrite is re-architecting at the highest possible level.

In chapter 4, I'll introduce a number of refactoring patterns that I've often used or seen used successfully. In chapter 5, I'll provide a case study of splitting a monolithic Java application into a number of interdependent modules, and I'll also touch on the comparative merits of monoliths and microservices. Finally, in chapter 6 I'll provide tips for achieving a successful rewrite of a large piece of software.

Preparing to refactor

In this chapter we'll tackle some of the nontechnical issues that you'll often face when carrying out a major refactoring on a real-world codebase. In an ideal world, you'd have complete freedom and unlimited amounts of time to craft beautiful code, but the reality of software development often demands compromise. When you're working as a member of a team, which in turn is part of a larger organization with plans and goals, budgets and deadlines, you'll need to hone your negotiating skills in order to achieve consensus from both your fellow engineers and nontechnical stakeholders on the best way to proceed.

After that I'll give you a friendly reminder that refactoring should always be done with the goals of the organization in mind. In other words, don't forget who pays your salary! Refactoring should be done only if you can prove that it provides long-term value to the business.

An important question to answer before embarking on a major improvement project is refactor or rewrite? Can you realistically raise the software's quality to an acceptable level using refactoring alone, or is the code so far gone that a greenfield rewrite is the more sensible option? Ultimately this is a question that you and your team will have to answer for yourselves, but I'll try to provide pointers to help you make your decision. I'll also discuss a hybrid approach that can reduce the risk inherent in a full rewrite.

Tales from The Site

A warning: this chapter will be light on technical content and will tend toward the abstract in places. To bring things back down to earth, I'll be referring throughout the chapter to an actual legacy application that I maintained, refactored, and eventually helped to rewrite. Let's simply call it The Site.

The Site was a large Java web application built with raw servlets and Java Server-Pages (JSP), backed by an SQL DB. When I joined the company, it had already been in production for about 10 years. The company's main product was a portal site comprising a large number of services and minisites of various size and popularity, and The Site was the home of a few of the major ones.

3.1 Forming a team consensus

If you're planning to carry out a substantial refactoring, you don't want to be doing it on your own. If possible, the whole team should work together to make the changes, reviewing each other's work and sharing the information gleaned from the refactoring. Even if the rest of the team are busy with other work and you're doing most of the refactoring yourself, you at least want them to support you by reviewing your changes.

For this to happen, you need to make sure everybody on the team is on the same page, in agreement about what you want to achieve and how you plan to achieve it. Reaching consensus on the team's goals and working style may take a while, and it depends largely on how well the team communicates. It's essential to nurture an environment in which frank, open discussion and sharing of useful information are the norm.

Every team is unique, and how you get your team communicating depends on what kinds of people you're working with. Let's look at a couple of the characters you might encounter on your team, and see how you could get them working effectively together.

Before we continue, let me make clear that these are exaggerated caricatures, and we all probably have a little of each of them in us. Most developers are hopefully a little more well-rounded than the hypothetical characters in figure 3.1.

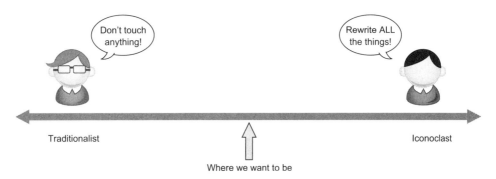

Figure 3.1   The spectrum of developer attitudes towards legacy code

3.1.1   *The Traditionalist*

The Traditionalist is a developer who's strongly averse to changes of any kind. They don't enjoy working on those clunky legacy systems any more than the next guy, but at the same time they see refactoring as an unnecessary risk. "If it ain't broke, don't fix it" is their motto. Perhaps they've been bitten once too often by a regression caused by a bad change to a legacy system. Or maybe they've been around the block with this legacy system and observed it running fine for years, so they don't see why it needs to be fixed all of a sudden.

The Traditionalist may also think of refactoring as a distraction from the real work that we developers are paid to do, namely adding features and fixing bugs. They want to get their assigned task done as quickly as possible and with the minimum of fuss, and they don't see how unnecessarily altering the codebase is going to help with that.

Here are a few ways you can work with the Traditionalist to help them stay integrated with the team and its refactoring efforts, and hopefully convince them that refactoring is worth it in the long run.

PAIR PROGRAMMING

Asking the Traditionalist to pair up with you while you improve the codebase can be useful. For example, after setting up FindBugs (as explained in the previous chapter), you could work together to fix a particular FindBugs warning. It's most impressive if you can find a really nasty bug to fix, such as a potential null pointer dereference. First, demonstrate how a null pointer can occur, and then show how it can easily be fixed by adding a null check. Finally, once you've committed the fix and Jenkins has run the build, you can show how the FindBugs warning has disappeared. This should give the Traditionalist a clear idea of what this FindBugs thing is all about, and give them the confidence and motivation to tackle FindBugs warnings on their own.

Later you could move on to performing simple refactorings as a pair. If you have many fragments of duplicated code, you could extract a method to replace them all. Along the way, you'd explain that this will make new features and bug fixes easier to implement and less error-prone, because now you only have to change one part of the codebase instead of many.

Pair programming can be difficult to get used to at first. Although some people take to it like a fish to water, the Traditionalist may be hesitant to try it. This is totally understandable, and the worst thing you can do is force pair programming on somebody who's not happy with it. Start gradually, perhaps limiting your pairing sessions to 15 minutes, and try to extend them from there.

The Traditionalist is probably more interested in getting their own work done, so you could start with them as the driver and you as the navigator. Let them get on with fixing a bug or whatever work they happen to be doing. Meanwhile, you can help by looking up documentation, writing tests for the code they're working on, or suggesting other ways to write the code.

Tales from The Site

The team in charge of maintaining The Site was quite close to the Traditionalist end of the spectrum. When I joined the team, for example, they hadn't upgraded the application's dependencies for years, because they were worried about the possible side effects of upgrading. There was also a lack of communication within the team, with each developer knowing little about what their neighbor was working on.

To try to tackle both of these problems, I started by setting up continuous inspection using Jenkins (as described in chapter 2), before instituting a policy of code reviews and eventually introducing pair programming to the team.

The results were, on the whole, pretty positive. Nowadays the team is a heavy user of Jenkins and performs code reviews as a matter of course. Pair programming didn't go down that well, and I eventually stopped my efforts to promote it, but I feel like it resulted in developers communicating more than they used to, even if they didn't do it in a pair programming setting.

EXPLAIN TECHNICAL DEBT

If the Traditionalist doesn't see the point in refactoring a legacy system and claims that the status quo is working just fine, it may be worth explaining to them the concept of *technical debt*.

> **TECHNICAL DEBT** Debt as a metaphor for the accumulation of unresolved issues in a software project is an idea first noted by Ward Cunningham, who is also the inventor of the wiki.

Most likely the Traditionalist has been working on the system for years, so they haven't noticed that the accumulated technical debt has been gradually slowing down their development speed. Every quick hack, every copy-pasted fragment of code, every good-enough-for-now bug fix is a new piece of technical debt, which increases the amount of interest that the team has to pay. In other words, whenever the team wants to make a new change to the codebase, they have to spend a disproportionate amount of time working around quirks in the codebase rather than focusing on what they're actually trying to do. But because this process is gradual and cumulative, it's hard to notice it happening if you work with the same code every day. It sometimes takes a fresh pair of eyes to see just how glacial a project has become.

It's easiest to drive the point home if you have some hard data. If you keep records in your issue-tracking system of when a bug was registered and when it was fixed, try comparing the time to fix a bug a few years ago to how long it takes to fix a similar bug now. Most likely you'll find evidence that development speed is decreasing.

Of course, technical debt is not only about development speed. Accumulated debt also negatively affects a project's flexibility. For example, imagine that your biggest competitor just added shiny new feature X to their product. Your boss, in a panic, asks you how quickly you can add similar functionality to your own product. You sit down with your team and start sketching out a design, but it turns out that, given the complexity and fragility of the existing codebase, adding feature X is practically impossible. This is not what your boss wants to hear, but it's a direct consequence of accumulated technical debt.

3.1.2 *The Iconoclast*

The Iconoclast is a developer who abhors legacy code. They're not satisfied until they've fixed every file in the codebase. They can't bear to see a poorly written piece of code, and their definition of poorly written often approximates written by somebody else.

Ironically, the Iconoclast is sometimes also a dogmatist. For example, if they happen to be a zealous adherent of test-driven development (TDD), they may make it their personal mission to work through the whole of a legacy codebase and rewrite it using TDD.

The Iconoclast is obviously passionate about improving the quality of code, which is a good thing, but if left unchecked and allowed to proceed with their rogue refactoring missions, they can cause havoc.

Refactoring is an inherently risky business, even when done right. Every time you make a change to the code, there's the possibility of human error leading to a bug. And when the Iconoclast starts rewriting so much of the code that it's impossible to properly review, then there's a high probability of a regression creeping in somewhere. It goes without saying that creating new bugs is exactly the opposite of what we want to achieve with refactoring.

Excessive refactoring and rewriting of other people's code can have unintended social effects as well as technical ones. When other developers see the Iconoclast ruthlessly and indiscriminately rewriting their code, it can lead to resentment and a deterioration of the team's morale. They'll become less inclined to communicate with the Iconoclast, so less knowledge will be shared within the team.

Here are a few ways you can channel the Iconoclast's passion into more useful activities, without adversely affecting their motivation to improve the code.

CODE REVIEW

Make it a rule that no changes can be merged into your master branch without first passing code review. Then make it clear that you'll only review changes of a sensible size, and any changes that are too large will be rejected. After having their changes rejected a few times, the Iconoclast will soon learn to dial it down and split their changes into more manageable chunks.

AUTOMATED TESTS

Another good rule to introduce is that all changes must be accompanied by automated tests. Having to write a test for every change will slow down the Iconoclast's rampage, and the tests will help to reduce the probability of regressions, especially if combined with code review. Don't forget, of course, that you need to review the tests as well as the production code.

PAIR PROGRAMMING

Pair programming can work equally well for the Iconoclast as for the Traditionalist. With the Iconoclast as the driver doing the refactoring, you as navigator can guide them toward the most useful places to refactor and prevent them from spending excessive time on refactoring unimportant parts of the codebase.

DEMARCATE AREAS OF CODE

When it comes to refactoring, not all code is equal. Some components of the codebase are more valuable to the team than others, and some are also more risky than others. For example, refactoring to improve (make more readable and easier to maintain and extend) a commonly updated part of the codebase is more valuable than refactoring a piece of code that was scheduled to be replaced anyway. Similarly, a small, self-contained piece of code is less risky to refactor than one that's depended on by many other components, because any regression introduced by refactoring will have a smaller effect on the overall system.

Deciding whether and how to refactor a given piece of code requires an understanding of this balance between value and risk that the Iconoclast may lack. Discussing as a team which areas of the codebase are most important and which are most risky may help the Iconoclast to focus their efforts on more useful, less risky refactorings.

Tales from The Site

To be honest, I was the most Iconoclastic member of the team maintaining The Site, and I introduced code reviews partly to save me from myself. I was desperate to refactor the mountains of legacy code that I encountered, but I knew that overzealous refactoring could be dangerous. I introduced a code review policy partly so that developers could check my changes, but also to deliberately slow myself down.

3.1.3 *It's all about communication*

When you're working to achieve consensus on a team's goals and refactoring plans, by far the most important factor is having a team that communicates well. Many development teams find it surprisingly difficult to communicate useful information about the code that they work on, even if the team's members work in the same office and interact with each other on a daily basis.

Although every team is unique, and there's no silver bullet to get people communicating, here are a few techniques that I've used in the past.

CODE REVIEW

Although code review is often thought of as a technique to check for mistakes in code, it also has a couple of other benefits, arguably just as important.

First, it's a chance for the reviewer to share their knowledge. For example, a reviewer might point out that the code's input-validation logic, while correct, is not consistent with how validation is done elsewhere in the codebase. Or they may suggest a more efficient algorithm for the data processing that the code performs.

Second, it allows the code author to show the rest of the team what they've written. This keeps everybody in the loop about what kind of code is being added to the codebase, which helps to reduce unnecessary code duplication. If I see in a review that somebody has written a utility class to help with data caching, I may decide to reuse that class in my own code later. Without the review, I probably wouldn't know that the class existed, so I'd end up writing my own class to do exactly the same thing.

PAIR PROGRAMMING

Pair programming, in which two developers sit side-by-side and write code together, can be a great way to get people communicating. Its real-time conversational nature can engender a more uninhibited exchange of ideas than the more formal setting of a code review.

Conversely, pair programming is exhausting! I usually find that I can only last an hour or two before the stress of having somebody watch me write code becomes too much to bear. Some people take to it more than others, and some pairs work better than others, so it's best to leave it up to individual developers whether and how they want to pair up. Speaking from experience, any attempt to enforce mandatory pair programming is likely to end in failure.

SPECIAL EVENTS

Any kind of event outside of the normal work routine is often a good stimulus to communication. It could be a hackathon, a regular study meeting, or maybe just going for a drink after work occasionally.

One company that I worked at had a regular biweekly event called Tech Talk. This was a one-hour event, usually on Friday afternoons, at which developers could give presentations about any kind of technology, work-related or otherwise. The sessions were short (ranging in length from 5 to 20 minutes), and the atmosphere was very laid-back, so there was no pressure to put in a lot of effort preparing slides. The event was a great success, becoming popular not only with engineers but also with designers and testers, and even friends from nearby companies occasionally attended.

3.2 *Gaining approval from the organization*

Once you and your team have agreed on what you want to refactor and how you want to do so, it's time to bring the rest of the organization on board.

3.2.1 *Make it official*

It's tempting to imagine that refactoring can be done for free. You're just tweaking code that's already been written, so it shouldn't take that long. Just do it a little at a time, whenever you have an hour to spare.

In reality, it doesn't work like this. Although it's true that you should be performing minor refactorings on a daily basis in order to keep your code in good shape, this way of working doesn't scale to larger refactorings. If you're talking about a major overhaul of a legacy application, or maybe even a full rewrite, you need dedicated time and resources.

You may also find yourself having to convince people in suits that refactoring is a worthwhile activity and in the interests of the organization. By definition, refactoring aims to preserve the existing behavior of the system, which, put another way, means that it results in zero new features, not even any bug fixes. This can make it difficult for stakeholders on the business side of things to understand the value of refactoring, and thus make them reluctant to assign resources to it.

You'll have to put on your diplomacy hat and explain to the business stakeholders why refactoring provides long-term value to the organization, but don't expect them to get it in one go. You might have to go through the process a few times. And even if you can convince them to assign resources to refactoring, be prepared for managers to try to pull the plug later when project deadlines start looming and they're looking for low priority tasks to cancel.

Even if a refactoring doesn't directly result in any new features, that doesn't necessarily mean it provides no value to the business. It's important to identify the expected business value before you start the project, making it as clear and specific as possible. For example, your value proposition might look something like this.

> *The goals of this refactoring project are to*
> - *Make it possible to implement new feature X in the future*
> - *Improve the performance of feature Y by 20%*

This not only helps when you're negotiating with stakeholders to allocate resources; it also fixes the scope of the project and acts as a reference to keep you and your team on track. Print it in massive letters and stick it to the wall of the office, tattoo it on your forehead, and write a bot to tweet it to you once a day. This reminder of the project's high-level goals will help to combat the inevitable feature creep a few months down the line.

Notice how in the preceding example I referred to specific features X and Y, rather than merely claiming that the refactoring would make it easier to implement any and all new features. Goals related to new features that are already in the pipeline are more useful to business stakeholders than nebulous assertions about improving code quality or maintainability. If you have already been asked to implement feature Z, perhaps you could make a case for a preliminary refactoring phase in order to make the implementation of that feature easier, before embarking on the actual implementation. (Splitting the project into two phases like this is usually much easier and less error-prone than trying to implement and refactor at the same time.)

> **Tales from The Site**
>
> After about six months of day-to-day refactoring, code quality was reaching a plateau, and I decided that a more drastic approach was needed. I started a project to rewrite part of The Site from scratch using new technologies. Unfortunately, setting clear goals for the project was one thing that I spectacularly failed to do, and consequently the project scope ballooned. The rewrite ended up taking over a year and spanning multiple teams and systems.

3.2.2 *Plan B: The Secret 20% Project*

If the refactoring you're planning is reasonably small, going through the process of making it official can be overkill. In cases like this, it's often faster to just go ahead and do it, rather than hemming and hawing about business value or technical minutiae. A good rule of thumb is that if a refactoring can be completed by one developer in less than a week, it's a candidate for this method.

The idea of a Secret 20% Project is simple.

1 Start working on a refactoring, without seeking authorization first.
2 Work on it a little at a time, making sure not to spend so much time on it that it interferes with your other work. (This is the meaning of the 20% in the name—you should aim to spend less than 20% of your time on it.)
3 Once you've got some results worth sharing, reveal the secret and open up your work to the team for review.
4 Bask in your teammates' praise for a job well done. Improve your work based on their feedback, until the whole team is satisfied with the quality.

Of course, there's no real need for secrecy here, and developers actively hiding information from each other on a regular basis is not a sign of a healthy team! Rather, the point is that excessive discussion before any facts are known can sometimes hinder progress, whereas building a functioning prototype and then reviewing it can be a much faster way to proceed.

I once used this method when my team decided to migrate a large codebase's version control system from Subversion (SVN) to Git. At that time the team wasn't very familiar with Git, so there was a lot of uncertainty about how difficult and risky the migration would be. People had a lot of meetings and discussions, and various rumors got started, such as that Git wouldn't be able to handle our source code's non-UTF8 encoding, or that all commits more than a few years old would be lost. These false rumors triggered more discussions, such as about whether or not the loss of ancient commits was really a problem.

Progress was slow, and when people started having meetings about meetings, I decided it was time to take matters into my own hands. After a few days of research and hacking, I was able to successfully migrate the SVN repository to Git (using the `svn2git` tool) on my local machine, and I managed to get Git wired up to our issue tracker and Jenkins server. It was easier than expected, and all the pessimistic rumors turned out to be false. When I showed my results to the team, their fears evaporated. After adding a little polish to the scripts, we were ready to perform the migration for real.

3.3 *Pick your fights*

As I mentioned when we were discussing the Iconoclast earlier in this chapter, not all refactorings are equal. Most refactorings can be categorized along three axes: value, difficulty, and risk.

Value is a measure of how useful the refactoring is to the team, and indirectly to the organization as a whole. For example, imagine a script for sending emails. It was written many years ago by a Perl guru who has now left the company and consists of 2,000 lines of mind-bending Perl code. For the most part it works well, but every few months somebody has to volunteer to dive in and add a new feature. This code isn't causing the team too much trouble, so it shouldn't be a high priority for refactoring.

Now imagine that the build script for your software is broken, meaning that developers have to manually copy files from one directory to another every time they compile the code. Fixing this should obviously be a higher priority than the mailer script.

Difficulty is, of course, a measure of how easy or hard it is to perform a given refactoring. Deleting dead code and splitting up long methods are relatively easy tasks, whereas more substantial refactorings such as removing a large piece of global state requires more effort.

Risk is often related to the amount of code that depends on the code you want to refactor. The more dependents a piece of code has, the more likely it is that a change will have an unexpected side effect.

There are a couple of standard categories of refactorings that I recommend focusing on. You should be able to use the data you collected in chapter 2, such as Find-Bugs warnings, to help you find them.

- *Low-hanging fruit (risk = low, difficulty = low)*—These are a good place to start.
- *Pain points (value = high)*—Fix enough of these, and your team will treat you like a hero!

Figure 3.2 shows where these categories of refactorings lie on the three axes: value, difficulty, and risk.

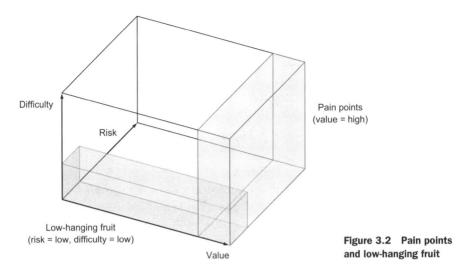

Figure 3.2 **Pain points and low-hanging fruit**

3.4   *Decision time: refactor or rewrite?*

The most important decision that you and your team will have to make when you decide to revitalize any piece of legacy software is whether to refactor or rewrite. Is it possible to pull the code's quality back up to a reasonable level using refactoring methods, or is it faster and easier to throw the code away and write a replacement from scratch?

Refactor, rewrite, or replace

You may have noticed that I just presented you with a false dichotomy. In fact, when you're looking to improve or replace a piece of legacy software, refactoring and rewriting aren't the only options available.

Before you commit to rolling your own solution to a problem, remember that every line of code you write will need to be maintained for years to come. Make sure you've also thoroughly investigated the feasibility of replacing your in-house software with a third-party solution, either commercial or open source. In terms of maintenance cost, the best code is no code at all, as explained in the excellent "The Best Code is No Code At All" blog post by Jeff Atwood: http://blog.codinghorror.com/the-best-code-is-no-code-at-all/.

A lot of in-house software was written because there was no third-party alternative at the time it was developed, but the marketplace may have changed dramatically since then. For example, many websites use a homegrown pageview tracking system, whereby a beacon (usually an <img> tag) is placed on every page. The tracking system may include scripts to parse the web server log files, a database to store the parsed events, and more scripts to query that DB, calculate aggregates, and produce a variety of reports.

> **(continued)**
> All of this adds up to a lot of code that needs to be maintained. At the time the system was developed, it was probably a reasonable solution, but if you were to build a similar site nowadays you'd most likely use a third-party system such as Google Analytics. Because it's hosted on Google's servers, it requires virtually zero maintenance on your side, and it probably provides far more functionality than your homegrown scripts.

Assuming that you've decided against a third-party solution, it's often tempting to opt for the rewrite. After all, writing a brand new system from scratch is more fun than refactoring an old one, right? Rewriting gives you complete freedom to design the perfect architecture, unencumbered by existing code, and correct all the mistakes of the previous system. Unfortunately life is never that simple, and there are plenty of downsides to rewriting as well. Let's go through some of the arguments for and against a full rewrite, so that you can hopefully make an informed and unbiased decision.

3.4.1   *The case against a rewrite*

Let me make it clear right from the start: I believe that a full rewrite is almost always a bad idea. But don't just take my word as gospel—let me try to convince you. Let's look at some detailed arguments against rewriting.

RISK

Rewriting a legacy system is a major software development project. Depending on the size of the original system, it could take months or even years to complete. All development projects of this scale carry a certain amount of risk. Any number of things can go wrong.

- The software might have an unacceptably high bug count.
- Even if the software is stable and bug-free, it might not do what users want.
- The project might take longer to complete than originally planned, and thus overrun its budget.
- You might discover halfway through the project that the architecture is fundamentally unworkable and end up scrapping all the code you've written so far.
- Even worse, you might not discover these architectural weaknesses until you release the software to users, and it turns out to be totally unstable under load.

These risks are inherent to all software projects, and although there are software development best practices that can help to mitigate them, it's undeniable that they exist. In comparison, making changes to an existing codebase is much less risky. The existing system has likely been running in production for years, so you're working against a foundation that has already proven itself to be reasonably trustworthy.

If you look at a rewrite from the perspective of the business stakeholders, it's quite an unappealing prospect. In general, the rewritten system will work pretty much the same as the old one, so it's a huge chunk of risk with no perceivable benefit.

In addition to the preceding examples, a rewrite of an existing system comes with its own particular risk: the risk of regressions. The existing software encodes, in program source code, the entire specification of the system, including every business rule. Unless you can guarantee to find every single one of these business rules and accurately port them to the new system, the behavior of the system will change as a result of the rewrite. If this change in behavior is significant to even one end user, you have a regression on your hands.

The existing source code also contains many years' worth of bug fixes, which you'll need to find, understand, and port if you want to avoid regressions. If you're not careful, you're likely to make exactly the same mistakes that the developers did when they wrote the original software many moons ago.

For example, developers often think only about the *happy path* of the code, and fail to provide sufficient handling for error cases. Imagine you're rewriting a system that makes an API call to a remote service. The developer of the original system never considered the case where the remote system takes a very long time to respond, so they didn't add a timeout to the network request. One day, a few years later, this very case occurred in production, prompting them to add a timeout. Now, if you repeat his original mistake and forget to include a timeout in your new code ... congratulations, you've created a regression.

It's sobering to think that a bug that was first created ten years ago, and successfully fixed five years ago, could rear its ugly head again thanks to your rewrite.

Refactoring can also lead to regressions, but the risk is generally lower. A disciplined refactoring in which you perform a sequence of small, well-defined transformations (some of which we'll look at in the next chapter) against an existing codebase should in theory preserve the behavior of the software. After each step of the refactoring you can stop, perform code reviews, and run automated tests to check that the behavior hasn't changed before moving on to the next transformation. In a rewrite, on the other hand, you're starting with nothing and attempting to build something that perfectly emulates the behavior of the original software. Which do you think is easier: taking the ceiling of the Sistine Chapel and swapping some of the frescoes around, or trying to recreate Michelangelo's handiwork from scratch?

OVERHEAD

Engineers often underestimate the amount of overhead involved in setting up a new software project from scratch. There's a lot of uninteresting boilerplate to be written to get a piece of software off the ground: build files, logging utilities, database access code, utilities to help with reading configuration files, and many other bits and pieces that you never really notice when you're working with a project that's already mature. Of course, you'd probably use a variety of open source libraries to take care of this stuff (for example, you might use Logback as your logging library for a Java project).

But configuring these libraries, writing wrappers and helpers for them, and wiring them all together takes time and effort. If you're using Spring MVC to build a web application, it's easy to waste a whole day on setting up the various XML files and pro-grammatic configuration needed to get Spring up and running, for example.

It might be possible to alleviate some of the burden of writing boilerplate code by borrowing code from the codebase that you're replacing. If you're planning to reuse the same database, you might be able to lift the DB access code and model classes directly from the old project and use a mishmash of bridges, wrappers, and adapters to squeeze them into the new codebase. This can be useful as a stopgap measure, allowing you to get up and running quickly and move on to more interesting work. But you should always have a plan to remove or refactor this code later. If you never get around to refactoring out this legacy code, or if you find yourself transplanting huge swaths of legacy code into your new codebase, then you may actually be doing a very roundabout and inefficient refactoring, disguised as a rewrite.

There's also a checklist of administrative tasks to be performed, such as registering a new project on the issue tracker, setting up jobs on the continuous integration server, and maybe creating a new mailing list. If the software is a service, such as a web-site or a backend system, then there's also a variety of ops-related work to be done: you need to provision a machine on which to run the service, set up databases and caches, write rollout scripts, set up monitoring and add a health-check API, manage log files, and sort out backups ... the list is surprisingly long. Oh, and don't forget that you probably need to do this for three or four different environments!

It's also worth remembering that the operations cost of a new service is ongoing, not just a one-off payment at the start of the project. In the long term, at least until you manage to completely switch off the old system, you have one extra system to maintain, monitor, and keep running smoothly.

ALWAYS TAKES LONGER THAN EXPECTED

Even taking account of the overhead just described, and factoring in developers' ten-dency to wildly underestimate the amount of work required, rewrites still invariably overrun.

Estimating the size of a software project is notoriously difficult, and the larger the project, the more difficult it becomes. A colleague of mine once showed me an inter-esting visual analogy to this problem. If I show you a standard A5 notepad and ask you how much bigger it is than an iPhone, you could probably take a guess and be reason-ably confident in your answer. (I would say an A5 notebook is the size of three or four iPhones.) Now repeat the experiment, this time with a cinema screen instead of a notepad. How many times bigger is a cinema screen than an iPhone? A thousand times? Ten thousand? I have no idea!

In this analogy, the iPhone is a known, easy-to-estimate unit of work, such as a devel-opment task that takes one engineer one day to complete. The notepad is a small proj-ect that's easy to split into iPhone-sized tasks, whereas the cinema screen is a much larger project as shown in figure 3.3. The project is so large that it's difficult to see from the start how it will be split up into tasks, or how big each of those tasks will be.

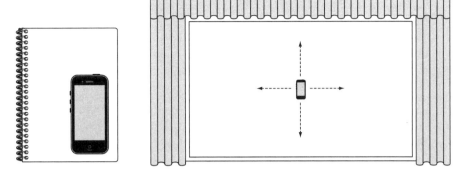

Figure 3.3 Estimating the size of a project: how many iPhones fit in a cinema screen?

A while ago I ported the UI portion of a reasonably large application from one Scala web framework to another. I estimated that it would take about two days, but in fact it took over a week. The main reason that it took so much longer than expected was that it involved a large number of small tasks. I underestimated how long an average task would take, and my estimation error was multiplied by the number of tasks.

Because rewrites are usually long-running projects, and even more so because they tend to overrun, you'll need a plan to handle any changes that occur in the original software while the replacement is being developed. There are three options here, none of them ideal.

- *Freeze all development on the original software for the entirety of the rewrite.* This is likely to make users unhappy.
- *Allow development to continue, and do your best to keep up with the constantly changing specs.* This can dramatically slow down your rewrite project, because you're working against a moving target.
- *Allow development to continue, but don't try to implement any changes in the rewrite.* Instead, implement against a snapshot of the spec when you started, and keep track of all changes that need to be implemented. Once the rewrite is nearly complete, freeze development on the original software and port the entire backlog of changes over to the new version.

Major refactoring projects can be equally difficult to estimate and thus can also overrun, but the key difference is that it's easier to gain incremental benefits from refactoring. Even if your refactoring overruns and you decide to stop halfway through, it's likely that you'll have made some useful improvements to your codebase. A full rewrite provides no value until it's finished, so once you commit to it, you have to see it through to the bitter end, even if it overruns.

GREENFIELD DOESN'T STAY GREEN FOR LONG

A lot of rewrites tend to go something like this:

1 Start with a fresh, clean design and well-organized models, free from the implementation cruft that has built up in the legacy code.

2 Implement a few features and start to realize that your model doesn't work quite as well as you expected. It's too abstract, requiring a lot of boilerplate, so you add helper code to handle a few common cases.

3 Remember that crazy, obscure feature that everybody said was no longer needed? Well it turns out that some users still rely on it, so you'll have to add support for it.

4 Stumble across some data in the DB that, as far as you know, can't possibly exist. After a bit of detective work, you discover that it was caused by a bug that was fixed a few years ago. Even though it shouldn't exist, you'll need to add a check for it.

5 Take a step back and compare your implementation with the code you're trying to replace. In many cases you'll find that they are eerily similar.

It often turns out that what first appeared to be "implementation cruft" is in fact "complicated spec," and there's not much you can do about it.

3.4.2 *Benefits of rewriting from scratch*

Of course, rewriting software from scratch also provides some benefits over refactoring.

FREEDOM

Writing new code from scratch gives you the freedom to slay some sacred cows—code in the original codebase that you were too afraid to touch. Psychologically, refactoring or deleting a piece of existing code, in the knowledge that this might cause a regression, is very difficult to do, whereas you'll be less inhibited when writing replacement code from scratch.

I once worked on a site whose authentication logic was infamous among developers for being extremely complex and fragile. Nobody wanted to touch it, for fear of causing regressions. Creating an authentication bug, resulting in users not being able to log in to the site, is pretty much the worst thing you can do, short of deleting user data. But when we came to rewrite the site, the actual authentication spec turned out to be quite simple. A lot of complexity in the existing code was related to a legacy spec that was no longer needed, but we could only discover this by rewriting from scratch. Sometimes when working with legacy code, it's hard to see the wood for the trees.

On a broader level, writing from scratch allows you to avoid being unduly influenced by the existing code. When you write code within the paradigm of an existing codebase, it's natural to be constricted by the design and implementation of the surrounding code, for better or for worse. I once worked on a legacy Java application that made heavy use of a so-called God class, a 3,000-line monster filled with static utility methods. When adding new code to this application, it was practically impossible to avoid using this class, even though I shed a tear every time I referenced it. It was also tempting to keep adding more crud to the God class, and the existing design made it virtually impossible to write the code any other way.

TESTABILITY

A lot of legacy code has very few automated tests and was not designed with testability in mind. Once code has been written, it's very difficult to retroactively add testability, so writing tests for legacy code can take a prohibitive amount of developer time and effort.

When writing from scratch, on the other hand, you can build testability into the design from the start. While there's plenty of scope for debate about the true value of unit testing and how much testability should be allowed to influence design, having the freedom to make your code as testable as you like is certainly useful.

In chapter 4 we'll talk more about how to test when refactoring legacy code.

3.4.3 *Necessary conditions for a rewrite*

Given the preceding pros and cons, and based on personal experience, I strongly recommend erring on the side of refactoring by default. The considerable risk and overhead associated with starting a new project often outweigh the potential benefits. But there's always a point at which a codebase becomes impossible to salvage using refactoring alone, and a rewrite becomes the only option. I believe there are two necessary conditions that must both be fulfilled before a rewrite should be considered.

REFACTORING TRIED AND FAILED

Before attempting a rewrite, refactoring should always be your first option. Some legacy codebases are more amenable to refactoring than others, and it's hard to know in advance how successful a refactoring will be. The best way to find out is to dive into the code and try it. Only once you've spent a considerable amount of time and effort on refactoring, without a noticeable improvement in quality, is it time to start considering a full rewrite.

Even if you do opt for a rewrite in the end, it's still worth attempting a refactoring first. It's a great way to learn about the codebase, and it can throw up some valuable insights about how best to design and implement the replacement system.

PARADIGM SHIFT

If you've decided that a fundamental change in technology is in the best interests of the team and the organization, a rewrite is often the only option. The most common change associated with a rewrite is a change in implementation language. For example, you may want to port a COBOL mainframe app to Java because COBOL engineers are becoming too rare and expensive. Or your company may be making a strategic move from technologies such as Spring MVC to a more lightweight framework such as Ruby on Rails in the hope of improving developer productivity.

Tales from The Site

We thought long and hard before deciding to rewrite The Site. We had been gradually refactoring for about six months, with visible improvements to code quality as a result. But development was still a constant struggle, and velocity was low. It was obvious that we needed to take drastic measures in order to make the system more maintainable and allow us to keep up with the pace of modern web development.

At that time the Scala programming language was gaining momentum within the company. A lot of developers, including myself, were interested in Scala and the productivity benefits it promised. We decided that the time was right to bite the bullet and rewrite The Site, and that Scala was the right tool for the job.

3.4.4 *The Third Way: incremental rewrite*

Sometimes you'll really want to rewrite at least some of an application, but a full rewrite carries too much risk and doesn't provide any value to the business until the big-bang cutover at the end of the project. In this case, it's worth considering whether the rewrite could be performed incrementally.

The Third Way

The Third Way is a branch of political theory that attempts to find a compromise between the extremes of socialism and capitalism by advocating a combination of right-wing economic and left-wing social policies.

It is relevant to us inasmuch as it preaches moderation between two extremes. Refactoring is low-risk but provides limited benefits, while a full rewrite is risky but more powerful. If we find a middle path between the two then we can get the best of both worlds.

The basic idea is to split the rewrite into a number of smaller phases, but it's important to stress two points:

- Each individual phase should provide business value.
- It should be possible to stop the project after any given phase, and still reap some benefits.

If you can structure the rewrite in this way, it substantially decreases the amount of risk you face. Instead of a monolithic year-long rewrite project, which requires a lot of faith and patience from the business stakeholders, even though it may fail in myriad ways, you now have a series of month-long mini-rewrites, which are less risky and more manageable. After each phase is complete, you can perform a release, providing value to the organization. The developers also get their hands on the shiny new code more quickly, so they're happier too.

With a traditional rewrite, once you've committed to the rewrite you have to see it through to the bitter end. If you stop halfway, you've wasted months of developer time, and usually you have nothing to show for it. Splitting the rewrite into self-contained phases, however, allows you to stop the project before completion and still end up with some useful results.

One way to split up a rewrite is to divide the legacy software into a number of logical components and then rewrite them one at a time. As an example of how to do this, let's look at an imaginary e-commerce site, Orinoco.com. The site is implemented as a monolithic Java servlet application, and its main features include

- *Listings*—Shows a list of products, organized by category
- *Search*—Allows the user to search for products by keyword
- *Recommendations*—The machine-learning algorithm for deciding what products to recommend to users
- *Checkout*—Payment, gift wrapping, delivery address, and so on
- *My Page*—Lets users view their past orders and recommended purchases
- *Authentication*—User logins and logouts

ORINOCO The Orinoco is one of the longest rivers in South America. It's also the name of my favorite Womble (http://en.wikipedia.org/wiki/The_Wombles).

Because the site already has a list of self-contained features, it makes sense to split it into components along the same lines, with one component per function. Note that this approach also allows you to blur the line between refactoring and rewriting. Some parts of the application may be in better shape than others, so once you have a well-defined public interface for each component, you can decide on a per-component basis whether to refactor the implementation or rewrite it completely.

In cases like this it's common to re-architect the monolithic site into a service-oriented architecture consisting of one front end and a number of back-end services. We'll discuss that approach in detail in chapter 5, but for the purposes of this example let's keep the monolithic design. Instead of splitting into services, we'll have one Java library (JAR) per component, with all of them running inside the same JVM.

Table 3.1 shows a possible plan for the first few phases of an incremental rewrite of Orinoco.com.

Table 3.1 Rewriting Orinoco.com

Phase	Description	Business value
0	Preliminary refactoring. Define component interfaces, split components into separate JARs.	Clear interfaces increase code maintainability.
1	Rewrite Authentication component. Change the way passwords are stored.	Better compliance with data security regulations.

Table 3.1 Rewriting Orinoco.com *(continued)*

Phase	Description	Business value
2	Rewrite Search component. Switch to different search engine implementation.	Better quality search results. Easier for users to find products.
3	Refactor Recommendations component.	Can test different recommendation algorithms more quickly.

The rest of the components could be dealt with one by one in much the same way. The project could be continued for as long as the stakeholders feel it's providing value, and the order of the phases could be chopped and changed depending on business priorities. As you can see, splitting up a rewrite like this provides stakeholders with a lot more control.

> **Strangler**
>
> At this point it would be remiss of me not to mention Martin Fowler's Strangler pattern, as it bears a lot of similarities to the incremental method described here. In a Strangler rewrite, the new system is built around the outside of the existing one, intercepting its inputs and outputs and gradually assuming responsibility for more and more functionality, until eventually the original system quietly dies.
>
> Martin Fowler can explain it much better than I, so I'll simply direct you to his website for further reading: http://martinfowler.com/bliki/StranglerApplication.html.

3.5   *Summary*

- Improving a legacy codebase has to be a team effort, so you need to make sure your team is communicating well and working toward common goals before you start.
- Refactoring can't be done just for the sake of it. It must provide business value, and all stakeholders must be on board. The project should also be given clear goals, so that everybody knows when it's finished and whether it succeeded.
- Any major change to a codebase should be evaluated in terms of value, difficulty, and risk.
- As a rule of thumb, consider your options in the following order: replace (purchase a third-party solution), refactor, rewrite.
- Make large changes incrementally, applying them to one component of the software at a time instead of attacking the entire codebase at once.

Refactoring 4

This chapter covers

- Methods for maintaining discipline when refactoring
- Common smells found in legacy code, and refactoring techniques for removing them
- Using automated tests to support refactoring

In this chapter we'll look at your most important weapon in the fight against legacy, namely *refactoring*. I'll introduce some general tips for effective refactoring, as well as a few specific refactorings that I often use in real-world code. We'll also look at techniques for writing tests for legacy code, which is vital if you want assurance that your refactoring work hasn't broken anything.

4.1 Disciplined refactoring

Before we start looking at specific refactoring techniques, I want to talk about the importance of discipline when refactoring code. When performed correctly, refactoring should be perfectly safe. You can refactor all day long without fear of introducing any bugs. But if you're not careful, what started out as a simple refactoring can rapidly spiral out of control, and before you know it you've edited half the files in the project, and you're staring at an IDE full of red crosses. At this point you have to make a heart-wrenching decision: should you give up and revert half a day's work, or keep going and try to get the project back into a compiling state? Even if you can reach the other side, you have no guarantee that the software still works as it's supposed to.

The life of a software developer is stressful enough without having to make decisions like that, so let's look at some ways to avoid getting into that situation.

4.1.1   *Avoiding the Macbeth Syndrome*

> *I am in blood*
> *Stepped in so far that, should I wade no more,*
> *Returning were as tedious as go o'er.*
>
> —Macbeth, act 3, scene 4

When Macbeth uttered these words, he'd already done away with his beloved King Duncan, two innocent guards, and his best friend Banquo, and he was debating with himself whether to stop the carnage or to carry on slaughtering people until he had no enemies left. (In the end he chooses the latter path, and, suffice it to say, it doesn't work out.)

Now, if I'm interpreting the text correctly, and this may come as quite a shock to the Shakespeare scholars among you, the Scottish play was actually intended to be an allegory about undisciplined refactoring. Macbeth, spurred on by a feature request from his wife and Project Manager, Lady Macbeth, starts out with the simple aim of removing a piece of global mutable state called King Duncan. He succeeds in this, but it turns out that there were some implicit dependencies that also needed to be refactored. Macbeth tries to tackle all of these at once, leading to excessive amounts of change, and the refactoring rapidly becomes unsustainable. In the end, our hero is attacked by trees and decapitated, which is pretty much the worst result I can imagine for a failed refactoring.

So what can we do to avoid ending up like poor Macbeth? Let's look at a few simple techniques.

4.1.2   *Separate refactoring from other work*

Often you realize that a piece of code is ripe for refactoring when you're actually trying to do something else. You may have opened the file in your editor in order to fix a bug or add a new feature, but then decide that you may as well refactor the code at the same time.

For example, imagine you've been asked to make a change to the following Java class.

```
/**
 * Note: This class should NOT be extended -- Dave, 4/5/2009
 */
public class Widget extends Entity {
    int id;
    boolean isStable;
```

```
    public String getWidgetId() {
        return "Widget_" + id;
    }

    @Override
    public String getEntityId() {
        return "Widget_" + id;
    }

    @Override
    public String getCacheKey() {
        return "Widget_" + id;
    }

    @Override
    public int getCacheExpirySeconds() {
        return 60; // cache for one minute
    }

    @Override
    public boolean equals(Object obj) {
        ...
    }

}
```

The specification for widgets has changed so that the cache expiry of a widget should depend on the value of its isStable flag. You've been asked to update the logic in the #getCacheExpirySeconds() method accordingly. But as soon as you glance at the code, you notice a number of things you'd like to refactor.

- There's a comment from some guy called Dave saying the class shouldn't be extended, so why not mark it as final?
- The fields are mutable and they have package-private visibility. This is a dangerous combination, as it means other objects might change their values. Maybe they should be private and/or final?
- There is redundancy among the various ID/key-generating methods. The ID generation logic could be factored out into one place.
- The class overrides #equals(Object) but not #hashCode(). This is bad form and can lead to some nasty bugs.
- There's no comment explaining the meaning of the isStable flag. It might be nice to add one.

The actual change to the cache expiry logic is quite simple, so it's tempting to combine it with a spot of refactoring. But be careful! Some of the refactorings in the preceding list are more complex than they first appear.

- Even though Dave says we shouldn't extend Widget, maybe somebody already did. If there are any subclasses of Widget anywhere in the project, then marking the class as final will cause compilation errors. You'll have to go through the subclasses one by one and decide what should be done about them. Is it OK to extend `Widget` after all? Or should those subclasses be fixed to remove the inheritance?

- What about those mutable fields? Is anybody actually mutating them? If so, should they be? If you want to make them immutable, you'll have to change any code that is currently relying on their mutability.
- Although the lack of a `#hashCode()` method is generally a Bad Thing in Java code, there might be some code somewhere that actually relies on this behavior. (I've seen code like this in the wild.) You'll have to check all code that deals with `Widgets`. Also, if the person who wrote `Widget` (Dave?) also wrote any other entity classes, the chances are that they're all missing this method. If you decide to fix all of them, it might become a much larger job.

If you try to take on all this refactoring at the same time as the change you were originally planning, that's a lot of stuff to fit in your head. Maybe you're a refactoring wizard, in which case go for it, but I wouldn't trust myself to handle that kind of cognitive load without making any mistakes.

It's much safer to split the work into stages: either make the change, then refactor, or vice versa. Don't try to do both at the same time. Splitting refactoring work and other changes into separate commits in your version control system also makes it easier for you and other developers both to review the changes and to make sense of what you were doing when you revisit the code later.

4.1.3   *Lean on the IDE*

Modern IDEs provide good support for the most popular refactoring patterns. They can perform refactorings automatically, which obviously has a number of benefits over performing them by hand.

- *Faster*—The IDE can update hundreds of classes in milliseconds. Doing this by hand would take a prohibitively long time.
- *Safer*—They're not infallible, but IDEs make far fewer mistakes than humans when updating code.
- *More thorough*—The IDE often takes care of things that I hadn't even thought of, such as updating references inside code comments and renaming test classes to match the corresponding production classes.
- *More efficient*—A lot of refactoring is boring drudge work, which is what computers were designed to do. Leave it to the IDE while you, rock star programmer that you are, get on with more important things!

To give you a taste of what the IDE is capable of, figure 4.1 shows a screenshot of IntelliJ IDEA's Refactor menu for a Java project. (Your menu might look slightly different, depending on what IDE you use and what plugins you have installed.) It's definitely worth the time to go through each of your IDE's refactoring options, try them out on some real code, and see what they do.

Figure 4.1   IntelliJ's Refactor menu

As an example of what your IDE can do for you, let's use IntelliJ IDEA to help us replace a large and unwieldy constructor using the Builder pattern. Figure 4.2 shows a Java class that represents a tweet. As you can see, the large number of fields results in a constructor that's frankly ridiculous.

Figure 4.3 shows an example of using the class's constructor directly. It's very hard to read, and a lot of the fields are optional, so this is an ideal candidate for using the Builder pattern.

```java
public final class Tweet {
    private final Coordinates coordinates;
    private final boolean favorited;
    private final boolean truncated;
    private final Date createdAt;
    private final Entities entities;
    private final Long inReplyToUserId;
    private final List<Contributor> contributors;
    private final String text;
    private final int retweetCount;
    private final Long inReplyToStatusId;
    private final long id;
    private final Geo geo;
    private final boolean retweeted;
    private final boolean possiblySensitive;
    private final String place;
    private final User user;
    private final String inReplyToScreenName;
    private final String source;

    public Tweet(Coordinates coordinates, boolean favorited, boolean truncated, Date createdAt,
                 Entities entities, Long inReplyToUserId, List<Contributor> contributors, String text,
                 int retweetCount, Long inReplyToStatusId, long id, Geo geo,
                 boolean retweeted, boolean possiblySensitive, String place,
                 User user, String inReplyToScreenName, String source) {
        this.coordinates = coordinates;
        this.favorited = favorited;
        this.truncated = truncated;
        this.createdAt = createdAt;
        this.entities = entities;
        this.inReplyToUserId = inReplyToUserId;
        this.contributors = contributors;
        this.text = text;
        this.retweetCount = retweetCount;
        this.inReplyToStatusId = inReplyToStatusId;
        this.id = id;
        this.geo = geo;
        this.retweeted = retweeted;
        this.possiblySensitive = possiblySensitive;
        this.place = place;
        this.user = user;
        this.inReplyToScreenName = inReplyToScreenName;
        this.source = source;
    }

    // getters, other methods ...

}
```

Figure 4.2   A Java class representing a tweet

```java
private final Tweet myTweet = new Tweet(
    null, false, false, new Date(), new Entities(),
    null, Collections.<Contributor>emptyList(),
    "hello world", 123, null, 456789, null, false,
    false, null, new User(), null, "twitter.com"
);
```

Figure 4.3   Using the Tweet constructor directly

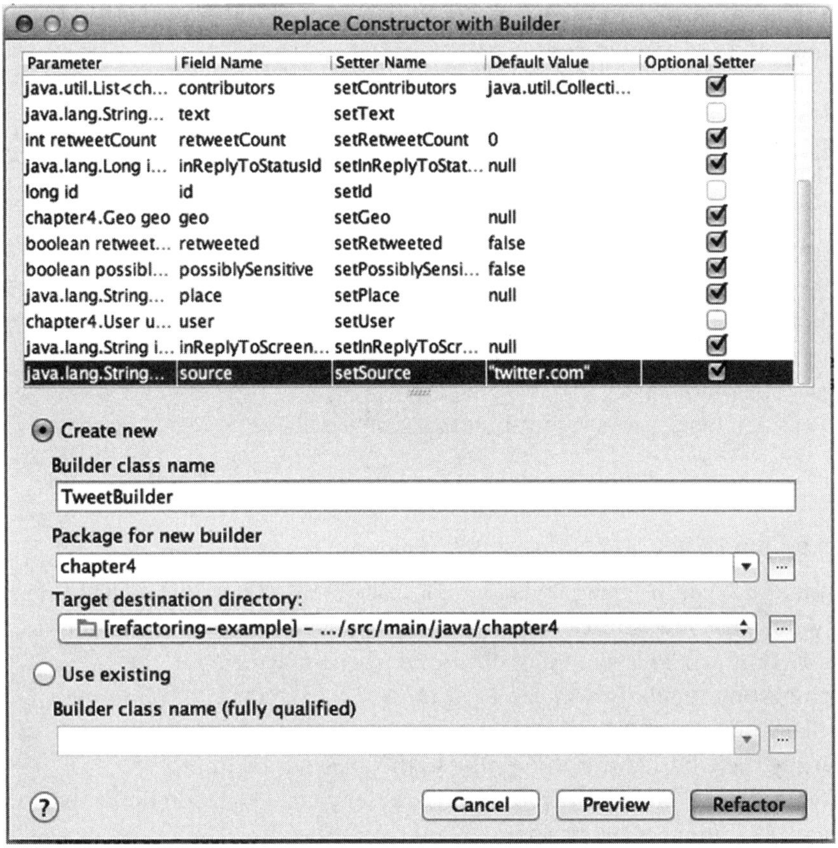

Figure 4.4 The Replace Constructor with Builder wizard

Let's ask IntelliJ to create a Builder to fix this mess. Figure 4.4 shows the Replace Constructor with Builder wizard, where I can set default values for optional fields.

When I click the Refactor button, the IDE generates a new class called `Tweet-Builder`. It also automatically rewrites any code that's calling the `Tweet` constructor, updating it to use `TweetBuilder` instead. After a little manual reformatting, the code to create a new `Tweet` now looks like figure 4.5. Much better!

```
private final Tweet myTweet = new TweetBuilder()
        .setId(456789)
        .setText("hello world")
        .setRetweetCount(123)
        .setUser(new User())
        .createTweet();
```

Figure 4.5 Creating a `Tweet` using `TweetBuilder`

IDEs make mistakes too

Occasionally the IDE can get it wrong. Sometimes it's overzealous, trying to update files that are completely unrelated to the change you want to make. If you rename a method called `execute()`, the IDE might try to update an unrelated code comment such as "I will execute anybody who touches this code." Sometimes it doesn't update a file that it should. For example the IDE's dependency analysis is often foiled by the use of Java reflection.

With this in mind, it's best not to trust the IDE unconditionally:

- If the IDE offers a preview of a refactoring, inspect it carefully.
- Check that the project still compiles afterward, and run automated tests if you have them.
- Use tools like grep to get a second opinion.

4.1.4   *Lean on the VCS*

I assume that you're using a version control system (VCS) such as Git, Mercurial, or SVN to manage your source code. (If not, put this book down and go and fix that situation right now!) This can be really useful when refactoring. If you get into the habit of committing regularly, you can treat the VCS as a giant Undo button. Any time you feel like your refactoring is getting out of control, you have the freedom to back out by hitting the Undo button (reverting to the previous commit).

Refactoring is often an exploratory experience in which you don't know whether a particular solution will work out until you try it. The safety net of the VCS gives you the freedom to experiment with a number of solutions, safe in the knowledge that you can back out whenever you want. In fact, effective use of branches means that you can have a few different solutions on the go at the same time, while you explore the pros and cons of each approach.

Figure 4.6 shows an example of the Git commits and branches that might be left after a session of experimental refactoring. The newest commits are at the top. You can see that there were a couple of experimental branches that didn't end up getting merged into the master branch.

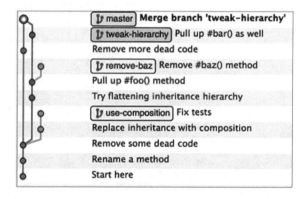

Figure 4.6   An example of using Git branches to aid refactoring

4.1.5 *The Mikado Method*

One method that I have recently been using with great success to implement large changes, including refactoring, is called the Mikado Method. It's very simple but effective. Basically it involves building up a dependency graph of all the tasks you need to perform, so that you can then execute those tasks more safely and in an optimal order. The dependency graph is constructed in an exploratory manner, with plenty of backtracking and leaning on the VCS.

For more details on the method itself and the motivations behind it, I highly recommend Ola Ellnestam and Daniel Brolund's book *The Mikado Method* (Manning, 2014).

Figure 4.7 shows an actual Mikado graph that I drew recently when I was porting the UI layer of a large application from one web framework to another.

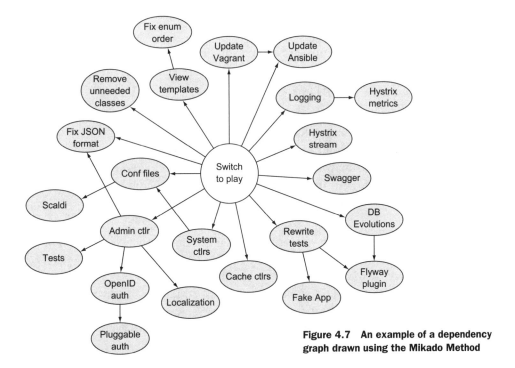

Figure 4.7   An example of a dependency graph drawn using the Mikado Method

4.2   *Common legacy code traits and refactorings*

Every legacy codebase is different, but a few common traits tend to surface time and time again when reading through legacy code. In this section we'll take a look at a few of these traits and discuss ways in which we can remove them. It's possible to devote entire books to this subject, but I only have one chapter to play with, so I've picked just a few representative examples of problems that have been especially prevalent in my own experience.

Imagine that you maintain World of RuneQuest, an online fantasy RPG. You're planning to start development on a new version of the game, but recently you've noticed that the code has become bloated and disorganized, and development velocity has dropped as a result. You want to give the codebase a thorough spring clean before you start developing the new version. Let's look at some areas you could tackle.

4.2.1 Stale code

Stale code is any code that remains in the codebase even though it's no longer needed. Deleting this unneeded code is one of the easiest, safest, and most satisfying refactoring tasks you can hope for. Because it's so easy, it's often a good way to warm up before embarking on more serious refactoring.

Removal of stale code has a number of benefits:

- It makes the code easier to understand, because there's now less code to read.
- It reduces the chance of somebody wasting time on fixing or refactoring code that isn't even used.
- As a satisfying bonus, every time you delete some code, the project's test coverage increases.

Stale code can be divided into a few categories.

COMMENTED-OUT CODE

This is the lowest of all low-hanging fruit. If you see a block of code that has been commented out, don't think twice, just delete it! There's absolutely no reason to leave commented-out code lying around. It's often left deliberately as a record of how the code was changed, but that's exactly what the version control system is for. It's pointless noise, making the surrounding code more difficult to read.

DEAD CODE

Dead code is any code in your software that will definitely never be executed. It might be a variable that's never used, a branch of an `if` statement that's never taken, or even a whole package of code that's never referenced.

In the following simple example of dead code, the `armorStrength` variable can never have a value greater than 7, so it's always less than 10 and the `else` block will never run. It's dead code and thus can and should be removed.

```
int armorStrength = 5;
if (player.hasArmorBoost()) {
    armorStrength += 2;
}
...
if (armorStrength < 10) {
    defenceRatio += 0.1;
} else {
    defenceRatio += 0.2;
}
```

Armor strength is always 7 or less, so this branch will always run.

This branch is dead code.

There are many tools that can help you find and remove dead code from your code-base. Most IDEs will point out fields, methods, and classes that aren't referenced, and tools such as FindBugs (discussed in chapter 2) also include relevant rules.

ZOMBIE CODE

Some code that's actually dead may look very much alive. I call this zombie code. Its liveliness (or lack of) is impossible to discover just from reading the surrounding source. Examples include

- Code that branches based on data received from an external source such as a database, in which some of the branches are never triggered
- Pages of a website or screens of a desktop application that are no longer linked from anywhere

As an example of the first point, let's alter the previous code sample so that the value of `armorStrength` is read from a DB. Just by reading the code, you have no idea what value `armorStrength` might have, so the code looks alive and reasonable.

```
int armorStrength = DB.getArmorStrength(play.getId());
...
if (armorStrength < 10) {
    defenceRatio += 0.1;
} else {                          Is this branch dead or alive?
    defenceRatio += 0.2;
}
```

But when you look at the actual data in the DB, you might find that all 5 million players have an armor strength of less than 10, so in fact the `else` will never run.

In this case, you should check all the places that are setting this value in the DB (to make sure that a strength of 10 or more is impossible), and then add a DB constraint to act as documentation for your understanding of the model, before finally deleting the unneeded `else` block.

In the case of pages or screens that aren't linked from anywhere, it's often difficult and time-consuming to confirm that a given page of a web application is dead. Even if there are no links to it, users might still be accessing it directly, perhaps via browser bookmarks, so you may have to trawl through web server access logs to check that the page is safe to delete.

I was affected by a real-world example of zombie code when I joined a team that maintained a large legacy web application. Before I joined the team, they'd been A/B testing a major update to the site's top page. There were two separate versions of the page, and users were directed to one or the other based on a per-user flag in the DB. Little did I know, the A/B test had already finished (the flags in the DB had all been set to the same value) but nobody had deleted the losing version of the page. So every time I had to make a change to the top page, I faithfully replicated my changes across both versions, wasting a lot of time in the process.

A/B TESTING   A/B testing is a commonly used process to investigate the effect that a change to a website will have on users' behavior. The basic idea is to introduce the change to only a limited segment of the site's users at first. Users are separated into two buckets, A and B, and one group is served the normal site, while the other is served a version of the site that includes the change. You then measure key metrics (page views, attention time, scroll depth, and so on) for each user segment and compare the results.

EXPIRED CODE

It's common for business logic to apply only within a certain timespan, especially in web applications. For example, you might run a particular ad campaign or A/B test for a few weeks. In World of RuneQuest, perhaps you run half-price sales on in-game purchases occasionally. This often requires corresponding date-specific logic in the code, so it's common to see code that looks like this:

```
if (new DateTime("2014-10-01").isBeforeNow() &&
    new DateTime("2014-11-01").isAfterNow()) {
  // do stuff ...
}
```

While there's nothing wrong with temporary code like this, developers often forget to go back and delete it after it has served its purpose, leading to a codebase littered with expired code.

There are a couple of ways of avoiding this problem. One is to file a ticket in your issue tracker to remind yourself to delete the code. In this case, make sure that the ticket has a deadline and is assigned to a specific person; otherwise it's easily ignored.

A smarter solution is to automate the check for expired code.

1 When writing code that has a limited lifespan, add a code comment in a specific format to mark it as expiring code.

2 Write a script that can search through the codebase, parse these comments, and flag any expired ones.

3 Set up your CI server to run this script regularly and fail the build if it finds any expired code. This should be much harder to ignore than a ticket in the issue tracker.

The following code shows an example of one of these comments.

```
// EXPIRES: 2014-11-01
if (new DateTime("2014-10-01").isBeforeNow() &&
    new DateTime("2014-11-01").isAfterNow()) {
  // do stuff ...
}
```

AUTOMATING EXPIRY CHECKS USING MACROS   In languages that support macros (running code at compile time), it's possible to make the project fail to compile if there's any expired code lying around. I know of a couple of Scala libraries that can do this for you: Fixme (https://github.com/tysonjh/fixme) and DoBy (https://github.com/leanovate/doby).

4.2.2 *Toxic tests*

When you're handed a legacy project to maintain, you might count yourself lucky if it includes some automated tests. They can often act as a good substitute for documentation, and the presence of tests gives a hint that the code quality might be reasonable. But be careful: there are some kinds of tests that are worse than no tests at all. I call these toxic tests. Let's have a look at some of them.

TESTS THAT DON'T TEST ANYTHING

The basic template for a good software test, no matter whether it's manual or automated, unit, functional, system, or whatever, can be summed up in just three words: given-when-then.

- *Given* some preliminary conditions and assumptions,
- *when* I do this
- *then* this should be the result.

Surprisingly often I encounter tests in legacy projects that don't fit this simple pattern. I see a lot of tests that are missing the "then" part, meaning that they don't include any assertions to check the result of the test against what was expected.

Imagine that World of RuneQuest uses an event bus to manage in-game events and their corresponding notifications. For example, when a player proposes a treaty with another player, an event is posted to the event bus. A listener might pick up this event and send a notification mail to the player in question. The event bus is implemented using a bounded queue data structure that automatically discards the oldest element when it becomes full, in order to bound the amount of memory used. Here's the JUnit 3 test that the original developer wrote to check that the bounded queue worked as expected.

```
public void testWorksAsItShould() {
    int queueSize = 5;
    BoundedQueue<Integer> queue =
            new BoundedQueue<Integer>(queueSize);
    for (int i = 1; i <= 20; i++) {
        queue.enqueue(i);
    }
    while (!queue.isEmpty()) {
        System.out.println(queue.dequeue());
    }
}
```

Most likely the test was written before the days of CI, so the author never expected it to be run more than once. They ran the test, manually verified that the numbers printed to the screen matched what they expected, and then forgot about it.

But these days that kind of testing just doesn't cut the mustard. We want our automated tests to guard against regressions, but the preceding test doesn't. Even if you accidentally change the behavior of the `BoundedQueue` class, the test won't fail; it will simply spit out a different set of numbers to the console.

Tests like this one are particularly toxic because they look and feel like a test, even though they aren't testing anything at all. They falsely inflate the project's test count and test coverage, giving developers a false sense of security. The solution is simple: either fix the test by adding proper assertions, or delete it. (In this particular case, an even better solution would be to delete both the test and the BoundedQueue class itself, replacing it with a trustworthy third-party implementation such as Guava's EvictingQueue.)

BRITTLE TESTS

Good unit tests can prove valuable when refactoring, by providing assurances that the behavior of given parts of the codebase is preserved. But if you find that tests often break when you refactor, it may be a sign that the tests are too brittle. In this case, the tests become a hindrance, as you end up spending more time fixing them than refactoring.

A common cause of fragility is unit testing at too fine-grained a level. Continuing our BoundedQueue example, imagine you wrote a test for it like the following (this time using JUnit 4 syntax).

```
@Test
public void wibbleFlagIsSet() throws Exception {
    int queueSize = 5;
    BoundedQueue<Integer> queue =
            new BoundedQueue<Integer>(queueSize);

    Field wibble =                                      ←── Expose the private
            BoundedQueue.class.getDeclaredField("wibble");    field "wibble"
    wibble.setAccessible(true);
                                                        ←── Flag should
    assertThat(wibble.getBoolean(queue), is(false));        start off
                                                            false
    for (int i = 1; i <= queueSize; i++) {              ←── Fill the queue
        queue.push(i);
    }
                                                        ←── Flag should
    assertThat(wibble.getBoolean(queue), is(true));         now be true
}
```

This test uses Java reflection hackery to expose a private field and check its value. So if you ever remove or rename this field in the course of a refactoring, the test will break.

In general there's no need to write tests like this. We should be testing the behavior that components expose to each other, not any internal state they might be holding. If you ever find a test that's accessing private members of a class, or you find yourself wanting to write one, it might be a hint that the class contains too much state or is doing too much. You should consider splitting it into smaller classes that are easier to test.

RANDOMLY FAILING TESTS

A good test is completely deterministic, meaning that its result shouldn't be affected by changes in CPU load, thread scheduling, network congestion, other tests running in parallel, or any other external factor. But some tests don't achieve this gold standard and will fail occasionally. Examples include concurrency tests that depend on processing completing within a certain timeout, and integration tests that depend on the contents of an external database or filesystem.

These tests are dangerous, as they lead developers to start treating a test suite with a few failing tests as normal. Your test suite should be as simple as possible to understand: zero failing tests = GOOD, anything else = THE SKY IS FALLING! It's difficult to maintain this sense of urgency if two or three tests in your suite fail occasionally. Consequently, any randomly failing tests should be

- *Fixed*—If it is easy to do so
- *Disabled*—If they can be fixed but you don't have time to do so right now
- *Deleted or rewritten*—If they look very difficult to fix

4.2.3 *A glut of nulls*

Tony Hoare, the inventor of the null reference, calls the following his "billion-dollar mistake."

```
if (x == 0) {
    return null;                ◄——— NOOOOOOO!!!
}
```

Null references are the bane of the programmer's existence, and my heart sinks every time I see a `NullPointerException` (or .NET's equivalent `NullReferenceException`).

The use of `null` makes it more difficult to read and write code because nullability is not made explicit, at least in languages like Java. When reading a block of code, it's not obvious that a given variable might be `null`, so the reader must remember to keep the implicit nullability of references in mind at all times.

Modern languages strive to make developers' lives easier concerning `null`. Kotlin, for example, builds the concept of nullability into its type system, so that `String` and `String?` are separate types (non-nullable and nullable strings, respectively). The compiler is also smart enough to know whether you've performed a `null` check on a nullable reference, so that this will fail to compile:

```
print(player.getCharacterId())    ◄——— Assuming player is
                                        of type Player?
```

In contrast, the next example will compile just fine:

```
if (player != null) {
    print(player.getCharacterId())
}
```

Scala provides an `Option` type in its standard library to reduce the need for `null`. A value with `Option` type can be either a `Some(thing)` or a `None`, where `None` assumes the role for which `null` is used in other languages. You might wonder if there's actually any benefit to replacing a `null` with a `None`, but the point is that the `Option` type makes the "there was no result" case more explicit and forces the developer to deal with it, whereas a null result can be easily overlooked.

Compare the following Java and Scala code for retrieving a Player from a database. First the Java:

```
Player player = playerDao.findById(123);
System.out.println("Player name: " + player.getName());
```

Returns null if player with ID 123 does not exist

In the Java case, the developer has forgotten to include a null check, so if player 123 isn't found in the database, this code will throw a NullPointerException.

Now let's look at the same code written in Scala.

```
val maybePlayer = playerDao.findById(123)
// Do a pattern-match on the result
maybePlayer match {
  case Some(player) => println("Player name: " + player.getName())
  case None => println("No player with ID 123")
}
```

Returns an Option[Player]

In this case, because the DAO gives us an Option, both the "player exists" and "player does not exist" cases are obvious, and we're forced to handle both cases appropriately.

In Java it's possible to emulate the approaches used in languages such as Scala. If you're using Java 8 (which is unlikely, if you're working with legacy code), you can use the java.util.Optional class. Otherwise, Google's Guava library contains, among a host of other useful utilities, a class called com.google.common.base.Optional. The following code shows one way you could rewrite the previous code using Java 8's Optional.

```
Optional<Player> maybePlayer = playerDao.findById(123);
if (maybePlayer.isPresent()) {
    System.out.println("Player name: " + maybePlayer.get().getName());
} else {
    System.out.println("No player with ID 123");
}
```

If you have a lot of legacy Java code that uses null extensively and you don't want to rewrite it all to use Optional, there's a simple way to keep track of null-ness and thus make your code more readable. JSR 305 standardized a set of Java annotations that you can use to document the nullability (or otherwise) of various parts of your code. This can be useful purely as documentation, to make the code more readable, but the annotations are also recognized by tools such as FindBugs and IntelliJ IDEA, which will use them to aid static analysis and thus find potential bugs.

To use these annotations, first add them to your project's dependencies:

```
<dependency>
    <groupId>com.google.code.findbugs</groupId>
    <artifactId>jsr305</artifactId>
    <version>3.0.0</version>
</dependency>
```

Once you've done that, you can add annotations such as `@Nonnull`, `@Nullable`, and `@CheckForNull` to your code. It's good to get into the habit of adding these annotations whenever you read through legacy code, both to aid your own understanding and to make life easier for the next reader. The following sample shows a method with JSR 305 annotations added.

```
@CheckForNull
public List<Player> findPlayersByName(@Nonnull String lastName,
                                      @Nullable String firstName) {
    ...
}
```

Here the `@CheckForNull` annotation means that the method might return `null` (perhaps if there are no matches or if an error occurred), the `@Nonnull` annotation means that the first parameter must not be `null`, and the `@Nullable` annotation means that it's OK to pass `null` as the second parameter.

Null in other languages

Languages other than Java treat `null` in different ways. Ruby, for example, has the `nil` object, which acts in a "falsey" way, so you often don't need to check whether a variable is `nil` before referencing it.

Regardless of the language, you can generally use the Null Object pattern, whereby you define your own object to represent the absence of a value, instead of relying on the language's built-in `null`. Wikipedia has some simple examples of the Null Object pattern in various languages here: https://en.wikipedia.org/wiki/Null_Object _pattern.

4.2.4 *Needlessly mutable state*

Unnecessary use of mutability ranks alongside overuse of `null` in terms of making code difficult to read and debug. In general, making objects immutable makes it easier for a developer to keep track of the state of a program. This is especially true in multithreaded programming—there's no need to worry about what happens when two threads try to alter the same object at the same time, because the object is immutable and can't be altered in the first place.

Mutable state is common in legacy Java code for a couple of reasons:

- *Historical*—Back in the day when Java Beans were cool, it was standard practice to make all model classes mutable, with getters and setters.
- *Performance*—Using immutable objects often results in more short-lived objects being created and destroyed. This object churn caused early Java GCs to struggle, but it usually isn't a problem for modern GCs such as HotSpot's G1.

Mutability certainly has its place (for example, modeling a system as a finite state machine is a useful technique that entails mutability), but I usually design code to be immutable by default, only introducing mutability if it makes the code easier to reason about or if profiling has shown the immutable code to be a performance bottleneck.

Taking an existing mutable class and making it immutable usually goes something like this.

1 Mark all fields as `final`.
2 Add constructor arguments to initialize all fields. You may also want to introduce a builder, as shown earlier in the chapter.
3 Update all setters to create a new version of the object and return it. You might want to rename the methods to reflect this change in behavior.
4 Update all client code to make it use instances of the class in an immutable fashion.

Imagine that players of World of RuneQuest can acquire and use magic spells. There are only a few different spells, and they're large, heavyweight objects, so for memory efficiency it would be nice if you could have only one singleton object in memory for each spell, and share them among many different players. However, the spells are currently implemented in a mutable fashion, whereby the `Spell` object keeps track of how many times its owner has used it, so you can't share a given spell object between multiple users. The following sample shows the current, mutable implementation of `Spell`.

```
class Spell {
    private final String name;
    private final int strengthAgainstOgres;
    private final int wizardry;
    private final int magicalness;                    ← Lots more fields

    private int timesUsed = 0;                         ← Only this field is mutable

                                                       Constructor, other
    public void useOnce() {                            methods ...
        this.timesUsed += 1;
    }
}
```

If, however, we move the `timesUsed` field out of `Spell`, the class will become completely immutable, and thus safe to share among all users. We could create a new class `SpellWithUsageCount` that holds the `Spell` instance and the usage count, as shown in the following sample. Note that the new `SpellWithUsageCount` class is also immutable.

```
class SpellWithUsageCount {
    public final Spell spell;                          Spell#timesUsed
    public final int timesUsed;                        field has been
                                                       removed
    public SpellWithUsageCount(Spell spell, int timesUsed) {
        this.spell = spell;
        this.timesUsed = timesUsed;
```

```
    }
    /**
     * Increment the usage count.
     * @return a copy of this object, with the usage count incremented by one
     */
    public SpellWithUsageCount useOnce() {
        return new SpellWithUsageCount(spell, timesUsed + 1);
    }

}
```

This is an improvement over the original code for a couple of reasons. First, we can now share the heavyweight `Spell` objects between all players in the system, with no danger of one player's actions accidentally affecting another player's state, so we can save a lot of memory. We're also safe from any potential concurrency bugs whereby two threads try to update the same `Spell` at the same time, resulting in corrupted state. Immutable objects are safe to share both between multiple objects and between threads.

> ### Immutability in other languages
> Mainstream languages other than Java provide differing degrees of support for immutability.
>
> - C# has good support for immutability. It has the `readonly` keyword to mark a specific field as write-once (meaning it's immutable once it has been initialized), and anonymous types are an easy way to create immutable objects. The standard library also contains some immutable collections.
> - Dynamic languages such as Python, Ruby, and PHP don't provide much support for immutability, and idiomatic code written in those languages tends to be written in a mutable style. Python at least provides the ability to "freeze" instances of some built-in types, such as `set`. For Ruby, Hamster (https://github.com /hamstergem/hamster) is a nice library of immutable collections.

4.2.5 Byzantine business logic

The business logic in legacy applications can often seem very complicated and difficult to follow. This is usually for a couple of reasons.

- The business rules really are complicated. Or rather, they started off simple and gradually became more complicated over time. Over the years that the system has been in production, more and more special cases and exemptions have been added.
- Business logic is intertwined with other processing such as logging and exception handling.

Let's look at an example. Imagine that World of RuneQuest generates some of its revenue from banner ads, and the following class is responsible for choosing a banner ad to display to a given player on a given page.

```java
public class BannerAdChooser {
    private final BannerDao bannerDao = new BannerDao();
    private final BannerCache cache = new BannerCache();

    public Banner getAd(Player player, Page page) {
        Banner banner;
        boolean showBanner = true;

        // First try the cache
        banner = cache.get(player, page);

        if (player.getId() == 23759) {
            // This player demands not to be shown any ads.
            // See support ticket #4839
            showBanner = false;
        }

        if (page.getId().equals("profile")) {
            // Don't show ads on player profile page
            showBanner = false;
        }

        if (page.getId().equals("top") &&
            Calendar.getInstance().get(DAY_OF_WEEK) == WEDNESDAY) {
            // No ads on top page on Wednesdays
            showBanner = false;
        }

        if (player.getId() % 5 == 0) {
            // A/B test - show banner 123 to these players
            banner = bannerDao.findById(123);
        }

        if (showBanner && banner == null) {
            banner = bannerDao.chooseRandomBanner();
        }

        if (banner.getClientId() == 393) {
            if (player.getId() == 36645) {
                // Bad blood between this client and this player!
                // Don't show the ad.
                showBanner = false;
            }
        }

        // cache our choice for 30 minutes        ← Dozens more checks
        cache.put(player, page, banner, 30 * 60);      and conditions ...

        if (showBanner) {
            // make a record of what banner we chose
            logImpression(player, page, banner);
        }

        return banner;
    }

}
```

All of these special cases that have accumulated over the years have made the method very long and unwieldy. They're all necessary, as far as we know, so we can't just delete them, but we can refactor the code to make it easier to read, test, and maintain. Let's combine a couple of standard design patterns, Decorator and Chain of Responsibility, to refactor the BannerAdChooser. The plan is as follows.

1 Use the Chain of Responsibility pattern to separate business rules into their own testable unit.

2 Use the Decorator pattern to separate the implementation details (caching and logging) from the business logic.

Once we're finished, a conceptual view of our code should look something like figure 4.8.

First, we'll create an abstract Rule class that each of our business rules will extend. Each concrete subclass will have to implement two methods: one to decide whether the rule applies to a given player and page, and another to actually apply the rule.

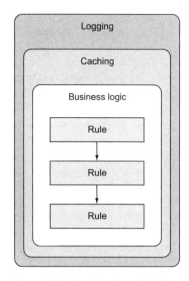

Figure 4.8 Our plan for refactoring the BannerAdChooser class using the Chain of Responsibility and Decorator patterns

```
abstract class Rule {
    private final Rule nextRule;

    protected Rule(Rule nextRule) {
        this.nextRule = nextRule;
    }

    /**
     * Does this rule apply to the given player and page?
     */
    abstract protected boolean canApply(Player player, Page page);

    /**
     * Apply the rule to choose a banner to show.
     * @return a banner, which may be null
     */
    abstract protected Banner apply(Player player, Page page);

    Banner chooseBanner(Player player, Page page) {
        if (canApply(player, page)) {
            // apply this rule
            return apply(player, page);
        } else if (nextRule != null) {
            // try the next rule
            return nextRule.chooseBanner(player, page);
        } else {
            // ran out of rules to try!
            return null;
        }
    }
}
```

Next, we'll write a concrete subclass of `Rule` for each of our business rules. I'll show a couple of examples.

```
final class ExcludeCertainPages extends Rule {

    // Pages on which banners should not be shown
    private static final Set<String> pageIds =
        new HashSet<>(Arrays.asList("profile"));

    public ExcludeCertainPages(Rule nextRule) {
        super(nextRule);
    }

    protected boolean canApply(Player player, Page page) {
        return pageIds.contains(page.getId());
    }

    protected Banner apply(Player player, Page page) {
        return null;
    }
}

final class ABTest extends Rule {
    private final BannerDao dao;

    public ABTest(BannerDao dao, Rule nextRule) {
        super(nextRule);
        this.dao = dao;
    }

    protected boolean canApply(Player player, Page page) {
        // check if player is in A/B test segment
        return player.getId() % 5 == 0;
    }

    protected Banner apply(Player player, Page page) {
        // show banner 123 to players in A/B test segment
        return dao.findById(123);
    }
}
```

Once we have our `Rule` implementations, we can chain them together into a Chain of Responsibility.

```
Rule buildChain(BannerDao dao) {
    return new ABTest(dao,
        new ExcludeCertainPages(                    ◄──────  Only showing a few links
        new ChooseRandomBanner(dao)));                       of the chain, for brevity
}
```

Whenever we want to choose a banner to show, each rule will be tried in turn until a matching one is found.

Now that we have our business rules cleanly isolated from each other, the next step of our plan is to move the caching and logging code into decorators. First let's extract an interface from the `BannerAdChooser` class. Each of our decorators will implement this interface.

We'll use the name `BannerAdChooser` for the interface and rename the concrete class to `BannerAdChooserImpl`. (This is a horrible name, but we're about to replace this class anyway.)

```
interface BannerAdChooser {

    public Banner getAd(Player player, Page page);

}

final class BannerAdChooserImpl implements BannerAdChooser {

    public Banner getAd(Player player, Page page) {
        ...
    }

}
```

Next we'll split the method into a base case and a couple of decorators. The base case will be the main Chain of Responsibility-based implementation.

```
final class BaseBannerAdChooser implements BannerAdChooser {
    private final BannerDao dao = new BannerDao();
    private final Rule chain = createChain(dao);

    public Banner getAd(Player player, Page page) {
        return chain.chooseBanner(player, page);
    }
}
```

We'll also have decorators that transparently take care of caching and logging respectively.

The following code shows a decorator for wrapping the existing banner ad logic with caching. When asked for an ad, it first checks if it already has an appropriate ad in its cache. If so, it returns it. Otherwise, it delegates the choice of ad to the underlying `BannerAdChooser`, and then caches the result.

```
final class CachingBannerAdChooser implements BannerAdChooser {
    private final BannerCache cache = new BannerCache();
    private final BannerAdChooser base;

    public CachingBannerAdChooser(BannerAdChooser base) {
        this.base = base;
    }

    public Banner getAd(Player player, Page page) {
        Banner cachedBanner = cache.get(player, page);
        if (cachedBanner != null) {
            return cachedBanner;
        } else {
            // Delegate to next layer
            Banner banner = base.getAd(player, page);
            // Store the result in the cache for 30 minutes
            cache.put(player, page, banner, 30 * 60);
            return banner;
        }
    }
}
```

The next code segment shows another decorator, this time for adding logging. The choice of ad is delegated to the underlying `BannerAdChooser`, and then the result is logged before being returned to the caller.

```
final class LoggingBannerAdChooser implements BannerAdChooser {
    private final BannerAdChooser base;

    public LoggingBannerAdChooser(BannerAdChooser base) {
        this.base = base;
    }

    public Banner getAd(Player player, Page page) {
        // Delegate to next layer
        Banner banner = base.getAd(player, page);
        if (banner != null) {
            // Make a record of what banner we chose
            logImpression(player, page, banner);
        }
        return banner;
    }

    private void logImpression(...) {
        ...
    }
}
```

Finally, we need a factory to take care of wiring up all our decorators in the correct order.

```
final class BannerAdChooserFactory {

    public static final BannerAdChooser create() {
        return new LoggingBannerAdChooser(
                new CachingBannerAdChooser(
                    new BaseBannerAdChooser()));
    }

}
```

Now that we've separated each business rule into a separate class and separated the implementation concerns of caching and logging from the business logic, the code should be easier to read, maintain, and extend. Both the Chain of Responsibility and Decorator patterns make it very easy to add, remove, or reorder layers as needed. Also, each business rule and implementation concern can now be tested in isolation, which was not possible before.

4.2.6 *Complexity in the view layer*

The Model-View-Controller pattern is commonly used in applications that provide a GUI, especially web applications. In theory, all business logic is kept out of the view and encapsulated inside the model, while the controller takes care of the details of accepting user input and manipulating the model.

In practice, however, it's easy for logic to infect the view layer. This is often a consequence of trying to reuse the same model for multiple purposes. For example, a model that's designed for easy serialization to a relational database will directly reflect the DB schema, but this model is probably not suitable for being passed as-is to the view layer. If you try to do so, you'll end up having to put a lot of logic into the view layer to transform the model into a form suitable for showing to the user.

This accumulation of logic in the view layer is a problem for a few reasons:

- The technologies used in the view layer (such as JSP in a Java web application) are usually not amenable to automated testing, so the logic contained within them can't be tested.
- Depending on the technology used, the files in the view layer might not be compiled, so errors can't be caught at compile time.
- You might want people such as visual designers or front-end engineers to work on the view layer, but this is difficult if the markup is interspersed with snippets of source code.

We can alleviate these problems by introducing a transformation layer between the model and the view. This layer, as shown in figure 4.9, is sometimes called a *presentation model* or a *ViewModel*, but I tend to call it a *view adapter*. By moving the logic out of the view and into the view adapter, we can simplify the view templates, making them more readable and easier to maintain. This also makes the transformation logic easier to test, because the view adapters are plain old objects, with no dependencies on the view technology, and can thus be tested just like any other source code.

Let's look at an example. World of RuneQuest has a `CharacterProfile` object that holds information about a player's character: name, species, special skills, and so

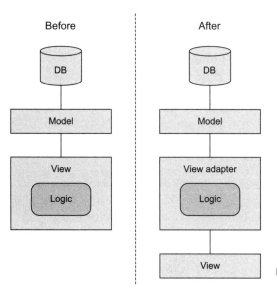

Figure 4.9 Introducing a view adapter

on. This model is passed to a JSP in order to render the character profile page. The `CharacterProfile` is shown here.

```
class CharacterProfile {
    String name;
    Species species;
    DateTime createdAt;
        ...
}
```

The following code is a snippet of the JSP.

```
<table>
  <tr>
    <td>Name</td>
    <td>${profile.name}</td>
  </tr>

  <c:choose>
    <c:when test="${species.name == 'orc'>
      <c:set var="speciesTextColor" value="brown" />
    </c:when>
    <c:when test="${species.name == 'elf'>
      <c:set var="speciesTextColor" value="green" />
    </c:when>
    <c:otherwise>
      <c:set var="speciesTextColor" value="black" />
    </c:otherwise>
  </c:choose>
  <tr>
    <td>Species</td>
    <td style="color: $speciesTextColor">${profile.species.name}</td>
  </tr>

  <%
    CharacterProfile profile = (CharacterProfile)(request.getAttribute("profile"));
    DateTime today = new DateTime();
    Days days = Days.daysBetween(profile.createdAt, today);
    request.setAttribute("ageInDays", days.getDays());
  %>
  <tr>
    <td>Age</td>
    <td>${ageInDays} days</td>
  </tr>
</table>
```

This JSP is horrible! It has logic jumbled together with presentation, making it very hard to read. Let's introduce a view adapter and pass that to the JSP, instead of passing the `CharacterProfile` model directly.

In the following code, I've extracted all the logic from the JSP and put it into a view adapter. I could have called the class `CharacterProfileViewAdapter`, but that's a bit of a mouthful. For brevity's sake I usually follow the view adapter class for a `Foo` model as `FooView`.

```
class CharacterProfileView {
    private final CharacterProfile profile:

    public CharacterProfileView(CharacterProfile profile) {
        this.profile = profile;
    }

    public String getName() {
        // return the underlying model's property as is
        return profile.getName();
    }

    public String getSpeciesName() {
        return profile.getSpecies().getName();
    }

    public String getSpeciesTextColor() {
        if (profile.getSpecies().getName().equals("orc")) {
            return "brown";
        } else if (profile.getSpecies().getName().equals("elf")) {
            return "green";
        } else {
            return "black";
        }
    }

    public int getAgeInDays() {
        DateTime today = new DateTime();
        Days days = Days.daysBetween(profile.createdAt, today);
        return days.getDays();
    }

        ...

}
```

The next code snippet shows how the JSP looks when we make use of the view adapter.

```
<table>
  <tr>
    <td>Name</td>
    <td>${profile.name}</td>
  </tr>
  <tr>
    <td>Species</td>
    <td style="color: ${profile.speciesTextColor}">${profile.speciesName}</td>
  </tr>
  <tr>
    <td>Age</td>
    <td>${profile.ageInDays} days</td>
  </tr>
</table>
```

There, that's better! The logic is now contained in a testable Java class, and the template is much more readable than before.

It's worth noting that if you don't trust yourself to keep logic out of the view layer, you can force yourself to do by choosing a logic-less template technology for your views. I've had success with logic-less template languages such as Mustache for building simple, readable views for web applications. The templates can be written and maintained by web designers, allowing the developers to focus on the business logic.

APPLICABILITY TO OTHER LANGUAGES   The View Adapter pattern is not specific to Java and JSP templates. It's useful no matter whether you're using Ruby and ERB, ASP.NET, or any other technology. Whenever you have an application with a UI of some kind, you can and should keep complex logic out of the view layer.

Further reading

I've just scratched the surface in this brief foray into refactoring. If you'd like to learn more about refactoring, there are plenty of excellent books dedicated to the subject. Here are three recommendations.

- *Refactoring: Improving the Design of Existing Code* by Martin Fowler et al. (Addison-Wesley Professional, 1999). Although it's getting a little dated (it was written when Java was at version 1.2), it's a classic and still a great reference. It takes a pattern-based approach, describing in what situation you might want to use a particular refactoring.
- *Refactoring to Patterns* by Joshua Kerievsky (Addison-Wesley Professional, 2004). This book cleverly shows how you can take legacy code that lacks a clear structure, and migrate it toward well-known design patterns using the refactorings described in Martin Fowler's book. If you want to brush up on design patterns before reading this book, read *Design Patterns: Elements of Reusable Object-Oriented Software* by Erich Gamma, Richard Helm, Ralph Johnson, and John Vlissides (Addison-Wesley Professional, 1994), also known as the Gang of Four book.
- *Principle-Based Refactoring* by Steve Halladay (Principle Publishing, 2012). This book is full of useful refactoring techniques, but it takes more of a "teach a man to fish" approach, promoting the value of studying the underlying principles of software design rather than slavishly learning dozens of rules by rote.

4.3   *Testing legacy code*

When refactoring legacy code, automated tests can provide valuable assurances that the refactoring has not inadvertently affected the behavior of the software. In this section I'll talk about how to write these automated tests, and what to do when you're faced with untestable code.

4.3.1   *Testing untestable code*

Before you start refactoring, you want to have unit tests in place. But before you can write unit tests, you need to refactor the code to make it testable. But before you start refactoring, you want to have unit tests in place ...

This chicken-and-egg situation is something we often face when trying to retroactively add tests to legacy code. If we insist on having unit tests in place before refactoring, then it seems like an unbreakable paradox. But it's worth remembering that if we can manage to get a few tests in place, we can start refactoring, making the software more testable, allowing us to write more tests, in turn allowing more refactoring, and so on.

Think of it like peeling an orange. At first it seems perfectly round and impenetrable, but once you apply a little force to break the skin, the thing practically peels itself. So we need to lower our standards temporarily in order to break the skin and get our first few tests in place. When we do this, we can use code review to make up for the lack of tests.

Our first priority when trying to make code testable is to isolate it from its dependencies. We want to replace all of the objects that the code interacts with, with objects that we control. That way we can feed it whatever inputs we like and measure its response, whether it consists of returning a value or calling methods on other objects.

Let's look at an example of how we can refactor a piece of legacy code in order to get it into a test harness. Imagine we want to write tests for the Battle class, which is used when two players fight each other in World of RuneQuest. Unfortunately, Battle is riddled with dependencies on a so-called "God class," a 3,000-line monster of a class called Util. This class is filled with static methods that do all kinds of useful things, and it's referenced from all over the place.

> **BEWARE THE UTIL** Whenever you see a class with Util in the name, alarm bells should start ringing in your head. It may well be a good candidate for refactoring, if only to rename it to something more meaningful.

Here's how the code looks before we start.

```
public class Battle {
    private BattleState = new BattleState();
    private Player player1, player2;

    public Battle(Player player1, Player player2) {
        this.player1 = player1;
        this.player2 = player2;
    }

        ...

    public void registerHit(Player attacker, Weapon weapon) {
        Player opponent = getOpponentOf(attacker);
        int damageCaused = calculateDamage(opponent, weapon);
        opponent.setHealth(opponent.getHealth() - damageCaused);

        Util.updatePlayer(opponent);

        updateBattleState();
    }
```

```
    public BattleState getBattleState() {
        return battleState;
    }

    ...

}
```

The class has a nice, simple constructor, so we can easily construct an instance in order to test it. It also has a public method exposing its internal state, which should be useful for our tests. We have no idea what that suspicious call to `Util.updatePlayer` `(opponent)` is doing, but let's ignore it for now and try writing a test.

```
public class BattleTest {

    @Test
    public void battleEndsIfOnePlayerAchievesThreeHits() {
        Player player1 = ...;
        Player player2 = ...;
        Weapon axe = new Axe();
        Battle battle = new Battle(player1, player2);

        battle.registerHit(player1, axe);
        battle.registerHit(player1, axe);
        battle.registerHit(player1, axe);

        BattleState state = battle.getBattleState();
        assertThat(state.isFinished(), is(true));
    }

}
```

OK, let's run the test, and ... whoops! It turns out that the `Util.updatePlayer` `(player)` method not only writes the `Player` object to a database, it may also send an email to the user to inform them that their character is unhealthy/lonely/running out of gold. These are side effects that we definitely want to avoid in our tests. Let's see how we can fix this.

Because the `Battle` class's dependency is on a static method, we can't use any tricks such as subclassing `Util` and overriding the method. Instead, we'll have to create a new class with a method that wraps the static method call, and then have `Battle` call the method on the new class. In other words, we'll introduce a layer of indirection between `Battle` and `Util`. In tests, we'll be able to substitute our own implementation of this buffer class, thus avoiding any unwanted side effects.

First, let's create an interface.

```
interface PlayerUpdater {

    public void updatePlayer(Player player);

}
```

We'll also create an implementation of this interface for use in production code:

```
public class UtilPlayerUpdater implements PlayerUpdater {

    @Override
    public void updatePlayer(Player player) {
        Util.updatePlayer(player);
    }

}
```

We now need a way to pass the `PlayerUpdater` to `Battle`, so let's add a constructor parameter. Notice how we create a `protected` constructor for use in tests, and we avoid changing the signature of the existing `public` constructor.

```
public class Battle {
    private BattleState = new BattleState();
    private Player player1, player2;
    private final PlayerUpdater playerUpdater;

    public Battle(Player player1, Player player2) {
        this(player1, player2, new UtilPlayerUpdater());
    }

    protected Battle(Player player1, Player player2,
                     PlayerUpdater playerUpdater) {
        this.player1 = player1;
        this.player2 = player2;
        this.playerUpdater = playerUpdater;
    }

    ...

    public void registerHit(Player attacker, Weapon weapon) {
        Player opponent = getOpponentOf(attacker);
        int damageCaused = calculateDamage(opponent, weapon);
        opponent.setHealth(opponent.getHealth() - damageCaused);

        playerUpdater.updatePlayer(opponent);

        updateBattleState();
    }

    ...

}
```

PROTECTED METHODS IN JAVA Because we added the new constructor with `protected` visibility, it will only be visible to subclasses of `Battle` or classes in the same package. We should put our test class in the same package as `Battle` so that it can call the constructor we added.

So far we've made changes to the `Battle` class, but we think we've maintained the existing behavior. Now is the time to pause, commit what we have so far, and ask a colleague for a code review, just to check that we haven't done anything silly. Once that's complete, we can move on to fixing our test.

In the test, we could create a dummy implementation of `PlayerUpdater` that does nothing, and pass it to the `Battle` constructor. But actually we can do better. If we use a mock implementation, we can also check that `Battle` calls our `updatePlayer()` method as we expected. Let's use the Mockito library (http://mockito.github.io/) to create our mock implementation.

```java
import static org.mockito.Mockito.*;

public class BattleTest {

    @Test
    public void battleEndsIfOnePlayerAchievesThreeHits() {
        Player player1 = ...;
        Player player2 = ...;
        Weapon axe = new Axe();

        PlayerUpdater updater = mock(PlayerUpdater.class);

        Battle battle = new Battle(player1, player2, updater);

        battle.registerHit(player1, axe);
        battle.registerHit(player1, axe);
        battle.registerHit(player1, axe);

        BattleState state = battle.getBattleState();
        assertThat(state.isFinished(), is(true));

        verify(updater, times(3)).updatePlayer(player2);
    }

}
```

Passes the mock to the Battle instance →

Creates a mock implementation of **PlayerUpdater** interface

Checks that the updatePlayer() method was called 3 times

Yay, we've broken the skin and our first working test is in place. Not only did we break the dependency on the `Util` class, we also managed to verify the test subject's interactions with other classes.

> **Further reading**
>
> For a whole book dedicated to examples like this one, as well as detailed explanations of the reasoning behind the approach taken in each case, I highly recommend *Working Effectively with Legacy Code* by Michael Feathers (Prentice Hall, 2004).

4.3.2   *Regression testing without unit tests*

Here's a deliberately inflammatory statement for you:

Writing unit tests before refactoring is sometimes impossible and often pointless.

Of course I'm exaggerating, but I wanted to get two points across here:

- "Sometimes impossible" is a reference to the difficulty of retroactively adding unit tests to legacy code that wasn't designed with testability in mind, as seen in the previous section. Although you can try to exploit a seam in order to inject mocks and stubs and test a piece of code in isolation, in practice this often requires a lot of effort.

- Writing tests is "often pointless" because refactoring isn't always restricted to an individual unit (a single class, in object-oriented languages). If your refactoring affects multiple units, then the very refactoring that you're about to perform can wipe out the value of the unit tests you're writing.

  For example, if you're about to perform a refactoring that combines existing classes A and B into a new class C, then there's little point in writing tests for A and B beforehand. As part of the refactoring, A and B will be deleted, so their tests will no longer compile, and you'll have to write tests for the newly created class C anyway.

UNIT TESTS ARE NOT A SILVER BULLET

If your refactoring is going to break unit tests, you need to have a backup—functional tests for the module that contains those units. Likewise, if you're planning a larger-scale refactoring of a whole module, then you need to be prepared for your refactoring to break all of that module's tests. You'll need to have tests in place at a higher level, that can survive the refactoring. As a general rule, you should make sure that you have tests at a level of modularity *one level higher* than the code that will be affected by your refactoring.

For this reason, it's important to build up a suite of tests at multiple levels of modularity (see figure 4.10). When working with legacy code that wasn't designed for testability, it's often easiest to start at the outside, writing system tests, and then working your way in as far as you can.

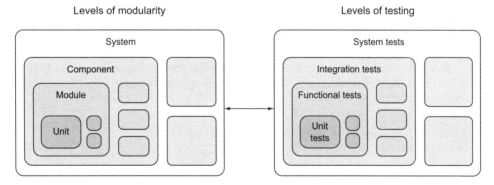

Figure 4.10 Levels of modularity and their corresponding tests

DON'T GET HUNG UP ON COVERAGE

Because test coverage is easy to measure, and increasing it is quite a satisfying pastime, it's easy to focus on it too much. But when you've inherited code with a very low test coverage, and you're trying to add tests retroactively to untestable code, getting test coverage up to what you consider an acceptable level can require a mammoth effort. I've seen a number of teams inherit code with test coverage of less than 10%, spend weeks trying to increase the coverage, and then give up at around 20% with no notice-able improvement in quality or maintainability. (I also saw a team inherit a large C# codebase with no tests, and 18 months later they had achieved their goal of 80% cov-erage, so there are exceptions to every rule!)

The problem with setting an arbitrary goal of improved test coverage is that you'll start by writing the easiest tests first. In other words, you'll write dozens of tests for

- Code that happens to be easily testable, neglecting more important but less test-able parts of the codebase
- Code that is well written and easy to reason about, even though a code review might be enough to verify that this code works as expected

AUTOMATE ALL YOUR TESTS

Most developers would agree that unit tests should be fully automated, but the level of automation for other kinds of tests (such as integration tests) is often much lower. Although we want to run these tests as often as possible when refactoring, in order to spot regressions quickly, we can't do so if they rely on manual labor. Even if we had an army of willing testers to rerun the whole integration test suite every time we made a commit, it's possible that they would forget to run a test, or misinterpret the results. Plus it would slow down the development cycle. Ideally we want all of our regression tests, not just the unit tests, to be 100% automated.

One area that cries out for automation is UI testing. Whether you're testing a desk-top application, a website, or a smartphone app, there's a huge selection of tools avail-able to help you automate your tests. For example, tools such as Selenium and Capybara make it easy to write automated web UI tests. The following code sample shows a Capybara script that you could use to test World of RuneQuest's player profile page, which you saw earlier in the chapter. This simple Ruby script opens a web browser, logs in to World of RuneQuest, opens the My Profile page, and checks that it contains the correct content, all within a matter of seconds.

```ruby
require "rspec"
require "capybara"
require "capybara/dsl"
require "capybara/rspec"

Capybara.default_driver = :selenium
Capybara.app_host = "http://localhost:8080"

describe "My Profile page", :type => :feature do
    it "contains character's name and species" do
        visit "/"
        fill_in "Username", :with => "test123"
        fill_in "Password", :with => "password123"
        click_button 'Login'

        visit "/profile"
        expect(find("#playername")).to have_content "Test User 123"
        expect(find("#speciesname")).to have_content "orc"
    end
end
```

Login as a known test user — (annotation pointing to the login section)

Opens the 'My Profile' page and checks its content — (annotation pointing to the profile section)

This test can easily be run by a developer on their local machine or by a CI server such as Jenkins. It could also be configured to run in headless mode instead of opening and manipulating a web browser, in order to speed up the test execution.

Of course, it's not possible to test everything in your application using UI tests alone, but they make a valuable addition to your test suite, especially when working with legacy code that may be difficult to test by other means.

4.3.3 *Make the users work for you*

You've done pair programming, you've conducted code reviews, you've run your unit tests, functional tests, integration tests, system tests, UI tests, performance tests, load tests, smoke tests, fuzz tests, wobble tests (OK, I made that last one up), and they've all passed. This means your software has no bugs, right?

No, of course not! No matter how much testing you do, there will always be a pattern you haven't managed to check. Every test that you run before release is, in a sense, an attempt to emulate the actions of a typical user, based on your best guess about how users will use the software. But the quality and rigor of this simulacrum will never match the real thing—the users themselves. So why not put this army of unwitting testers to good use?

You can make use of user data to help ensure the quality of your software in a few ways.

- *Perform gradual rollouts of new releases, while monitoring for errors and regressions.* If you start to see unusually high error counts, you can stop the rollout, investigate the cause, and either roll back to the previous version or fix the problem before continuing the release. Of course, error monitoring and subsequent rollback can be automated. Google is one company known for its dedication to gradual rollouts, with major releases of Android taking many weeks to reach all devices.
- *Gather real user data and use it to make your tests more productive.* When load testing a web application, it's difficult to generate traffic that reflects real usage patterns, so why not record the traffic of a few real users and feed that into your test scripts?
- *Perform stealth releases of new versions, whereby software is released into the production environment but not yet visible to the users.* All traffic is sent to both the old and new versions, so you can see how the new version works against real user data.

4.4 *Summary*

- Successful refactoring takes discipline. Perform refactorings in a structured way and avoid combining them with other work.
- Removal of stale code and low-quality tests is a nice way to get the refactoring ball rolling.
- Use of `null` pointers is a very common source of bugs, no matter what language you're using.

- Prefer immutable state over mutable.
- Use standard design patterns to separate business logic from implementation details or to make complex business logic more manageable and composable.
- Use the View Adapter pattern to keep complex logic out of your application's view layer.
- Beware any class or module with `Util` in the name.
- Introduce a layer of indirection in order to inject mock dependencies in tests.
- Unit tests aren't a silver bullet. You need tests at multiple levels of abstraction to protect against regressions caused by refactoring.
- Automate as many tests as possible—not only the unit tests.

Re-architecting 5

> **This chapter covers**
> - Splitting a monolithic codebase into multiple components
> - Distributing a web application into a collection of services
> - The pros and cons of microservices

In the previous chapter we looked at techniques for refactoring—making improvements at the source code level. But refactoring can get you only so far, and sometimes you need to think bigger. In this chapter we'll look at ways to improve the structure of the software as a whole by splitting it into smaller, more maintainable components. I'll also discuss the pros and cons of splitting an application into multiple services, micro or otherwise, communicating over the network.

5.1 What is re-architecting?

Don't worry too much about the difference between refactoring and re-architecting. They're really two sides of the same coin. The point of both refactoring and re-architecting is to change the structure of your software for the better without affecting the externally visible functionality.

Re-architecting is refactoring at a higher level than that of methods and classes. You can think of it as refactoring in the large. For example, when refactoring, you might move some classes into a separate package, whereas re-architecting might involve moving them out of the main codebase and into a separate library.

The main goals of splitting up an application, into either component modules or full-blown services, are as follows.

- *Quality through modularity.* Small software generally has a lower defect density than large software. (See Yashwant K. Malaiya and Jason Denton, *Module Size Distribution and Defect Density,* www.cs.colostate.edu/~malaiya/p/denton_2000.pdf, for an academic study of the relationship between module size and defect density.)

  If you split a large piece of software into a number of smaller parts, and you assume that the quality of the software as a whole is equal to the quality of its parts, then in theory the quality should increase. (Of course, that's a big assumption and things aren't always that simple. You'll need to wire the modules together and make them interact with each other, which can introduce a new class of bugs.)

- *Maintainability through good design.* By splitting an application, you can promote the design goal of separation of concerns. Each component is small, it only does one thing, and its interface (what other components expect it to do) is well-defined, making the code easier to understand and change than a large application with many moving parts.

- *Autonomy through independence.* Once you've split an application into components, each component can be maintained by a separate team of developers, using the tools of their choice. In the case of (micro)services, each service might even be implemented in a different language, so teams have the freedom to choose whatever technology works best for them. Teams can also choose to release new versions of their components at a pace that suits them.

  This autonomy, along with the obvious parallelization associated with having multiple teams working on the same application, can increase development velocity and result in new features reaching users faster.

The increased modularity that comes from splitting a large application is generally a Good Thing, but there are potential downsides. Although the complexity of the source code should decrease (because each module is small and self-contained compared with the original monolithic application), the management of that source code will become more complex, because there are now multiple modules instead of just one. You'll need to manage the building of all these modules, perhaps versioning them separately, and package them together, so your build scripts and workflows will become more numerous and/or complex. If you're splitting into distributed services, it becomes even more complex, as you'll need to write (or auto-generate) and maintain client code to allow each service to communicate with the others.

I'll discuss the pros and cons of each approach as we proceed through the chapter. We'll look first at the simpler approach, breaking a monolithic codebase into multiple modules. Then we'll move on to look at the more radical step of distributing those modules as separate services, communicating with each other via HTTP or some other network protocol.

Terminology

Before we go any farther, I want to make clear what I mean when I use certain words. Some of these words are quite ambiguous, so your definitions might be different from mine, but please bear with me.

- *Monolithic codebase*—A codebase in which all source code is managed in one folder and built as one binary file. In your IDE, everything is in one project. In Java terms, everything is in the same JAR file.
- *Module (or component)*—A part of an application's source code that's managed in a separate folder and built as a separate binary file. The module provides an interface to other modules, so that modules know nothing about each other's implementation. In Java terms, you usually have one JAR file per module, and put all the JAR files on the same classpath in order to run the application.
- *Monolithic application*—An application that runs entirely in one process on one machine. It may be built from either a monolithic codebase or a collection of modules.
- *Service*—A piece of software that's isolated from other parts of the application and can only communicate via messages over a network protocol such as HTTP or Thrift. Services usually send and receive messages using language-agnostic formats such as JSON or XML. A service runs in its own process, usually on a separate machine from other services. An application that's distributed across multiple services is often known as a service-oriented architecture (SOA).
- *Microservice*—An SOA with a particular focus on decoupling and bounded contexts. (Credit to Adrian Cockcroft, whose definition I've paraphrased here.) Don't worry about this for now—we'll discuss it in more detail later in the chapter.

5.2 *Breaking up a monolithic application into modules*

If you've tried fine-grained refactoring on the level of methods or classes, but you find that the software still lacks clarity and structure at a higher level, you can try breaking it into modules. Because each module has to provide an interface in order for other modules to interact with it, this partitioning process will force you to clarify the various parts of the application, as well as how these parts depend on and interact with each other.

5.2.1   *Case study—a log management application*

This section will take the form of a case study. I'll walk you through a modularization of a large Java application that I performed a few years ago.

The application in question was an integrated log management solution targeted at medium to large enterprises. It had several main features:

- *Log collection*—You could get log data into the system in various ways, such as by uploading log files via FTP or sending them using the syslog protocol.
- *Storage*—Logs were written to a custom-built database, optimized for storing and searching logs.
- *Real-time alerting*—Users could register alert conditions, so that, for example, they'd be notified by email if a large number of logs containing the word "error" occurred within one minute.
- *Search*—Once logs were written to the DB, you could search for logs of interest using conditions such as keyword, timestamp, and so on.
- *Statistics*—Users could generate tables and graphs to display statistics about their logs, such as a graph showing how many emails their mail server had processed in each hour of the previous day.
- *Reports*—Search results, alert results, and statistics could be combined into a single report in a format such as HTML or PDF. Reports could be scheduled to run regularly and be sent via email.
- *User interface*—There was a web application to allow users to use and configure the application from their browser.

STARTING POINT

The application was originally architected in a slightly unorthodox semi-monolithic fashion. The codebase was monolithic, but the application was deployed as two services communicating over Java RMI (Remote Method Invocation). Figure 5.1 shows the source code organization and architecture in more detail.

The source was split into three main packages: `core`, `ui`, and `common`. Subsets of this source code were then packaged as two services, the Core service (a command-line Java app) and the UI service (a Struts web app running on Tomcat). These services communicated using Java RMI.

The reason for splitting the code into two services was scalability. For large enterprises with a lot of log data, it was possible to deploy multiple instances of the Core service, making it possible to get more logs into the system at once. Because the Core service also contained the search engine, this made it possible to distribute searches across multiple machines in order to improve search performance. Having multiple instances of the UI didn't make much sense, so the system was designed to have one UI instance and one or more Cores.

Building and packaging was performed using a complicated Ant script, and dependency management consisted of a folder full of JAR files.

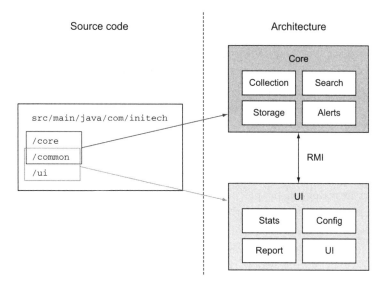

Figure 5.1 Log management application before modularization

BACKGROUND

Years earlier, the log management application had originally been written as an in-house utility, and from there had organically grown into a full-fledged business application, so some parts of the design were the result of historical accident rather than careful planning.

Although the application included a reporting engine for generating reports about logs, there was no single Java interface corresponding to this engine. Instead, the code for report generation was spread across a number of tightly coupled classes, and these classes were coupled to other parts of the application.

Some parts of the application were also very difficult to test, owing to excessive coupling, and test coverage was low. The development team had made efforts to improve test coverage, but had hit an impasse when faced with untestable code. A lot of code also depended on a few large God classes containing utility methods.

> **GOD CLASSES** A *God class* (or *God object*) is an anti-pattern in object-oriented programming in which an object does too much. It knows about everything in the system, and it's coupled with, and often controls, too many other objects.

Despite extensive refactoring efforts, development velocity had been steadily decreasing and code quality had reached a plateau. Developers were becoming increasingly frustrated with both the source code (particularly its lack of structure and testability) and the rather antiquated tool chain.

PROJECT GOALS

The goals of the modularization project were as follows:

- *Introduce explicit interfaces*—Introducing Java interfaces corresponding to each of the application's main features was not only an essential first step to modularization, but it would also make testing easier. Modules are only able to interact via these interfaces, so it becomes easy to inject mock implementations in tests.

- *Split the source code into modules*—As well as making the source code easier to work with, another important benefit is that the dependencies between modules become explicit.

- *Improve dependency management*—The "folder full o' JARs" wasn't ideal, so we wanted to introduce a proper dependency management system. This would become especially important once we had a collection of modules with dependencies between them.

- *Clean up and simplify the build script*—We wanted to do something about the complicated Ant script that was currently in use. Splitting up the codebase into modules would result in more build scripts being necessary, so we knew this goal would be difficult to achieve.

Equally importantly, we made clear a few things that were *outside* the scope of the project:

- *Changes to system architecture*—The separation into Core and UI services worked reasonably well, allowing the core to be scaled separately from the UI, so we decided to leave the architecture alone. However, when designing the modules, we kept in mind the possibility that the architecture might change in the future.

- *Changes in functionality*—Trying to add any new features or changes at the same time as a major reorganization of the codebase would be asking for trouble.

5.2.2 *Defining modules and interfaces*

The first step was to decide how we (the development team and I) wanted the codebase to look when the project was complete. The module structure fell into place quite naturally, with one module for each major feature of the application. Figure 5.2 shows how we envisaged the modules ending up.

> **Deciding an application's structure**
>
> When deciding how an application should be organized, whether designing the package structure or splitting the application into modules, I try to keep the end user in mind.
>
> Every component should have a single purpose that could easily be explained to a typical user in one sentence. For example, the `Storage` module could be described as "the component that takes care of storing log data reliably on disk." This method of defining components helps me to achieve the right level of granularity for components:

- No component has too much responsibility, as its purpose can be explained in only one sentence.
- Every component does one useful thing, so components are not too fine-grained.

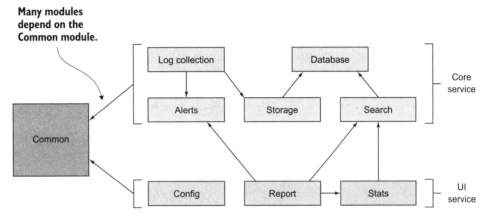

Many modules depend on the Common module.

Figure 5.2 The expected module structure. The arrows show the most important dependency relationships between modules (an arrow from one module to another represents a dependency).

The Core and UI services were also implemented as modules. Each service module would depend on all the modules in that service, take care of wiring them together, and provide the Java application's entry point.

Note that the Database module is separate from Search and Storage. This was a custom-built, highly optimized database designed for storing log data. Although it was good at its job, it was a burden to support and maintain. At the time there were a few interesting open source technologies emerging in the log management space, so we wanted to make it possible to migrate from the database to one of these open source offerings in the future.

There were a number of utility classes that were heavily depended upon by large parts of the codebase. Teasing apart these dependencies, while not impossible, would have taken a huge refactoring effort. Instead we decided to simply make a Common module, lump them all in there, and let all other modules depend on Common where necessary.

5.2.3 *Build scripts and dependency management*

With the planning out of the way, it was time to start getting our hands dirty. We began by defining a skeleton structure for all the modules, including the build scripts, dependency management files, and standard directory structure. Then we started moving code into the modules.

For the build scripts, we wanted to replace Ant with something more modern. The original Ant file was reasonably complex, mainly because it needed to build distributable packages for multiple platforms, each including bundled software such as a JRE, a Perl runtime, and an application server. It also had to copy license keys for a few proprietary libraries. Writing and maintaining all of this logic in Ant's restrictive XML DSL was pretty painful.

We experimented with a few different tools, including Maven, Gradle, and Buildr, but decided it was easiest to stick with Ant in the short term. We already had a lot of Ant tasks that we could reuse, so we could get up and running quickly, and revisit the problem later. After a bit of experimentation, we ended up with one common Ant file (build.xml) shared between all modules, plus a short build.xml in each module, referencing the common one and providing module-specific customizations. This situation was actually worse than the original Ant file, as it required more lines of XML in total and there was some redundancy in the per-module build files, but it was good enough to get us started on splitting up the codebase.

We also needed a dependency management tool so that we could specify each module's dependencies, both on other modules and on third-party libraries. We decided to use Apache Ivy for this. We wanted to package each module as a separate artifact (JAR file), so we set up Artifactory (https://www.jfrog.com/artifactory/), an in-house Ivy repository server. This allowed us to publish each module's artifacts to a central repository from which other modules could reference them.

For each module, we separated the interface and the implementation into separate artifacts, such as stats-iface.jar and stats-impl.jar. The former would contain only Java interfaces and model classes, whereas the latter contained the concrete implementation.

The point of separating interface and implementation into separate artifacts was that modules would only be able to depend on other modules' interfaces, not on their implementation classes. By splitting them into two artifacts, we could enforce this guarantee by including only the interface artifact on the compile-time classpath.

This may seem like more trouble than it's worth, but we did it for psychological reasons as much as technical ones. We wanted to make the point to ourselves that there was no way to make one component on the application depend on an implementation detail of another, no matter how tempting it might be.

The setup is summarized in figure 5.3. Artifacts were published to Artifactory, mainly for the benefit of Jenkins. We wanted separate Jenkins jobs for each module, so that they ran quickly, and Artifactory made it easy to share artifacts between jobs.

5.2.4   *Spinning out the modules*

Once the module framework was in place, defining the interfaces and moving the source code into the modules was comparatively easy. We started with the easiest, which happened to be the statistics engine. It was already reasonably self-contained and had a clear interface defined, so most of the code could be used as is.

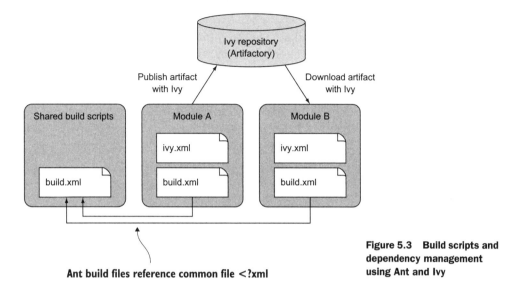

Ant build files reference common file <?xml

Figure 5.3   Build scripts and dependency management using Ant and Ivy

Other modules took more effort to extract because they didn't have interfaces defined and they had large numbers of dependencies, often cyclic. We made heavy use of dependency analysis tools to work out where the cycles were, and after a lot of patient refactoring, we managed to tease them apart.

In some places we ended up with quite unnatural interfaces, due to tight coupling between modules. The Report module's ReportEngine needed various pieces of information and assistance from the caller (the UI module) in order to create a report, so we ended up creating a ReportEngineHelper interface and making the caller supply its implementation. The method signature looked something like the following.

```
interface ReportEngine {

    ReportResult createReport(ReportRequest request, ReportEngineHelper helper);

}
```

Our first priority was to separate the code into modules, so we tolerated these idiosyncrasies as a means to an end. We were able to tidy up most of them later by adjusting the boundaries between modules.

5.2.5   *Giving it some Guice*

We now had a collection of nice, isolated modules, each with its interface cleanly separated from its implementation. This was great, but there was one problem: whenever you wanted to use a module, you needed detailed knowledge of that module's implementation. For example, to use the stats engine to calculate some statistics, you'd write code like the following.

```
StatsEngine statsEngine = new StatsEngineImpl(new SearchEngineImpl(), ...);
statsEngine.calculateStats(...);
```

This was suboptimal for two reasons:

- The client module had to take care of instantiating the StatsEngine's concrete implementation, including all the messy details of instantiating and passing all of its constructor parameters.
- It required a compile-time dependency on stats-impl.jar, so it was easy to accidentally depend on implementation classes that the client module wasn't supposed to know anything about.

To get around this problem and minimize the boilerplate needed to bind interfaces to implementations, we introduced Guice, Google's dependency injection library.

In this setup, each module of the application would provide a corresponding Guice module, which took care of binding that module's interfaces to its implementations. If the Stats module exposed a StatsEngine interface like this,

```
interface StatsEngine {

    StatsResult calculateStats(StatsRequest request);

}
```

and an implementation like this,

```
public class StatsEngineImpl implements StatsEngine {

    @Inject
    private SearchEngine searchEngine;

    public StatsResult calculateStats(StatsRequest request) {        Calculates
        SearchResult searchResult = searchEngine.search(...);        stats ...

        return result;
    }

}
```

then it would also expose the implementation binding in its Guice module:

```
public class StatsModule extends AbstractModule {

    @Override
    protected void configure() {
        bind(StatsEngine.class).to(StatsEngineImpl.class);
    }

}
```

This way, any module that wanted to use the Stats module only needed to depend on the interface and Guice module at compile time, while depending on the implementation at runtime.

A nice side effect of introducing Guice into the application was that it encouraged developers to write modular, testable code within modules as well. We found Guice to be a very all-or-nothing library—as soon as you add it to a codebase, it becomes difficult *not* to use Guice in your code, so it spreads like wildfire. Before you know it, your whole codebase has been Guice-ified!

5.2.6 Along comes Gradle

By this time the code was in good shape, but we still weren't happy with the Ant + Ivy setup for building and dependency management. We were very interested in switching to Gradle, but when we had evaluated it at the start of the project, it had been quite immature and had a few critical bugs that had prevented us from using it. It matured quickly, however, and by the time we re-evaluated it a few months later, all of the show-stopping bugs had been fixed and we felt confident enough to start using it. We switched our build tool from Ant to Gradle, with great success.

There were a few main benefits of switching to Gradle:

- *It's designed for multi-module projects*—Ant has no concept of modules, and although Maven can handle them, it doesn't do so elegantly. Gradle, in contrast, was specifically designed with multi-module projects in mind. We were able to get rid of the per-module Ant and Ivy files and consolidate everything into one build file. Dependencies between modules were easy to express, and everything just worked.
- *The Gradle DSL*—Writing everything in Gradle's concise, powerful DSL, as well as being able to write standard Groovy code inside the build file, was certainly preferable to expressing complex build logic in XML using Ant.
- *Plugins*—Gradle has a powerful plugin system, and we were able to write plugins to handle our more complex build tasks.

I'm still a big Gradle fan, and I'll be preaching its virtues again in chapter 9 when we talk about improving the development workflow.

5.2.7 Conclusions

By the end of the modularization project, we'd introduced a lot of new technologies to the stack: Gradle had replaced Ant, Guice was being used for dependency injection, and some developers were switching their IDE from Eclipse to IntelliJ (primarily because of its superior support for multi-module projects).

Trying to get to grips with all of this new technology at once was a problem for developers. We took various approaches to get developers on board.

- *Guice*—Organized a half-day study meeting and hands-on session to explain what it was, how it worked, and why we had introduced it.
- *Gradle*—Two developers were reasonably knowledgeable about Gradle by the end of the project. To the rest of the developers we gave basic training about how to install it, commonly used commands, and so on, leaving those who were interested to find out more for themselves. The two knowledgeable developers worked to spread their knowledge around the team gradually.

- *IDE*—We let developers choose freely between sticking with Eclipse and switching to IntelliJ.

Although it's difficult to quantitatively measure the effect of the project on developer productivity, verbal feedback received a few weeks after project completion suggested that developers found the code easier to work with than before. They were also motivated by the chance to work with new technologies.

Overall the project was a success in that it made the codebase more amenable to change in the future. For example, it gave developers the chance to experiment with major changes to the system architecture, such as moving to a full-blown SOA in which each module ran as a separate service. This would have been very difficult to achieve without the initial step of splitting the codebase into modules.

One point that could have been improved was coordination with other developers who were working on the existing codebase. Ordinarily I'd suggest either performing refactorings on the main development branch or regularly merging the development branch into the refactoring branch in order to avoid divergence and huge merges. But in this case, we were making such a fundamental change to the software's structure that this was very difficult.

We resorted to mentally keeping track of the changes on the development branch and regularly performing manual merges to keep the modularization branch up to date, which was pretty painful and quite dangerous. We also had to freeze development for about two days at the end of the project while we switched everybody over to the new codebase. With hindsight, we should have put more effort into making the transition smoother and more incremental.

5.3   *Distributing a web application into services*

In the previous section you saw a case study in which we divided up the codebase into several modules, but we didn't make any changes to the system architecture. This time around, let's look at a number of different architectures we could use to deploy and run an application in production. Specifically, we'll look at the pros and cons of re-architecting a monolithic web application into a SOA. Finally we'll discuss a concept that could be described as the purest distillation of SOA, namely microservices.

5.3.1   *Another look at Orinoco.com*

In chapter 3 we looked at Orinoco.com, a popular e-commerce site. We'll be using Orinoco.com again as an example in this section, so let's recap and give a little more detail about the current implementation.

Orinoco.com is an e-commerce site where you can buy anything from books to blueberries, and it receives traffic on the order of 100 million page views per month. This traffic is usually quite stable, but it peaks massively a few times a year, on days such as Black Friday and Cyber Monday. The main features of the site include product listings, search, recommendations, checkout, My Page, and user authentication.

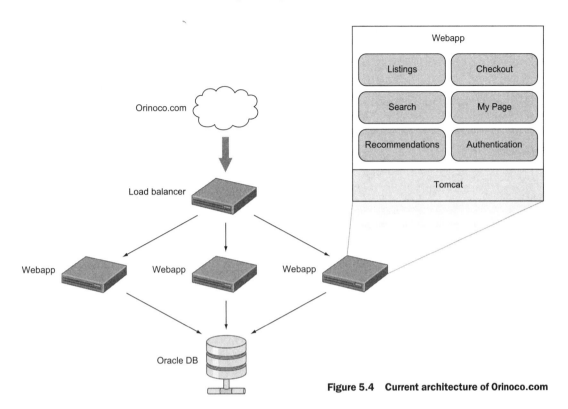

Figure 5.4   Current architecture of Orinoco.com

The site is currently implemented as a monolithic Java servlet application. To handle heavy traffic, and for redundancy purposes, there are several instances of the application running, fronted by a load balancer. The site is backed by an Oracle SQL database. This architecture is shown in figure 5.4.

The site is maintained by a couple of dozen full-stack developers, who take care of everything from the HTML, CSS, and JavaScript in the UI to the machine-learning algorithm used for product recommendations. There's also an operations team that keeps the site running smoothly, a quality assurance team, and a team of visual designers.

With such a large legacy codebase, and so many people committing changes to it, releases have to be performed with care. Currently the developers make a release every two weeks, but the testers are complaining that they don't have enough time to complete their manual tests, so they're considering a switch to a three-week release cycle. Development has gotten noticeably slower in the last couple of years as the site has grown more complex. And even with all the manual testing, critical bugs are sometimes introduced, so there are occasional emergency releases or rollbacks.

The product managers are desperate to develop and release a smartphone application for Orinoco.com, but that would require adding a REST API to the site, and the company can't spare the development resources to build it.

5.3.2 *Choosing an architecture*

The Orinoco.com developers are looking to re-architect the application, mostly to improve scalability in order to handle the heavy load on Thanksgiving weekends, and to increase development velocity. Table 5.1 compares some of the possible architectures they could choose.

Table 5.1   A comparison of various web application architectures

Architecture	Technical benefits	Technical challenges	Organizational benefits	Organizational challenges
Monolithic	• Low latency • Simple development • No duplication of models/validation	• Scaling • Complexity due to large codebase • Danger of unexpected interactions	• Low intra-feature comms overhead	• Fear of failure • High inter-feature comms overhead
Front end + back end	• Can scale FE and BE separately • Separate presentation from business logic • Can reuse BE and build more FEs	• Complexity due to network calls	• Specialization • Can iterate FE more quickly • Stepping stone toward SOA	• Communication overhead • Siloing • FE/BE devs blocking on each other
SOA	• Fine-grained scaling • Isolation • Encapsulation	• Ops overhead • Latency • Service discovery • Tracing/debugging/logging • Hotspot services • API docs, clients • Integration testing • Data fragmentation	• Autonomy	• Dilemma over extent of autonomy • Risk of duplicated work
Microservices	• Same as SOA, only more so!	• Same as SOA, only more so! • Risk of implicit coupling	• Even more autonomy due to bounded contexts	• Implies DevOps • Requires a platform team • Demands major shift in thinking

There's a lot of information packed into one table, so let's go through it in detail, one architecture at a time.

5.3.3 *Sticking with a monolithic architecture*

The easiest option for the Orinoco.com developers is, of course, to do nothing and keep their existing monolithic architecture. They're having some problems with it, but it also provides a number of benefits over distributed architectures.

TECHNICAL BENEFITS AND CHALLENGES

In a monolithic application, you never have to make a network call to get the data you need or to make something happen. Everything is only a method call (or at most a DB call) away. The cost of calling a method is on the order of nanoseconds, whereas a call to the REST API of a remote service elsewhere in the data center will take milliseconds or longer.

This provides two benefits: first, the site should be pretty fast, assuming your DB queries are well optimized and the code isn't doing anything too crazy. Second, development is relatively simple, as developers don't need to worry about the myriad challenges associated with calling remote APIs (which we'll discuss later). Instead, they simply call a method and get a result back.

For example, if an Orinoco.com developer wants to add a panel to a product page showing a list of similar products, with recommendations tailored to the particular user, they only have to call the appropriate method on the recommendation engine:

```
List<Product> similarProducts =
    recomEngine.getSimilarProductsForUser(productId, userId);
```

There are downsides to lumping the whole application together in one process. For one, scaling to handle load can only be done by deploying multiple replicas of the entire application. Although this heavy-handed approach has simplicity on its side, it's quite a wasteful use of hardware resources, because there are usually only a few hotspot areas within the application that need to be scaled. It would be more efficient to run large parts of the application on a few cheap machines, and run the power-hungry parts on better hardware or more machines.

A monolithic application is often powered by a monolithic codebase. This can be bad for development velocity, as the Orinoco.com developers have found, simply because there's too much code in one place. It's difficult to understand and reason about. This problem can be partially alleviated by clearly dividing the codebase into modules, as discussed earlier in the chapter.

But as long as you're deploying all those modules together in the same physical process, they can affect each other in unexpected and nasty ways. If, for example, Orinoco.com's search engine needs to run CPU-intensive processing every hour in order to update its indexes, this will slow down the whole site. Or perhaps two unrelated parts of the site accidentally start sharing a thread pool, resulting in a confusing degradation in performance. Worst of all, a bug in the recommendation engine causes an infinite loop, and suddenly the whole site is down!

Because these problems are caused by unexpected interactions between features, they are unlikely to be picked up by unit tests. In fact, because a unit test should be mocking everything apart from the feature under test, it shouldn't discover them! If you have integration tests, you have a better chance of finding problems caused by interactions between features. But some of the bugs that can occur in large codebases, especially those involving threading or resource leaks, are so obscure and complex that you're unlikely to find them until they happen in production.

The perils of reuse

Although quantitative data on this stuff is hard to come by, in my experience a large proportion of bugs is caused by a piece of code being reused in a way that it was not originally designed for.

For example, a developer writes feature A, which includes a utility class, say for validating model objects. Six months later, another developer comes along to add feature B. They find the utility class and decide to reuse it. They move it to a common package and tweak it to suit their needs, slightly changing its behavior in the process. This causes the utility class's unit test to fail, so they update the test to match the new behavior. Feature A is now subtly broken, and nobody is any the wiser.

The more code you have in one place, the more likely this kind of regression through reuse is to occur. If you split features A and B into separate services, you might end up duplicating some code, but at least feature A's code will be isolated from any changes made for the sake of feature B.

The complete lack of isolation between features in a monolithic app can be a major burden, and it's probably the strongest argument in favor of moving to a more distributed approach. If Orinoco.com had search and recommendations running as separate services, they could fail as hard as they liked, and the rest of the site would still stay up.

ORGANIZATIONAL BENEFITS AND CHALLENGES

On the organizational side, communication between developers tends to happen in different ways depending on the system architecture. In the monolithic case, a single team (or even a single developer) will implement a given new feature, so there's little need to communicate about that feature.

If a developer wants to add a new A/B test to Orinoco.com, they can implement the whole thing: add a new DB table to hold the list of target users, add the back-end code to check a user's segment and record the page view, and update the UI to include both the A and B patterns. At no point do any other developers need to be consulted about the details of any interfaces. The developer can iteratively tweak the internal interfaces to suit as required, so development can proceed quickly.

This lack of communication can be dangerous. Because everybody's code has to run shoulder-to-shoulder in the same process, developers need to be intimately aware of everybody else's changes and what effects they might have on each other. Although at first glance it appears that developers don't need to communicate in order to get things done, in fact they spend a lot of time checking other developers' changes, discussing workarounds to unwanted interactions between features, and reading the codebase to build up an implicit knowledge of its various foibles. So there is actually plenty of communication going on, but it's unstructured, implicit, and fragmented.

Any time a developer needs to stray outside of the particular feature that they're working on and touch code that potentially affects other developers, the communication overhead suddenly explodes. If they want to change code that's used by many different parts of the application, such as the user authentication code in Orinoco.com, they may need to check with dozens of developers before they can proceed. Obviously this slows down development, and it gets worse as the number of developers sharing the codebase increases. And any time that a developer wants to perform a large-scale refactoring on the whole codebase, every other developer might be prevented from working for days at a time.

Finally, putting all their eggs in one basket by running the site as a monolithic app means that the Orinoco.com developers are burdened with a lot of risk. Even the smallest, most innocent-seeming bug can take down the whole site, which results in a culture of fear. No failure can be tolerated, so the team has to spend an inordinate amount of time and effort on testing before every release. This slows development and makes the release cycle longer, so it takes longer to get new features to market and get user feedback about those features. Splitting out less critical parts of the application, such as product recommendations, into separate services would be a way to improve the situation.

5.3.4 *Separating front end and back end*

Another common architecture for web applications is to run the front end and back end as separate services. The back end implements the business logic of the application and usually includes a relational DB or other datastore. The front end should be as thin as possible and contain no business logic, and its job is to present the application to the user. The front end might be a traditional web application, generating HTML pages on the server side, or a client-side front end running in JavaScript in the user's browser using a framework such as AngularJS or Backbone.js.

The back end will expose its functionality via an API, and the two services will communicate solely through this API, often sending messages in a language-agnostic format such as JSON over a protocol such as HTTP. This API encapsulates all the details of input validation, transaction management, database schemas, and so on, shielding the front end from this unnecessary knowledge.

TECHNICAL BENEFITS AND CHALLENGES

One benefit of splitting the application into two services is more fine-grained scalability. The front end is often much less power-hungry than the back end (especially if it's only serving static HTML and JavaScript), so it could be run on fewer servers.

More importantly, the main point of splitting the front end from the back end is separation of concerns. By separating the business logic (the guts of the application) from the presentation layer, the code should become easier to understand and the application more amenable to change. The two services are conceptually (and physically) isolated by an API, so each side is free to make internal changes as long as that interface is respected. For example, the Orinoco.com developers are free to tweak the algorithms used in the recommendation engine inside the back end, without having to worry about how it might affect the UI.

Another benefit of having a back end that exposes an API is that it can be used by more than one front end. For example, the Orinoco.com developers want to build an API for use by smartphone applications. They could implement this as a separate front-end service, talking to the same back end as the website does. Because all of the business logic is implemented in the back end, the front ends are relatively simple and a new front end can be implemented quickly. Figure 5.5 shows how Orinoco.com could look in the future after multiple front ends have been implemented.

But there is a price to pay when isolating the front end and back end from each other. Interactions between them become an order of magnitude more complicated than just calling a method. All communication is done over the network, so there's a whole new class of potential errors to handle, and the probability of one of these errors occurring is reasonably high. API calls might fail to connect to the remote server, or they might take an unreasonably long time to return. Even worse, they might hang forever, if there's a problem with the network and you forgot to set a time-out on the client side.

Even if the back end manages to respond to the front end in a timely manner, the data it returns might not be what the front end expects. Back-end developers will need to be very careful not to make any breaking changes to their API, and front-end developers will have to program defensively, keeping in mind the possibility that any data returned from the back end might be invalid.

The developers will also need to write and maintain a client for the back-end API, or possibly several clients if they decide to implement multiple front ends in different languages. This client might include features such as automatic retry of API calls, a circuit breaker to avoid overloading the back end when it's struggling under load, and a service discovery mechanism to find an instance of the back end if there are multiple instances running.

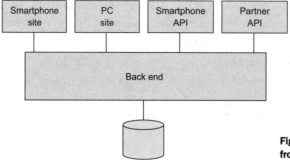

Figure 5.5 Orinoco.com with multiple front ends, each isolated from the others

ORGANIZATIONAL BENEFITS AND CHALLENGES

Given that the front end and back end have been split in order to separate the business logic from the presentation, it makes sense to split development along the same lines. Specialist front-end developers can concentrate on building a website that looks good and is easy to use, while back-end developers work on optimizing database queries and core algorithms to maximize performance.

Developing the front and back ends independently means that the development of each service can proceed at its own pace. The front-end team might want to iterate very quickly, releasing tweaks to the site's design every few days, or even multiple times per day, while the back-end team makes a release every week or so. Whatever release cycle each team decides upon, the important point is that they're not coupled to each other.

One implicit assumption when deciding to split the front and back ends is that there will never, or almost never, be any breaking changes in the API. If you introduce a breaking change, you immediately lose all the decoupling benefits, because the front and back ends will have to be deployed at exactly the same time. Even worse, if you can't afford a few minutes of downtime while you upgrade both services, it may be extremely difficult to deploy the change.

Unless the API is carefully designed for extensibility from the start, this inability to make breaking changes can be very restrictive to the back-end team. They may end up spending more time worrying about backward compatibility than building cool features. The problem is compounded when there are multiple front ends, each speaking a more or less out-of-date version of the API.

While the increased scope for specialization is a benefit, it can be a double-edged sword. It increases the risk of siloing, whereby the front-end developers end up knowing nothing about the internals of the back end, and vice versa. To think that developers only need an API as a common frame of reference and don't need to know anything about what's going on behind that interface is quite idealistic. In reality, developers will need some knowledge of the other side of the fence, and the organization will need to actively promote training and interteam communication, to make sure that developers don't become too ignorant of things that don't directly concern them.

Another problem I've often noticed when working with a split front end and back end is that it can make small changes excessively time-consuming. Remember the sole developer who was able to implement a new A/B test in the Orinoco.com monolithic architecture with a minimum of fuss? Well, with the new split architecture, that developer now has to do the following:

1 Add a DB table and corresponding query code in the back end.
2 Add a new endpoint to the back-end API.
3 Perform a rollout of the back end.
4 Add a new method to the API client corresponding to the new endpoint.
5 Release a new version of the API client.

6 Get the change implemented in the front end, either doing it personally or handing off the work to a member of the front-end team.

This need to coordinate work between the front-end and back-end teams can also lead to a situation where one team is blocked, waiting for the other team to finish a task. Imagine Orinoco.com wants to add a major new feature to the site to allow users to recommend products to their friends via email. This involves work on both the front end and back end, and ideally the teams would like to work in parallel. In theory, the teams first agree on an interface, and then the back-end team quickly writes a dummy implementation for the front end to work against. But in practice things rarely work this smoothly, and some blocking between teams is almost inevitable.

Despite these difficulties, the developers may still find that a distributed approach works better for them than a monolithic application. In this case, splitting the front end and back end is a great first step toward a fully distributed SOA. Once the tools and techniques for working with a remote API are in place, and developers have got used to the inherent challenges of distributed systems, it's easy to start experimenting with splitting the back end into more fine-grained services.

5.3.5   *Service-oriented architecture*

Many large-scale web applications use an SOA in which the application's functionality is distributed across many services. Many of these will be back-end services, exposing data in a machine-readable format such as JSON, which the front end then renders for display to the user. The front end may also be made up of a number of services, with each service rendering one or more components designed to be embedded inside a web page.

TECHNICAL BENEFITS AND CHALLENGES

The technical benefits of SOA are quite similar to those of splitting the front and back ends, but because the services are more finely separated, the benefits are correspondingly greater.

Because the application has been split into many different services, it's easy to scale each part of the application according to requirements. For example, the top page of Orinoco.com will receive much more traffic than the "Change my credit card details" page, so their scaling requirements are completely different. If they are running as separate services, they can be independently scaled.

Each service runs on a separate machine, so they're physically isolated from each other. Thus, assuming the application is correctly designed to handle service-level failures, a bug in any given service will not affect any other. Even if Orinoco.com's product recommendations service responds with an error, a product detail page will still render correctly, albeit without the Similar Products panel.

Running an SOA entails deploying a large number of services, which brings a number of operational and architectural challenges:

- *Operational overhead*—An SOA might include dozens or even hundreds of services, along with an assortment of datastores and message queues, all of which need to be provisioned, deployed, monitored, and maintained.

- *Latency*—In an SOA, one user request might result in dozens of interservice API calls. This might include chained calls, whereby service A calls service B, which calls service C, and so on. Without careful application design, the latencies of these requests can quickly add up, resulting in a very unresponsive user experience.

- *Service discovery*—With dozens of different services, and multiple instances of each service running, services need an easy way to find the service that they want to talk to. These days this is pretty much a solved problem, with open source solutions such as Eureka available.

- *Tracing, debugging, logging*—When something goes wrong in your application (or even when everything is fine and you just want some insight into how well your application is performing), it can be difficult to work out what the heck is going on. You'll need a way to collect logs from all of your services and store them centrally (tools such as Fluentd or Logstash can help here), and tools like Zipkin to help you trace the path of a single user request across your services.

- *Hotspot services*—There may be a few services that are relied on by nearly all other services. The user authentication/identity service is a common example. Service A is passed a user ID, uses the authentication service to look up the user, performs some processing, and then passes the user ID on to service B, which also contacts the authentication service, and so on. These hotspot services can end up receiving huge amounts of traffic and thus can become both a single point of failure and a scalability bottleneck.

- *API documentation and clients*—With so many services exposing APIs to each other, teams will spend a lot of their time writing documentation and clients for those APIs. These need to be kept up to date for them to be of any use. If they can be automatically generated from the source code, they're less likely to rot. Swagger is a popular tool for automatically generating API documentation.

- *Integration testing*—Checking that all the services interact with each other correctly and that the application works as a whole can be very difficult. For a start, you'll need a staging environment containing instances of all the services. If you have a mechanism in place to automatically spin up and tear down such an environment on demand, all the better.

  Testing that multiple versions of services work together correctly (ensuring that a change to a given service's API hasn't broken any services that are using older versions of the API client) can be quite fiddly. This is mainly due to the combinatorial explosion of version combinations that need to be tested. Version 2.3 of service A, version 3.4 of service B, and version 4.5 of service C work together, but how about versions 2.4, 3.5, and 4.6? If you need to test multiple version combinations like this, you'll need to invest in automation so that your testing framework can deploy a whole stack of services, with the appropriate versions, populate those services with data, and then run the integration tests.

Testing at the level of individual services can also be difficult. Although you can mock the data returned by requests to other services, you need to continuously maintain this mock data to make sure that it accurately reflects what the latest version of the service's API would return. This maintenance can be quite laborious, and if the API being mocked is maintained by another team, then it might be difficult to keep track of the changes.

- *Data fragmentation*—A monolithic application generally has only one database, but an SOA is likely to have many small DBs dotted around. This can make reporting and data analysis difficult, because you need to fetch data from multiple DBs, massage it into a common format, and join it together. It may be worthwhile setting up a data warehouse to take care of all this data munging.

ORGANIZATIONAL BENEFITS AND CHALLENGES

Much like the technical pros and cons, the organizational benefits and challenges of SOA are similar to those of splitting the front and back ends, but multiplied by the number of services.

SOA gives developers a lot of freedom. Each service can be developed by a different team, working in isolation from other teams. They can choose how to develop it, what technologies they want to use, and how and when they want to release it. The only rule is that they must respect the other services that depend on their API, so they can't introduce breaking API changes willy-nilly.

Is it really wise to give developers absolute freedom to choose their technologies? If every team chooses to implement their service in a different programming language, it's impossible for them to share any code, and they will likely end up duplicating a lot of work. It will also be difficult for teams to read each other's code, and developers will get locked into their respective teams and find it difficult to move between them. To avoid this situation, it's wise to lay down ground rules, or at least guidelines, specifying two or three recommended languages and technologies.

Even if teams are using the same technologies, they'll still end up duplicating each other's work if they don't keep abreast of what other teams are doing. There needs to be some way of making sure that teams talk to each other regularly and share information. It's also worth setting up a Platform team, whose role is to watch for duplicated work between teams and build common tools for everybody to use.

The duplicated effort across teams might take the form of re-inventing the wheel (for example, two different teams expending effort on solving the same problem, such as implementing healthchecks for monitoring their services) or duplicated code (each team writing similar utilities to include HTTP request information in log messages). To avoid the former case, the Platform team should gather information on what each team is doing, and formulate it into a set of guidelines or recommendations for other teams to use as a reference. In the case of duplicated code, the Platform team should write a generic library for all teams to use.

5.3.6 *Microservices*

Microservices is a popular buzzword these days, and there's some confusion about its exact meaning. (This confusion is possibly compounded by a variety of software vendors who are keen to jump on the bandwagon.) But microservices are just a special case of SOA, with an especially strong focus on decoupling, bounded contexts, and developer autonomy and responsibility.

WHAT'S A MICROSERVICE?

Microservices are an SOA in which the independence of services is strongly emphasized.

Services must be decoupled, so that it's possible to deploy a new version of a service at any time without affecting any other services. This implies that

- There's no way for services to communicate except through their APIs.
- Breaking changes in APIs are avoided at all costs.

Each service acts as a context boundary for its own domain model. This means that any models defined by service A can only be used in the context of service A, and using service A's models when communicating with service B is meaningless. In Orinoco.com, even if the authentication service and the product recommendation service both define a User model, and these models are quite similar, they aren't the same thing. A translation layer is needed to convert from one to the other.

This concept of a bounded context originally comes from the field of domain-driven design. For more details, I recommend you read the DDD bible, *Domain-Driven Design: Tackling Complexity in the Heart of Software* by Eric Evans (Addison-Wesley Professional, 2003). In the context of microservices, making these context bounds explicit means that each service is free to alter its own model without fear of affecting other services.

A final characteristic of microservices is the role that they give developers. Microservices aim to give them as much autonomy as possible, but in return they must take ownership of their services. The developer is responsible for supporting the service, deploying new releases of it, and keeping it running smoothly. In other words, microservices go hand in hand with DevOps.

BENEFITS AND CHALLENGES

Because microservices are a subset of SOA, everything I mentioned about SOA also applies here.

In addition, when implementing microservices one has to be aware of the risk of accidental coupling between services. The whole point of microservices is that services should be independent and loosely coupled, only communicating through their APIs. But if you're not careful, it's easy to inadvertently introduce other methods of communication between services. The most common culprit is a database shared between multiple services, so in general services aren't allowed to share a DB. Every service is responsible for its own datastore.

On the organizational side of things, microservices present much the same challenges as SOA. They require a massive change in mindset for any organization trying to migrate from traditional monolithic development, and they also demand commitment, as any half-hearted attempt to switch to microservices is likely to fail.

The organization must also be prepared to invest a lot of development time in things not directly related to the product, such as tooling for automatic deployment and monitoring of services. In order to keep services from getting bloated, there should be a team whose sole job is to make it as easy as possible for other developers to create a new service and get it into production.

5.3.7   *What should Orinoco.com do?*

It goes without saying that any architectural decision involves a set of tradeoffs, and each of the architectures I've shown you comes with its own pros and cons. Unfortunately there's no silver bullet.

One factor that I haven't mentioned is ease of migration from an existing monolithic application. In the case of Orinoco.com, it's a large application, so it's probably unwise to try to refactor it into separate front and back ends in one go. A more incremental solution is needed. I'd suggest keeping the monolith, but experimentally spin out a couple of noncritical functions into separate back-end services. If it goes well, they could gradually move farther toward an SOA, moving more and more functionality into new services, while simultaneously working on getting the necessary tooling, experience, and processes in place to make SOA work.

Of course, the incremental approach also means that you don't have to commit yourself to SOA. After building a couple of services in the SOA style, the team could re-evaluate their options based on their experience. If the team decides that SOA is not for them, they're free to go back to the monolithic approach, or perhaps a middle ground involving a small number of medium-sized services.

For any other monolithic app that you're tempted to split into services, first ask yourself, is it really necessary? Take another look at that long list of SOA's technical challenges and decide if you're really ready to take on that kind of operational burden. If the answer is yes, then go for it. Good luck!

5.4   *Summary*

- Splitting a monolithic codebase into modules forces you to clearly define the inter-module dependencies, which makes the code easier to understand.
- Once a codebase has been modularized, you're free to combine those modules however you like: run them together as a monolithic application, run each module as a separate microservice, give some modules away for free and charge for others, and so on.
- Choosing an architecture for your application involves a number of tradeoffs, both technical and organizational. For example, choosing microservices instead of a monolith may result in higher request latencies (because servicing

a request may involve multiple network hops), but it will give the teams more autonomy, allowing them to reduce their time to market.

- Running a monolithic app means that every change you introduce has a risk of bringing down the whole application. This can make organizations fear changes and spend too much time testing.

- Any communication that happens over the network can fail in many different ways. Adding a network call between services introduces a whole new class of failures.

- Splitting teams along service lines gives those teams autonomy and lets them work quickly most of the time, but development can slow down massively when teams need to coordinate with each other.

The Big Rewrite 6

Before you embark on The Big Rewrite, I hope you've exhausted all other options. You tried refactoring the codebase, but you hit an impasse. You investigated the feasibility of replacing your legacy software with a third-party solution, but it would require so much customization that it would be more work than writing it from scratch. You concluded that there's no getting away from a rewrite, as much as it makes your skin crawl.

Before we move on, let's remind ourselves why our skin is crawling at the prospect of rewriting a legacy application from scratch.

First, the project will drag on interminably. I guarantee that it will take longer than you expect. At first, a rewrite can seem like a relatively simple task, as you only have to copy whatever the existing software does. But once you start implementing, you'll uncover all kinds of weird corner cases and rabbit holes in the existing software (both the implementation and the specification), all of which need to be investigated and documented. Not only does this slow down the project, it also gets pretty dull for developers after a while. Although developers are usually keen to write code, a large proportion of the work involved in a rewrite is laborious investigation and debate about how best to deal with some obscure behavior of the legacy software.

Second, rewrites often provide limited direct value to the end user of the software, despite the Herculean effort that goes into them. You might invest months of development time building an application that, to the end user, appears to work exactly the same as the old one. In fact, people may have grown accustomed to the bugs and foibles of the existing software and treat them as features, so you risk disappointing your loyal users if you don't faithfully recreate them. On top of that, your new implementation is almost guaranteed to introduce new bugs of its own.

Nevertheless, sometimes a rewrite really is the least worst option. In that case, there are a few things worth taking into consideration if you want your rewrite to proceed smoothly. In this chapter we'll look at how to decide the scope of the project, how much you should allow your new software to be influenced by the existing implementation, and strategies for dealing with a legacy database.

6.1 Deciding the project scope

The most important thing to do before embarking on a major software project is to make your goals clear. What do you want to achieve by rewriting the software? And, perhaps more importantly, what *don't* you plan to do as part of this project?

6.1.1 What is the project goal?

A rewrite usually takes one of three forms.

- *Black-box rewrite*—In a black-box rewrite, the goal is to keep the software's functionality exactly as it is now, but the internals are reimplemented from scratch. This may be to port the software to a new technology stack (if, for example, it's currently running on a mainframe that's due to be decommissioned), or to make the software easier to maintain in the future. In the ideal case, the end user doesn't notice that anything has changed.
- *Brush-up rewrite*—In a brush-up rewrite, an additional goal is to use the rewrite as an opportunity to document, update, and normalize the specification, so that the new software functions differently (hopefully better!) than the old one.
- *Quid pro quo rewrite*—In a quid pro quo rewrite, the goal is to develop some major new features as part of the rewrite project, in order to convince business stakeholders to green-light it. If it were up to developers, we'd merrily spend all our working time refactoring and rewriting things just for the sake of it, but the people who pay our salaries need to be given some incentive to let us spend weeks or months rebuilding something that already works.

Recall the online game that we looked at in chapter 4, World of RuneQuest. It's a Java servlet application that's been running for over 10 years. Its technology stack has hardly changed in that time, and it's become very difficult to work with. The UI is also starting to show its age. The developers are desperate to rewrite the application using modern technologies.

The product managers are also on board for a rewrite, as it will give them a chance to write a proper specification—a vast improvement on the current situation of the implementation is the spec. But upper management is loathe to assign resources to a project that they see as being by the developers, for the developers, unless it also provides some benefit to the players of World of RuneQuest.

In this case, it seems like a quid pro quo rewrite is the way to go. Perhaps they could brand the rewrite as a major new version of the game, and they could use the new technology stack to add new features that have hitherto been impossible to implement. These features, such as in-game audio chat and more sophisticated player stats, are often requested by players and are already offered by World of RuneQuest's competitors.

> **Adding new features in a rewrite**
>
> The idea of adding new features at the same time as reimplementing an existing piece of software, as is done in a quid pro quo rewrite, may be quite undesirable from a developer's perspective. The conflation of multiple concerns, namely maintaining the original behavior while also adding new functionality, may make project planning more difficult and the resulting software harder to reason about.
>
> But sometimes adding new features is the only way to provide the rewrite project with enough business value to get approval. And besides, isn't building new functionality more satisfying than implementing something that works exactly the same as what you already had?

Making it clear to the end users that the game is being rewritten also frees the developers from any obligation to perfectly emulate the legacy UI and gameplay, although they will certainly need to be careful to preserve certain core features of the game, to avoid risking a backlash from players.

6.1.2 *Documenting the project scope*

Once you've decided what kind of rewrite you're going to do, it's vital that you clearly document this fact, along with any other salient details about the scope of the project. The document should be short enough for all stakeholders to read, understand, and agree to, but also clear and detailed enough to be unambiguous. This document will be very valuable as a reference when feature creep starts to set in, a few months down the line, so it should be written and agreed to with that in mind. Everybody involved in the project should understand that this document will become the Single Source of Truth, so if they disagree with any part of it, they should speak now or forever hold their peace.

I recommend including the following information in the project scope document:

- *New features*—Are you going to add any? If so, list them. For each one, say whether it is a must-have (the new software can't be released until it's completed) or nice to have (it could be added after the first release).

- *Existing features*—Are there any features of the existing software that you're planning to remove? Are there any particular features that are must-have or nice to have?
- *Timeliness versus feature-completeness*—Are you more interested in releasing something by a certain date or in releasing a product with all the planned features?
- *Phased releases*—Are you planning to make multiple releases, adding more functionality in each release? If so, give a brief summary of the content of each phase.

The final point is quite important. If possible, I highly recommend taking an iterative approach, whereby you make a number of small releases, adding more functionality in each release. This is less risky than the alternative, an all-or-nothing Big Bang release at the end of the project, because it gives you the opportunity to get feedback from your users about the new software while you still have time to alter the project's direction. It also highlights any technical issues with the new software at an early stage, when you still have the time to fix them.

For an incremental rewrite to work, you'll need to run the old and new software side by side until the new software is complete. This can present some technical challenges, especially if the old and new software will need to communicate with each other. But in my opinion the effort is justified by the reduction of risk that comes from being able to release incrementally.

Figure 6.1 shows what a scope document for a rewrite of World of RuneQuest might look like.

World of RuneQuest rewrite - project scope

Mission: To replace the existing Java Servlet webapp with a Play application written in Scala.

Developer goals: More maintainable code; better performance; faster development

Product Manager goals: A full and clear specification; a modern, usable UI

End-user benefits: 2 major new features (see below)

Deadline: 1st release on 1st August 20XX

New features: We will add 2 new features to the software.
  1) In-game voice chat (must-have)
  2) Advanced player statistics (nice-to-have)
Both features to be fully specified later.
We will also design and build a brand new UI.

Existing features: All existing features are must-have, except for the Map Editor feature (nice-to-have) and the Daily Email feature (will not implement).

Timeliness: We prefer an on-time release, even if it means removing features from the first release

Phased releases: We plan to make 3 releases at 3-month intervals. After the 3rd release, we will be able to switch off the old system. We plan to build a tool to synchronize user data between the two systems until then.

Figure 6.1 An example scope document for a rewrite of World of RuneQuest

6.2   *Learning from the past*

One other thing worth discussing at the start of a project is the extent to which the current implementation should be treated as a specification for the new one. This becomes important when you find that you need a clarification of the specification before you can proceed with your implementation. Let's look at an example.

It's a few weeks since the developers started implementing the new version of World of RuneQuest. By now the developers have become used to using a new programming language and web framework, the project structure and tool chain are set up nicely, and the team has settled into a groove of implementing new features in two-week sprints.

Developer Sarah has just finished implementing a feature, so she takes a new card from the backlog. The card is called Implement Player Matching feature. The idea is that players who want to start a new game of World of RuneQuest can enter an online waiting room, where they're automatically matched with a player with similar skills and experience. This is a feature that exists in the legacy version of the software.

Sarah is not sure how the player-matching logic should work, so she looks it up in the new spec document that's being compiled for the rewrite project. Unfortunately she can only find a single sentence: "A waiting player should be matched with another player of similar ability." Obviously she'll need more detail to go on, so she picks up her laptop and wanders over to the desk of Phil, the product manager.

Phil is responsible for deciding the specification in cases like this, but he doesn't have any bright ideas about how this feature should work in detail. He asks Sarah, "Well, how does it work at the moment?" Sarah finds the relevant code in her IDE and they look through it together.

```
public void runWaitingRoom() {
    while (true) {
        List<Player> players = getAllPlayersInWaitingRoom();
        for (Player p1: players) {
            for (Player p2: players) {
                if (p1 == p2)
                    continue;
                if (p1.isWizard() && p2.isWizard())
                    continue;
                if (p1.isElf() && p2.isOrc())
                    continue;
                if (p1.hasWeapon("axe") && !p2.hasShield())
                    continue;

                ...

                if (Math.abs(p1.getSkill() - p2.getSkill()) < 100)
                    // players are quite evenly matched
                    foundMatchingPlayers(p1, p2);
            }
        }
        Thread.sleep(1000L);
    }
}
```

More conditions ...

"Hmm, looks pretty complicated. Do you think all these conditions are necessary?" asks Sarah. Phil isn't really sure. He feels like this logic could be simplified, and he'd love to write a brand new specification, reasoning from first principles rather than blindly following the existing implementation. But he can't shake the nagging feeling that all those conditions must have been added for a good reason.

This is the kind of dilemma that comes up time and again when implementing a rewrite. If you haven't prepared for it by establishing, as a team, where on the spectrum between follow the existing implementation and write the spec from scratch you want to be, you can end up spending a lot of time vacillating over every tiny feature.

In the end, Phil and Sarah decide to go through the SVN commit log and make notes about when each condition was added, along with any hints they can find about the reasons for the addition. Then Phil writes a new specification from scratch, using these notes as a guide. If there's evidence that a condition was added for a good reason, he includes it in the new spec, along with an explanation of why it's needed. If there's no record of why a particular piece of logic was added, he simply discards it.

This is an example of the kind of balanced attitude toward existing code that leads to a successful rewrite. Although it's tempting to treat a rewrite as a break from the past, the existing code should be respected for a couple of reasons:

- It contains many years of accumulated bug fixes, performance optimizations, and corner case handling that could be lost in a rewrite if you're not careful.
- It precisely defines the behavior of the existing software, which can be a useful reference when deciding how the new software should behave.

If you follow the original implementation too closely, then you're remaking exactly what you already have. It's better to treat the existing code as a reference that can be used to guide your decisions or act as a tie-breaker in debates, rather than the ultimate source of truth.

It's also worth making the distinction between low-level implementation details, about which the existing code is a useful source of information, and higher-level software design and architecture. When you're designing your software, it's usually wise to deliberately avoid emulating the design of the existing code. At the very least, you should be aware that you're likely to be subconsciously influenced by the existing design, so you should try to actively combat this effect. Always be on the lookout for signs that the new design is emulating the old one for no good reason, and take a moment to think about whether you could solve the same problem in a completely different way.

For example, a lot of processing in World of RuneQuest is based on tasks running periodically once a second or so, like the player-matching code shown earlier. But is this really the best way to design a multiplayer online game? It might make more sense to base the software on events and event handlers. A new player joining the waiting room, for example, would cause an event to be fired, which would trigger an event handler to try to find a partner for that player. Or perhaps you could make use of the

Actor model, with one actor representing each player. As long as you remember that you're not constrained by the legacy design, the sky's the limit!

6.3   What to do with the DB

The software you're replacing will most likely have some kind of datastore. It's often a relational database (RDB) such as Oracle, but it might be something more exotic such as an object database, or something as basic as a folder full of flat files. Whatever it is, it's full of useful data, and your users will probably need to access that data using your new system.

You have two options here, as shown in figure 6.2: either connect the new software to the existing datastore, so that both the old and new systems are sharing the same DB, or create a new datastore and migrate the existing data to it.

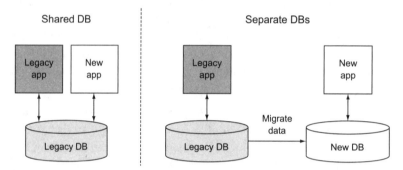

Figure 6.2   Two approaches to replacing legacy software that includes a database: share the existing DB or create a new DB and migrate the data

As usual, each approach has its own pros and cons. Let's look at each in turn.

6.3.1   Sharing the existing DB

If you're willing to accept the restrictions inherent in sharing the same datastore between multiple apps, this can be quite simple to implement compared to the complications of reliably replicating data between datastores.

Pros:

- *Simplicity*—There's no need to worry about migrating data between DBs, or how to recover when those DBs get out of sync, because there's only one DB.
- *No need to update other applications and scripts*—Sometimes the legacy application isn't the only software that interacts with the database. There might be all kinds of scripts, batches, and utilities that connect directly to the database and execute queries against it. If you keep using the existing DB, you won't have to touch any of these scripts.

Cons:

- *Can't choose the datastore technology*—You're stuck with whatever DB the legacy app happens to be using. If one of the goals of the rewrite is to migrate away from an expensive proprietary DB, then this is a show-stopper.
- *Can't re-architect*—As part of your rewrite, you might want to split a monolithic application into multiple smaller services, but this is unlikely to be effective unless you also split the DB into a number of isolated datastores.
- *Can't refactor the schema*—You might want to make major changes to the way data is structured inside the DB, either to make it more consistent with the models in your new application, or simply because the legacy DB hasn't been maintained and is a horrible mess. But making these changes isn't easy when the DB is being shared with another application. For every breaking change you want to make to the DB, you'll have to update the legacy software accordingly. There's also the risk of making a change that you believe to be harmless but that affects the behavior of the existing application.
- *Risk of corrupting data*—Once you release your new software, it will start writing new data to the DB. Ideally this data should be valid in both the old and new applications, so that you have the option of running both applications in parallel for a certain amount of time. This means you can release the new software incrementally, and you can switch to the old application if you find any problems with the new one in production. But if the data written by your new application can't be read correctly by the old one, this becomes impossible.

  You might become aware of the problem as soon as your new application starts writing bad data to the DB (if the old application starts throwing strange errors, for example). But you might be happily corrupting your DB for weeks before you notice. At that point, even if it's possible to salvage the data, you have a massive data recovery operation on your hands. You'll probably be forced to switch off the old application, so you no longer have it as a fallback for when things go wrong.

Clearly there are more cons than pros listed here, but in the right circumstances reusing the legacy database can be a reasonable approach. The simplicity gains of having only one DB to manage shouldn't be underestimated. If you decide to go down this route, I have a couple of recommendations.

INVEST HEAVILY IN THE PERSISTENCE LAYER

Since you're going to the trouble of a rewrite, you want the freedom to model your domain from scratch in your new application. But if you're using a legacy DB whose schema you can't change, it's easy to end up being constrained by the DB tables and the legacy models that led to their creation. You'll likely have a fundamental mismatch between your application's models and the DB in which you have to persist them.

To handle this mismatch, you'll need to include a translation layer in your application to convert from your domain-level models to the models that are persisted in the

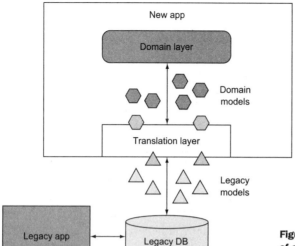

Figure 6.3   A translation layer takes care of converting between models in the domain layer and the data in the legacy DB.

DB, and vice versa. It's important to make this translation layer absolutely watertight, to avoid any risk of the legacy models escaping into your new application and corrupting your lovely new codebase. Be prepared to invest a lot of development time in building the translation layer early on in the project, as it will undoubtedly pay off in the end.

Figure 6.3 shows this translation layer sitting between the application and the DB, converting legacy models (nasty triangles) into models in the new domain (beautiful hexagons).

Let's look at an example of a translation layer for World of RuneQuest. In the original version of World of RuneQuest, no distinction is made between a Player (a human user) and a Character (that user's persona inside the game). In fact, there is no Character model at all, only Player. But in the rewrite, we want Players to be able to create multiple Characters and choose between them whenever they play.

In the legacy DB design, each Player is represented by a record in the player table. This record contains information about the human user (their username, hashed password, and so on) and about that user's persona in the game (such as species, strength, and magic points). Obviously we'll need to change this DB design if we want to support multiple Characters per Player, but how can we do this in a way that maintains compatibility with the legacy application?

One way would be to leave each Player's first Character in the player table, while putting all the Player's other Characters in a new character table. If a Player creates five Characters, one will be stored in the player table and the other four will be in the character table.

In terms of compatibility with the legacy application, this is a good solution. The legacy application will ignore the newly created table, and as far as it's concerned,

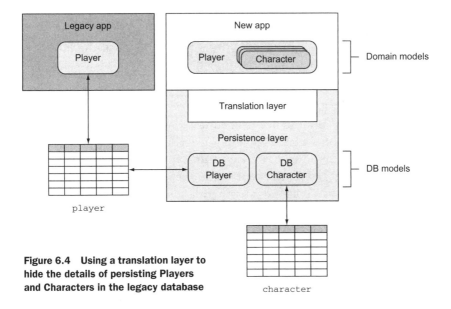

Figure 6.4 Using a translation layer to hide the details of persisting Players and Characters in the legacy database

nothing has changed. But in the context of our new application, this is a horrible hack. In our domain models, we don't want to know anything about the arbitrary split between first character and other four; we just want the Player model to contain a list of five Characters.

This is, of course, where the translation layer comes to the rescue. We can hide all the gory details of translating between DB models and domain models in the translation layer, so that hacks performed for the sake of legacy compatibility don't infect the core of our application. Figure 6.4 illustrates this.

It should be noted that in this example, a translation layer isn't the only possible solution. You might prefer to do the translation at the database level, using views, rather than in code. You could do the following:

1. Create the new character table and move the character-related fields out of player into character.
2. Create a view called `player_character` that contains the data the legacy app expects to find in the player table.
3. Make a small change to the legacy app so that it queries the new `player _character` view instead of the player table.
4. Make the view writable, if possible, so that the correct records are updated when the legacy app runs an SQL UPDATE against the view.

Personally, I tend to prefer keeping logic like this out of the DB and implementing it in code at the application layer, where it's easier to read, easier to test, and more visible to developers. When parts of a legacy application are implemented in DB triggers, stored procedures, shell scripts running as `cron` tasks on production servers, or anywhere else that can't be found just by looking through the source code, it can be very confusing for developers who come along to maintain the application later.

Performing translation at the application layer may involve multiple DB queries and can be much slower than doing it inside the DB using views, triggers, and so on. If performance is a priority, then translation at the DB layer can be more appropriate.

PLAN FOR THE DAY YOU GAIN CONTROL OF THE DB

As long as the legacy application is still running, you'll be restricted in the changes you can make to the DB schema. You can safely add new tables, as the legacy application will just ignore them, and you can probably add indexes to existing tables to improve performance, but that's about it. If there's anything you don't like about the current DB structure, you'll have to put up with it and work around it.

But as soon as you switch off the legacy system, you can take full control of the database. At this point you're free to alter the DB however you like and refactor all the parts that don't fit your new domain models or are simply a mess.

Because it might be months, or even years, before that day comes, it's a good idea to keep a running list of all the DB changes you want to make, just so you don't forget them. This could be a simple text file, stored in version control along with the project's source code, full of comments like "remove the `game.created_by` column because it's not used anymore" or "change `player.is_premium_member` from a `varchar` to a `boolean`." Or it could be a set of DB migration scripts, ready to run when the time comes.

For each change you want to make, you should leave some kind of record near any source code that's currently working around the problem, so you can find and update this source code once you've refactored the DB. This might take the form of a comment in the code, but depending on the language you may be able to take a more structured approach. In Java or C#, for example, you could define a custom annotation or attribute for marking such methods.

6.3.2   *Creating a new DB*

If you don't want to share the legacy application's database, the alternative approach is to create a brand new datastore for your new application.

The pros and cons of this approach are, of course, the opposite of those listed earlier. In short, you get the freedom to choose your datastore technology and schema according to the needs of your application, but you pay for it with the overhead of having to manage two datastores and synchronize data between them.

You'll need to build a number of tools to keep the data in your two datastores synchronized.

REAL-TIME SYNCHRONIZATION

Depending on your application's needs, you may need all writes in one DB to also appear instantly in the other, implying some kind of real-time notifications between the applications. This might be implemented using database triggers or in the application layer, as shown in figure 6.5.

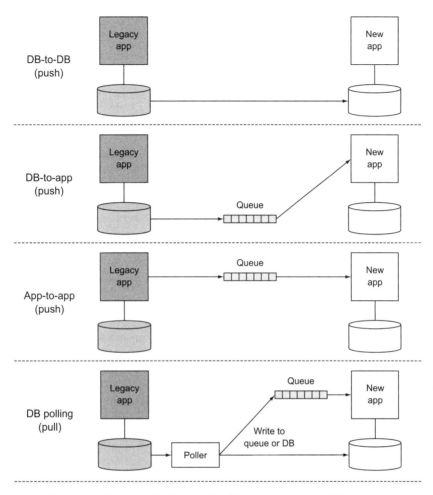

Figure 6.5 Different approaches for synchronizing DB writes in real time

In the first case, a DB trigger is used to copy writes directly from one DB to the other.

In the second case, a DB trigger writes the update to a queue, which is then consumed by the application. The reason for using a queue, rather than sending the data directly to an API endpoint on the application, is to avoid losing writes when the application is not running.

In the third case, the application writes to the queue whenever it updates data in the DB. The problem with this approach is that it requires implementation work on the legacy application side. You'll need to add code to the legacy application to send a message to a queue every time it writes to the DB, which is undesirable for a couple of reasons:

- The legacy application might be difficult to extend in this way. After all, you're rewriting it because it's difficult to maintain.

- Any change you make to the legacy code has an associated risk of introducing bugs.

If your requirements can allow for a slight lag in write replication, it might be to go for the fourth approach, building a tool that polls the DB regularly (such as once a second) and replicates writes to the new application in near real time. Pulling the data out of the legacy system like this, instead of pushing it, means you can avoid making too many changes to the legacy code.

BATCH SYNCHRONIZATION

As well as replicating new writes in real time (or near real time), you'll need a tool to copy a batch of existing updates from one datastore to the other. The tool should support both a full replication of the whole datastore and replication of only updates that match a certain query, such as all updates that occurred in the last hour. The former is useful when a bug in your new application corrupts its own datastore beyond repair, which *will* happen at least once during development, and the latter is useful for recovering quickly when some real-time updates are missed, which will also happen occasionally.

Note that if you go for the DB polling approach to real-time synchronization and build a tool that polls the legacy DB and replicates the latest writes, there's no need to build a separate tool for batch synchronization. You can use the same tool to do various kinds of synchronization, just by changing the query that the tool uses to find the writes it needs to replicate. Some examples are shown in table 6.1.

Table 6.1 Example queries to find writes matching different synchronization strategies

Synchronization type	Example PostgreSQL query fragment
Near real time	`WHERE last_updated > current_timestamp - interval '1 second'`
Batch (re-replicate last 24 hours' worth of data to recover from a bug)	`WHERE last_updated > current_timestamp - interval '1 day'`
Batch (replicate whole DB)	`WHERE 1 = 1`

MONITORING

You'll need monitoring tools to continuously check that the data replication is working as expected, ensuring both datastores contain the same data. When the monitoring system discovers that any updates have been missed, it should at least send an alert to the development team, and if possible recover automatically by triggering a re-replication of the affected data.

The monitoring tool might be as simple as a script run periodically by `cron`, but you might want to consider adding a graphical dashboard to reassure people that both the data replication and the monitoring system are actually doing something.

PUTTING IT ALL TOGETHER

Figure 6.6 shows an example of how the whole system might fit together, including the old and new applications, the batch replication scripts, and the monitoring tool.

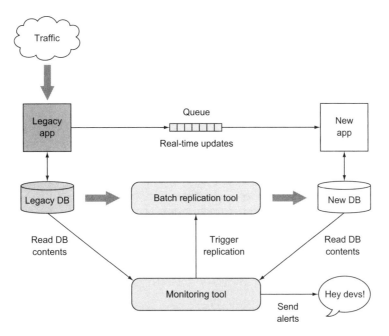

Figure 6.6 Infrastructure to reliably replicate data between a legacy application and its replacement during the migration period, when both applications are running

In this example, traffic is currently being directed to the legacy application. It sends notifications to the new application in real time, via a queue. There's also a separate tool that can replicate batches of updates. When the monitoring tool notices any missing updates, it sends an alert to developers and automatically triggers a replication of the missing data.

It's important to note that it should be possible to synchronize data, both in real time and in batches, in both directions. All data written using the old application must be visible to the new one, and vice versa. This gives you the freedom to run both applications for some time, switching traffic between them until you're sure that the new system is working correctly. Whenever you find a problem with the new application, you can switch the users back to the old one until it's fixed. This makes the migration process much less risky than a Big Bang cutover with no provision for failing over to the old system when things go wrong.

Figure 6.7 shows an example of how the process of migrating from the old system to the new one might look.

Before the cutover, traffic flows to the legacy application, which replicates writes to the new application. After cutting over, traffic is routed to the new application instead,

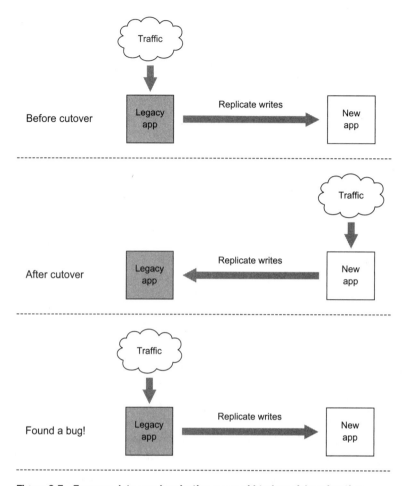

Figure 6.7   Two-way data synchronization as an aid to less risky migration

and write replication starts to flow the other way. The legacy application will have all the latest data in its database, so if you find a bug in the new application, you can switch traffic back to the legacy application while you fix it.

One thing that should be avoided, unless you're willing to take on an order of magnitude more complexity, is splitting the incoming traffic and sending some traffic to both applications at the same time. This implies that they're both writing to their respective DBs (or even to the same DB) simultaneously, and those writes are being synchronized both ways in real time, which leads to all kinds of difficulties. What do you do, for example, if one application tries to update a record that the other one is deleting? Although this kind of two-way synchronization isn't impossible, it's certainly non-trivial and the risk of a data-corrupting bug is high.

REPLICATING TRAFFIC

Replicating traffic—copying all incoming requests from clients and sending them to both applications (but, of course, returning only one application's responses)—is an alternative approach that can simplify things by obviating the need for one application to forward writes to the other. Each application will receive and process all requests and update its own database, caches, and so on, blissfully unaware of the other's existence. However, this approach is only applicable under certain conditions:

- The applications don't share a DB (otherwise they would both try to write the same data to it at the same time).
- The new application is relatively stable (it's running and able to receive traffic most of the time, and you have a way to recover any data that it missed out on whenever it wasn't running).

Figure 6.8 shows an example of performing replication at the level of incoming traffic rather than DB writes.

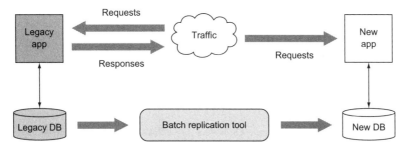

Figure 6.8 Replicating incoming traffic as an alternative to real-time write replication between the applications

As you can see, requests are sent to both applications, but only the responses from one application are returned to clients. There's a batch replication tool in place for recovery from bugs or downtime in the new application.

6.3.3 Inter-app communication

When you develop an application, you usually assume that it will be the sole writer of its own database. The software is designed with the implicit assumption that no data will ever change unless the application itself changes it. If you invalidate this assumption, then all kinds of things might start to break. If the application is performing any caching of DB query results, it may unwittingly be serving stale data from its cache because somebody else has updated the data in the DB. Even worse, if the application then performs a DB write based on that stale data, it may overwrite the data that was written by the third party.

When we run a legacy application and its replacement in parallel, they are no longer the sole writers of their respective DBs, so the assumption becomes invalid. If they're sharing the DB, then obviously they are both writing to it, so there are two writers. And even if they have separate DBs, the other application (or a batch replication tool) might be replicating writes directly to the DB.

The essence of the problem is that the applications have no way of knowing when somebody else has made a write to their DB. But if we notify the application whenever we make a write, it can take action accordingly. For example, if it receives a notification saying "I just updated User 123 in your DB," then it can remove all data about User 123 from its in-memory caches.

To support these notifications, we need to implement two things in both the existing legacy application and the new application, as shown in figure 6.9:

- A notifier that sends a notification to the other application every time it writes to the DB
- An endpoint that can receive notifications and act upon them

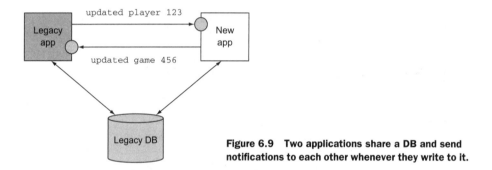

Figure 6.9   Two applications share a DB and send notifications to each other whenever they write to it.

On the legacy application side, it doesn't really matter how you implement this. As long as it works, the implementation can be as dirty as you like. But in the new application, the notification system should be implemented with an eye to the future, bearing in mind that it will become obsolete as soon as the legacy application is shut down. In other words, it should be implemented in a way that's easy to remove.

One design pattern that makes sense in this case is Event Bus (also known as Publish/Subscribe). Whenever the persistence layer writes data to the DB, it pushes an event onto the bus, which is then broadcast to all listeners. A listener then reacts to the event by sending a corresponding notification to the legacy application.

When the legacy application is shut down, all we need to do is remove the listener. We can leave the Event Bus system in place, as it may prove useful for other features in the future.

6.4   *Summary*

- All large software projects, including rewrites, should have a scope document.
- Make your rewrite as iterative as possible, even if it means more effort in total, in order to reduce risk.

- Resist the temptation to treat the existing implementation as the ultimate source of truth. Treat it as a valuable reference, but it's OK for the new spec to diverge from it.

- If your application has a DB, you need to choose between creating a new DB or letting the old and new implementations share the same datastore. Separating the DBs is more complex if you need to keep them in sync, but it gives you a lot more freedom.

- If your old and new applications share a datastore, you'll need to build a translation layer to translate between the old and new models.

- If you give your old and new applications separate datastores, be prepared to invest a lot of effort in tooling to synchronize the two DBs.

- If your DB synchronization mechanism writes directly to the DB, be careful you don't violate any assumptions the application makes about being the sole writer.

Part 3

Beyond refactoring— improving project workflow and infrastructure

In this third and final part of this book, we're going to shift our focus away from *what* software we should be writing and look at *how* we build and maintain that software.

This is a broad topic that includes setting up your local machine for efficient software development, managing the multiple environments in which the software needs to run, using a version control system effectively when working in a team, and deploying the software to production quickly and reliably.

I'll introduce quite a few tools over the course of the next three chapters, including Vagrant, Ansible, Gradle, and Fabric. Don't worry if you've never used these tools, or if you're already happily using a different set of tools to do the same things. I'm using them simply for the sake of providing concrete examples, so that you can learn the underlying techniques. Where applicable, I'll provide information about similar tools that you can use.

In the final chapter I'll give you some tips on how to prevent the software you write today from becoming tomorrow's legacy horror story.

Automating the
development environment

7

This chapter covers

- The value of a good README file
- Automating the development environment using Vagrant and Ansible
- Removing dependencies on external resources to make developers more autonomous

Nearly all software has some dependencies on its surrounding environment. The software (or rather the humans who developed it) expects certain other software to be running and some configuration to have been performed on the machine where it will run. For example, a lot of applications use a database to store their data, so they depend on a database server running somewhere and being accessible. As an example of a configuration dependency, the software might expect a certain directory to exist so it can save its log files inside it.

Discovering all of these dependencies, and provisioning the environment in order to satisfy them, can be quite tedious. The dependencies are often poorly documented, simply because there's no good place or standard format in which to document them.

In this chapter we'll look at how to make it as easy as possible for you and others to set up a development environment and get started on maintaining a piece of legacy software. We'll write scripts that not only automate the provisioning process, but also act as documentation, making it easy for later maintainers to understand the software's dependencies.

7.1   First day on the job

Congratulations, and welcome to your new job at Fzzle, Inc. Once the HR guy has given you the tour of the office, he takes you to meet your new boss. Anna is the tech lead of the User Services team, where you'll be working as a full-stack developer. She shows you your desk and fills you in on the details of the job.

First, a little background. Fzzle is a survivor of the dot-com bubble, a veteran of the social web sector. At its heart, it's a social network, but over the years it has accumulated a large number of auxiliary services and microsites. With a business model based on a combination of freemium membership and targeted ads, the company enjoys steady growth and boasts a few million users.

Fzzle.com's architecture is service-oriented, with a few dozen services of varying size, age, and implementation technology making up the site. As the vagueness of the User Services team's name suggests, the team is in charge of developing and maintaining a variety of these services. Unfortunately, there aren't enough developers in the team to properly maintain all the services they own, so Anna is really happy to have another pair of hands to share the workload. Currently she and the other developers are busy writing a brand new service, so you'll be tasked with maintaining some of the legacy services that they haven't had time to look after recently.

Your first job will be to add a new feature to the User Activity Dashboard (UAD). This is an in-house web application designed to be used by Fzzle's marketing department and advertising partners. It displays detailed information about how many users have been active on the site, what they've been viewing, which user segments are growing, and so on, so that advertisers can plan targeted ad campaigns. Unfortunately the UAD is quite old and hasn't received much development love recently, despite being critical to the business.

Anna tells you to start by cloning the Git repository and getting the UAD running on your local machine. She tells you to ask for help if you get stuck, but she looks really busy, so you decide to try your best to get things set up on your own, without bothering her. After all, how hard can it be?

7.1.1   Setting up the UAD development environment

As instructed, you clone the repository and take a look around. First stop, the README file. Hmm, no README? That's odd. I guess you'll have to do some detective work to find out how to build and run this thing.

Next you find an Ant build file, some Java source files, and a web.xml file. Now you're getting somewhere. It looks like it's a standard Java web app, so it should run on any web app container. You have experience with Apache Tomcat, so you grab a copy from the website and install it. You also head over to the Oracle website and download the latest Java package.

Once you've got Java and Tomcat installed, you open up the Ant build file in your editor and work out how to compile the application and package it into a WAR file, suitable for deployment on Tomcat. You find a target called package that seems to do what you want, so you go to the Ant website, download and install Ant, and then run ant package.

```
$ ant package
Buildfile: /Users/chris/code/uad/build.xml

clean:

compile:
    [mkdir] Created dir: /Users/chris/code/uad/dest
    [javac] Compiling 157 source files to /Users/chris/code/uad/dest

package:
    [war] Building war: /Users/chris/code/uad/uad.war

BUILD SUCCESSFUL
Total time: 15 seconds
```

Hey presto, it worked! You copy the resulting WAR file to your Tomcat webapps directory, start Tomcat, and point your browser to http://localhost:8080/uad/.

Unfortunately, you're met with a completely blank page. Checking the Tomcat logs, you find the following error message:

```
Cannot start the User Activity Dashboard. Make sure $RESIN_3_HOME is set.
```

Resin? You've heard of that, but never used it before. It's a Java web application container, just like Tomcat. Based on the error message, it looks like you need to install version 3. You head over to the Resin website, find a download page for Resin 3 (which turns out to be very old and deprecated, but luckily still available), download and install it. You do your best to configure it based on information you find in a blog post.

After copying the WAR file to the Resin webapps folder and starting Resin, you're immediately greeted with another error message:

```
Failed to connect to DB (jdbc:postgresql://testdb/uad)
Check DB username and password.
```

While you're ruminating on this error message, Anna comes over and says, "Sorry, I forgot to tell you, the instructions to set up UAD are on the developer wiki. Take a look at http://devwiki/ and you should be able to find it."

The wiki page, shown in figure 7.1, clears up a few mysteries. But it also appears to be unreliable and poorly maintained, so anything written on that page should probably be taken with a grain of salt.

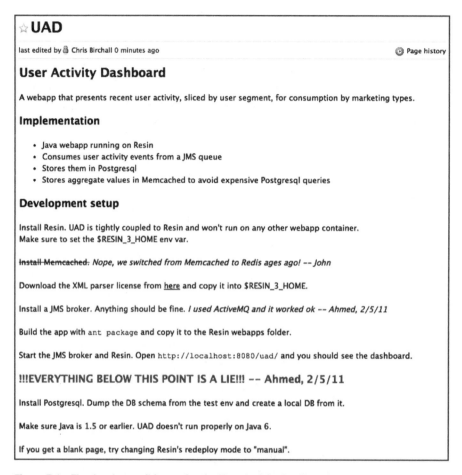

Figure 7.1   The developer wiki page for the User Activity Dashboard

Based on the wiki page, it looks like the application has a number of external dependencies, some of which you have already discovered.

- It needs a Java web app container, specifically Resin 3.
- It needs a Java Messaging Service (JMS) message broker to provide a message queue. It looks like Apache ActiveMQ is a good bet.
- It needs a PostgreSQL database in which to store its raw data.
- It needs a Redis instance in which to store aggregate data.
- Finally, it needs the license file for a proprietary XML parser to be installed.

You make a note of this and go back to trying to solve your DB connection issue. Looking at the error message in the logs again, it looks like the application is trying to connect to a PostgreSQL DB in the test environment. But where is it getting that JDBC URL from? There must be a configuration file somewhere. Looking in the Git repository again, you find a file called config.properties:

```
# Developer config for User Activity Dashboard.
# These values will be overridden with environment vars in production.

db.url=jdbc:postgresql://testdb/uad
# If you don't have a DB user, ask the ops team to create one
db.username=Put your DB username here
db.password=Put your DB password here

redis.host=localhost
redis.port=6379

jms.host=localhost
jms.port=61616
jms.queue=uad_messages
```

Following the instructions in the configuration file comment, you fire off an email to the ops team asking for a DB account for the test environment. By this time it's already past 3 p.m., so you're unlikely to get a response today.

In the meantime, you can get started on installing and configuring Redis and ActiveMQ, and working out where to put that XML parser license key ...

7.1.2   *What went wrong?*

That story got pretty long, but I wanted you to feel the frustration of the detective work that's often needed when starting work on a legacy codebase for the first time.

There were a few distinct, but interrelated, reasons why the experience of setting up the UAD project was so painful. Let's look at them in turn.

POOR DOCUMENTATION

The first problem with the documentation for the UAD project was that it wasn't discoverable. There's no point in writing documentation if people can't find it.

In general, the closer the documentation is to the source code, the easier it is for a developer to find. I recommend storing the documentation inside the same repository as the source code, preferably in the root directory where it's easy to spot. If you prefer to keep your documentation elsewhere, such as on a wiki, then at least add a text file to the repository with a link to the docs.

The second problem is that the wiki page appeared to have no proper structure. This meant that not only was it difficult to read, it was also difficult to update. There was no policy for how to update it, so over time it gradually become a mishmash of hints, corrections, and out-of-date or dubious information.

The key to making documentation easy to write, easy to read, and easy to update is pretty simple: give it some structure, and keep it short. We'll take a look at how to do this in the next section.

LACK OF AUTOMATION

As you probably noticed, there were a lot of tedious manual steps involved in getting the UAD working on a development machine. A lot of these steps were quite similar, something like this:

1 Download something.

2 Install it (unzip it and copy it somewhere).

3 Configure it (update some values in a text file).

This sort of procedure is just crying out to be automated. The benefits of automation are manifold:

- *Less developer time wasted*—Remember John and Ahmed who left notes on the wiki page? They, along with who knows how many others, had to go through exactly the same manual steps as you did.

- *Less verbose documentation*—This means it's more likely to be read and more likely to be kept up to date.

- *Better parity between developers' machines*—All developers will be running exactly the same versions of the same software.

RELIANCE ON EXTERNAL RESOURCES

You had to ask the ops team to create a PostgreSQL user for you. This sort of thing (a step that involves waiting for a human to respond) can really slow down the onboarding process, and it can be very frustrating to wait for somebody to reply to your email before you can finish setting up your development environment.

Ideally a developer should be able to install and run all necessary dependencies on their local machine. That way they have complete control over those dependencies. If they need to create a database user, for example, they can go ahead and do it. (Or, even better, have a script do it for them!) Doing everything you can to maintain developers' autonomy and remove blocking steps in workflows can really boost productivity.

Having developers run everything locally also reduces the scope for people to tread on each other's toes. You'll no longer hear developers saying things like, "Anybody mind if I change the time on this server? I need to test something" or "Oops, I just wiped the DB in the test environment. Sorry everyone!"

In the rest of the chapter we'll look at how to improve the onboarding process for UAD, first by improving the documentation and then by adding some automation.

7.2 *The value of a good README*

In my experience, a README file in the root folder of the source code's repository is the most effective form of documentation. It's highly discoverable, it's likely to remain up to date because it's close to the source code, and if written well it will make a new developer's onboarding process fast and painless.

Another bonus is that, because it's in the same repository as the source code, the README becomes a target for code review. Whenever you make a change to the software that alters the development environment's setup procedure, the reviewer can check that the README has been updated accordingly.

README FILE FORMAT The README should be a human-readable plain text file so that developers can open it in their editor of choice. There are a number of popular formats for structured text, but my preference is for Markdown. I find it easy to read and write, especially when including code samples, and sites such as GitHub can render it beautifully.

A README file should be structured as follows.

Listing 7.1　An example README file in Markdown format

```
# My example software

Brief explanation of what the software is.

## Dependencies

* Java 7 or newer
* Memcached
...

The following environment variables must be set when running:

* `JAVA_HOME`
...

## How to configure

Edit `conf/dev-config.properties` if you want to change the Memcached port, etc.

## How to run locally

1. Make sure Memcached is running
2. Run `mvn jetty:run`
3. Point your browser at `http://localhost:8080/foo`

## How to run tests

1. Make sure Memcached is running
2. Run `mvn test`

## How to build

Run `mvn package` to create a WAR file in the `target` folder.

## How to release/deploy

Run `./release.sh` and follow the prompts.
```

This example gives a new developer exactly the information they need to get started, and nothing more. The key to keeping the README file useful is to make it concise.

You may want to write more documentation about your software, such as to explain the architecture or how to troubleshoot when things go wrong in production, but this should not go into the README. You could write additional documentation on a wiki (making sure to link to it from the README) or perhaps add a docs folder to the repository and write it in separate Markdown files there.

Of course, if a lot of manual setup is needed to get the software running locally, it will be difficult to keep the README short. In the next section we'll look at how to automate the environment setup, which will solve this problem.

7.3   *Automating the development environment with Vagrant and Ansible*

There are a variety of tools available to help you automate the setup of a development machine. In the remainder of this chapter we'll use Vagrant and Ansible to perform this automation for the UAD project.

We'll look at both tools in detail soon, but here's a quick preview of what they do and why we want to use them.

- *Vagrant*—Vagrant automates the process of managing virtual machines (VMs), either on your local development machine or in the cloud. The point of this is that you can have one VM for each piece of software that you develop. The software's dependencies (Ruby runtimes, databases, web servers, and so on) are all kept inside the VM, so they're nicely isolated from everything else you have installed on your machine.
- *Ansible*—Ansible automates the provisioning of your application— the installation and configuration of all of its dependencies. You write down the steps needed in a set of YAML files, and Ansible takes care of performing those steps. This automation makes provisioning easy and repeatable and reduces the chance of incorrect provisioning due to human error.

7.3.1   *Introducing Vagrant*

Vagrant is a tool that allows you to programmatically build an isolated environment for your application and all of its dependencies.

The Vagrant environment is a VM, so it enjoys complete isolation from both the host machine and any other Vagrant machines you may be running. For the underlying VM technology, Vagrant supports VirtualBox, VMware, and even remote machines running on Amazon's EC2 infrastructure.

The vagrant command lets you manage your VMs (starting them, stopping them, destroying unneeded VMs, and so on), and you can log in to a VM simply by typing vagrant ssh. You can also share directories (such as your software's source code repository) between the host machine and the VM, and Vagrant can forward ports from the VM to the host machine, so you could access a web server running on the VM by accessing http://localhost/ on your local machine.

The main benefits of using Vagrant are as follows.

- It makes it easy to automate the setup of a development environment inside a VM, as you'll see shortly.
- Each VM is isolated from the host machine and other VMs, so you don't need to worry about version conflicts when you have many different projects set up on the same machine. If one project needs Python 2.6, Ruby 1.8.1, and PostgreSQL 9.1, while another needs Python 2.7, Ruby 2.0, and PostgreSQL 9.3, it can be tricky to set everything up on your development machine. But if each project lives in a separate VM, it can make life easier.

- The VMs are usually Linux machines, so if you're using Linux in production, you can exactly recreate the production environment.

If you want to get really fancy, Vagrant even supports multi-VM setups, so you could build the entire stack for your application (including web servers, DB servers, cache servers, Elasticsearch clusters, and what have you), exactly replicating the setup you have in production, but all running inside your development machine!

If you want to follow along with the rest of the chapter and you don't have Vagrant installed, head over to the Vagrant website (www.vagrantup.com/) and follow the installation instructions. It's pretty simple. Note that you'll also need a VM provider such as VirtualBox or VMware installed. For the remainder of the chapter I'll be using VirtualBox.

7.3.2 Setting up Vagrant for the UAD project

To add Vagrant support to the UAD, you first need to create a Vagrantfile. This is a file in the root folder of the repository named, unsurprisingly, `Vagrantfile`. It's a configuration file, written in a Ruby DSL, that tells Vagrant how to set up the VM for this project.

You can create a new Vagrantfile by running `vagrant init`. A minimal Vagrantfile is shown here:

```
VAGRANTFILE_API_VERSION = "2"

Vagrant.configure(VAGRANTFILE_API_VERSION) do |config|
  config.vm.box = "ubuntu/trusty64"
end
```

Note that you need to specify what box to use for your VM. A box is a base image that Vagrant can use as a foundation for building a new VM. I'll be using 64-bit Ubuntu 14.04 (Trusty Tahr) as the OS for my virtual machine, so I set the box to `ubuntu/trusty64`. There are many other boxes available on the Vagrant website.

> **WATCH OUT FOR SPACES IN THE PATH** The code shown in the remainder of this chapter won't work (and you'll get some confusing error messages) if you have spaces anywhere in the path of your working directory. If you want to follow along at home, make sure you don't get caught out by this.

Now you're ready to start your VM by typing `vagrant up`. Once it boots, you can log in by typing `vagrant ssh` and take a look around.

There's not much to see yet, but one thing to notice is that the folder containing the Vagrantfile has been automatically shared, so it's available as `/vagrant` inside the VM. This is a two-way share, so any changes you make in the VM will be reflected in real time on your host machine, and vice versa.

> **CODE ONLINE** You can see the complete code for this chapter in the GitHub repo (https://github.com/cb372/ReengLegacySoft).

So far Vagrant isn't doing anything very useful, as we have only an empty Linux machine. The next step is to automate the installation and configuration of the UAD's dependencies.

7.3.3   *Automatic provisioning using Ansible*

The installation and configuration of everything needed to run a piece of software is known as *provisioning*. Vagrant supports a number of ways of provisioning, including Chef, Puppet, Docker, Ansible, and even plain old shell scripts.

For simple tasks, a bunch of shell scripts is often good enough. But they're difficult to compose and reuse, so if you want to do more complex provisioning or reuse parts of the provisioning script across multiple projects or environments, it's a good idea to use a more powerful tool. In this book I'll be using Ansible, but you can achieve much the same thing using Docker, Chef, Puppet, Salt, or whatever tool you're happiest with.

In this chapter we're going to write a few Ansible scripts to provision the UAD application, and in chapter 8 we'll reuse those scripts so we can perform exactly the same provisioning across all our environments, from the local development machine all the way through to production.

Before we can provision with Ansible, we need to install it on the host machine. See the installation docs on the Ansible website for details (http://docs.ansible .com/intro_installation.html). (I appreciate the irony of manually installing all this stuff so we can automate the installation of other stuff, but I promise this is the last thing you'll need to install manually. And after you've installed VirtualBox, Vagrant, and Ansible once, you can use them for all your projects.)

> **ANSIBLE ON WINDOWS**   Ansible doesn't officially support running on Windows, but with a bit of work it's possible to get it running. The Azavea Labs blog has an excellent step-by-step guide on getting Vagrant and Ansible working on Windows: "Running Vagrant with Ansible Provisioning on Windows" (http://mng.bz/WM84).

Unlike other provisioning tools such as Chef or Puppet, Ansible is agentless. This means you don't need to install any Ansible agent on your Vagrant VM. Instead, whenever you run Ansible, it will execute commands on the VM remotely using SSH.

To tell Ansible what to install on your VM, you need to write a YAML file called a playbook, which we'll save as provisioning/playbook.yml. A minimal example is shown here.

```
---
- hosts: all
  tasks:
    - name: Print Hello world
      debug: msg="Hello world"
```

This tells Ansible two things. First, it should run the script on all hosts that it knows about. In our case, we only have a single VM, so this is fine for our purposes. Second, it should run a task that prints "Hello world".

THE YAML FORMAT Ansible files are all written in the YAML format. Indentation is used to represent the structure of your data, and you must use spaces (not tabs) for indentation.

You'll also need to add a couple of lines to your Vagrantfile to tell Vagrant to use Ansible for provisioning. Your Vagrantfile should now look like this.

```
VAGRANTFILE_API_VERSION = "2"

Vagrant.configure(VAGRANTFILE_API_VERSION) do |config|
  config.vm.box = "ubuntu/trusty64"

  config.vm.provision "ansible" do |ansible|
    ansible.playbook = "provisioning/playbook.yml"
  end
end
```

Now if you run `vagrant provision`, you should see output something like the following.

```
PLAY [all] ********************************************************************

GATHERING FACTS **************************************************************
ok: [default]

TASK: [Print Hello world] ****************************************************
ok: [default] => {
    "msg": "Hello world"
}

PLAY RECAP *******************************************************************
default                     : ok=2    changed=0    unreachable=0    failed=0
```

Now that you've got Ansible hooked up to Vagrant, you can use it to install the dependencies for the UAD. Recall that you need to do the following:

- Install Java
- Install Apache Ant
- Install Redis
- Install Resin 3.x
- Install and configure Apache ActiveMQ
- Download a license file and copy it to the Resin installation folder

We'll use the concept of Ansible roles, creating a separate role for each of these dependencies. This keeps each dependency cleanly separated, so we can later reuse them individually if we wish. Let's start with Java, as we need that before we can do much else.

OpenJDK can be installed using the `apt` package manager in Ubuntu, so our Java role will be quite simple. It will have just one task that installs the `opendjk-7-jdk` package.

Let's create a new file, provisioning/roles/java/tasks/main.yml (by convention this is where Ansible will look for the Java role's tasks), and write our task there:

```
---
- name: install OpenJDK 7 JDK
  apt: name=openjdk-7-jdk state=present
```

There are a couple of things to note, even in this very short file. First, apt is the name of a built-in Ansible module. There are loads of these, and it's worth becoming familiar with them so you don't accidentally reinvent the wheel when there's already a module that does what you want. You can see a list of them, with documentation and examples, on the Ansible website (http://docs.ansible.com/list_of_all_modules.html).

Second, you're not actually telling Ansible to install Java, but rather to ensure the Java package is present. Ansible is smart enough to check if the package is already installed before it tries to install it. This means that (well-written) Ansible playbooks are idempotent, so you can run them as many times as you like.

We need to tell the playbook to use our new Java role, so let's update the provisioning/playbook.yml file. It should now look like this.

```
---
- hosts: all
  sudo: yes
  roles:
    - java
```

Now if you run vagrant provision again, the output should look something like this.

```
PLAY [all] ****************************************************************
ATHERING FACTS ***********************************************************
ok: [default]

TASK: [java | install OpenJDK 7 JDK] *************************************
changed: [default]

PLAY RECAP ***************************************************************
default                     : ok=2    changed=1    unreachable=0    failed=0
```

If you want to check that it worked, SSH into the VM and run java -version:

```
vagrant@vagrant-ubuntu-trusty-64:~$ java -version
java version "1.7.0_79"
OpenJDK Runtime Environment (IcedTea 2.5.5) (7u79-2.5.5-0ubuntu0.14.04.2)
OpenJDK 64-Bit Server VM (build 24.79-b02, mixed mode)
```

Cool! You just installed your first dependency using Vagrant and Ansible.

7.3.4   *Adding more roles*

Let's continue in the same vein, adding another role for each of the dependencies. Next in the list are Redis and Ant, but they're pretty much the same as Java (just installing a package using apt), so I'll gloss over them here. Remember, you can view the complete code for this chapter in the GitHub repo (https://github.com/cb372 /ReengLegacySoft).

We'll try Resin next. The Resin role's tasks file is shown in the following listing. This file should be saved as provisioning/roles/resin/tasks/main.yml.

Listing 7.2 Ansible tasks to install Resin 3.x

```
---
- name: download Resin tarball
  get_url: >
    url=http://www.caucho.com/download/resin-3.1.14.tar.gz
    dest=/tmp/resin-3.1.14.tar.gz

- name: extract Resin tarball
  unarchive: >
    src=/tmp/resin-3.1.14.tar.gz
    dest=/usr/local
    copy=no

- name: change owner of Resin files
  file: >
    state=directory
    path=/usr/local/resin-3.1.14
    owner=vagrant
    group=vagrant
    recurse=yes

- name: create /usr/local/resin symlink
  file: >
    state=link
    src=/usr/local/resin-3.1.14
    path=/usr/local/resin

- name: set RESIN_3_HOME env var
  lineinfile: >
    state=present
    dest=/etc/profile.d/resin_3_home.sh
    line='export RESIN_3_HOME=/usr/local/resin'
    create=yes
```

This file is much longer than the previous one, but if you look at each task in turn, you'll see that it's not doing anything too complicated. The tasks, which will be run by Ansible in the order they're written, are doing the following:

1 Downloading a tarball from the Resin website
2 Extracting it under /usr/local
3 Changing its owner from root to the vagrant user
4 Creating a convenient symlink at /usr/local/resin
5 Setting up the RESIN_3_HOME environment variable that the UAD application requires

If you add the new Resin role to the main playbook file and run vagrant provision again, you should end up with Resin installed and ready to run.

The tasks for the next role, ActiveMQ, are similar to those for installing Resin (download a tarball, extract it, and create a symlink). The only task of note is the final one:

```
- name: customize ActiveMQ configuration
  copy: >
    src=activemq-custom-config.xml
    dest=/usr/local/activemq/conf/activemq.xml
    backup=yes
    owner=vagrant
    group=vagrant
```

This task uses Ansible's copy module, which copies a file from the host machine to the VM. You use this to overwrite ActiveMQ's configuration file with a customized one after the tarball has been extracted. This is a common technique, in which large files are downloaded from the internet onto the VM, but smaller files, such as configuration files, are stored in the repository and copied from the host machine.

The only remaining task is to download a license file for a proprietary XML parsing library from somewhere on the company's internal network, and store it in the Resin root directory. This task is quite specific to the UAD application and likely can't be reused anywhere, so let's create a role just for UAD-specific stuff and put it in there.

I'll leave the task definition as an exercise for the reader, in case you want to practice writing Ansible scripts. (Download any random text file from the internet to represent the hypothetical license file.) A solution is available in the GitHub repo.

7.3.5 *Removing the dependency on an external database*

This is going great so far. We've managed to automate almost the entire setup of the UAD development environment with just a few short YAML files, which should make the process a lot less painful for the next person who has to set this project up on their machine.

But there's one last issue that we haven't tackled. As things stand, the software depends on a shared PostgreSQL database in the test environment, so all new starters need to ask the ops team to create a DB user for them. If we could set up a PostgreSQL DB inside the VM and tell the software to use that one instead, it would solve the problem. It would also mean that each developer would have complete control over the content of their DB, without fear of somebody else tampering with their data. Let's give it a try!

We'll assume we have some credentials for the test environment and use those credentials to connect to the DB and take a dump of the schema:

```
$ pg_dump --username chris --host=testdb --dbname=uad --schema-only > schema.sql
```

Then we'll add some Ansible tasks to do the following: install PostgreSQL, create a DB user, create an empty DB, and initialize it using the schema.sql file we just generated. This is shown in the following listing.

Listing 7.3   Ansible tasks to create and initialize a PostgreSQL database

```
- name: install PostgreSQL
  apt: name={{item}} state=present
  with_items: [ 'postgresql', 'libpq-dev', 'python-psycopg2' ]

- name: create DB user
  sudo_user: postgres
  postgresql_user: >
    name=vagrant
    password=abc
    role_attr_flags=LOGIN

- name: create the DB
  sudo_user: postgres
  postgresql_db: >
    name=uad
    owner=vagrant

- name: count DB tables
  sudo_user: postgres
  command: >
    psql uad -t -A
    -c "SELECT count(1) FROM pg_catalog.pg_tables \
        WHERE schemaname='public'"
  register: table_count

- name: copy the DB schema file if it is needed
  copy: >
    src=schema.sql
    dest=/tmp/schema.sql
  when: table_count.stdout | int == 0

- name: load the DB schema if it is not already loaded
  sudo_user: vagrant
  command: psql uad -f /tmp/schema.sql
  when: table_count.stdout | int == 0
```

The psycopg2 library is needed to use the postgresql_* modules.

Uses the number of DB tables to decide if you have already loaded the schema

This task will not run if the DB schema already contains tables.

Note that this is a little more complicated than the Ansible tasks we've written so far, because we need to do a bit of trickery to achieve idempotency. This listing does some conditional processing so that you only load the DB schema if the number of tables in the DB is zero, meaning that you haven't already loaded it.

We've now automated the creation of a local PostgreSQL DB, so we've filled in the final piece of the automation puzzle. In the next section we'll look at how this automation effort pays off.

7.3.6   *First day on the job—take two*

Congratulations, and welcome to your new job at Fzzle, Inc. Once the HR guy has given you the tour of the office, he takes you to meet your new boss. Anna is the tech lead of the User Services team. She shows you your desk and fills you in on the details of the job.

Your first task is to add a new feature to an application called the User Activity Dashboard. You clone the Git repository and take a look at the README file to see how to get it running locally.

The README explains that you can set up a development environment using Vagrant and Ansible. As standard elements of the company's recommended tool chain, these tools are preinstalled on your development machine. You kick off the vagrant up command, which will build and provision your VM. It'll take a few minutes to complete, so you wander off to figure out how the coffee machine works ...

By the time you get back, the provisioning is complete and you get the application running with little fuss. By lunchtime you start work on implementing the new feature. By the end of the day you've completed the implementation and made your first pull request, and you've also made a note of a couple of places you'd like to refactor tomorrow. Not a bad first day on the job!

7.4   Summary

- The README is the most important file in the repository.
- Making it easy for a new developer to get started will make people more likely to contribute.
- Vagrant and Ansible are useful tools for automating the provisioning of a development environment for an application.
- Where possible, you should remove dependencies on shared developer DBs and other external resources. The Vagrant VM should contain everything the application needs, so that it's all under the developer's control.

Extending automation to test, staging, and production environments

8

This chapter covers

- Using Ansible to provision multiple environments
- Moving your infrastructure to the cloud

In the previous chapter we wrote an Ansible playbook to automatically provision the local development environment for the UAD application. In this chapter we'll build on that work, refactoring our Ansible scripts so that we can reuse them to provision all our environments, all the way from the developer's machine to the production servers.

Before we start, we should quickly go over what environments a piece of software needs to run on, and why we'd want to automate the provisioning process for those environments.

Every software application will have slightly different requirements about what environments are needed in order to develop and run it, but in general the list will look something like this:

- *Development*—The developers' local machines. I'll call this the *DEV* environment.
- *Testing*—A place in which to test the software against realistic data running on hardware similar to that found in production. Depending on your needs you might have multiple testing environments for different purposes: one for everyday manual testing, one for staging, another for performance testing, and so on. In this chapter I'll assume there's only one testing environment and I'll call it *TEST*. No matter how many environments you need to cater for, the same principles apply.
- *Production*—The production environment, where real users interact with the software. If the software is something like a native mobile app or a piece of business software that the users host themselves, this environment will be out of your control, so we needn't concern ourselves with it. But if it's something like a web application that you host yourself, then you control the production environment and are in charge of provisioning it. In this chapter I'll assume the latter, and I'll call it the *PROD* environment.

Of course there's also some software, such as libraries, that don't really run at all but rather form a part of some other piece of running software. But even in that case, it might be useful to have a separate TEST environment in which to run integration tests to check that the library functions correctly as part of an application.

8.1 Benefits of automated infrastructure

There are a number of benefits to extending automatic provisioning beyond the development machines and into all environments.

8.1.1 Ensures parity across environments

After many years of people logging in to servers and manually installing new software, updating existing software, and editing configuration files, the various environments will be hopelessly out of sync. (This phenomenon is sometimes known as *configuration drift*.) Not only that, but it's also difficult to tell exactly how they differ, so you can't even remedy the situation. If you have multiple servers in each environment, then even the different servers in the same environment are likely to have subtle differences between them.

This is a problem for a couple of reasons.

- The TEST environment no longer matches PROD, so code might work correctly and pass all the tests on TEST but turn out to be broken on PROD.

  I've seen a bug caused by clock skew on production servers. The servers weren't configured to use NTP (Network Time Protocol), so over a few months their system clocks drifted a few minutes apart. This caused unexpected behavior in a distributed database that assumed all data replicas were stored on machines with synchronized clocks. In a retrospective, it was discovered that the TEST servers were configured to use NTP but the PROD ones weren't.

  Forgetting to set up NTP is quite a fundamental mistake, but these things can happen when we rely on manual processes.

- Bugs might occur on one TEST server but not on the others, or on your development machine but not on anybody else's, leading to confusion and painful troubleshooting to work out why.

If you use provisioning scripts to automate all of your environments, you can achieve perfect parity between them. You can even run your provisioning scripts against those legacy servers that have been drifting out of sync for years, instantly bringing them back into line.

8.1.2 Easy to update software

Every time a new critical security patch for commonly installed software such as OpenSSL is released, operations teams around the world let out a collective groan. If they haven't automated their infrastructure, it means they'll have to manually patch all of their servers as quickly as possible.

With automation in place, of course, it's a different story. The ops team needs to write one short script to install the patched version of OpenSSL, and then let their provisioning tool run it against all of their machines simultaneously. Their entire system could be patched and secure within minutes of the vulnerability being announced.

8.1.3 Easy to spin up new environments

As you saw in the previous chapter, tools like Ansible make it very quick and easy to create a brand new, fully provisioned environment from scratch.

This can be very useful when recovering from hardware failure. If the hard disk in one of your PROD servers explodes at 3 a.m. on a Saturday, you won't need to spend hours working out what was installed where and manually provisioning a new server. Find a spare machine and run the provisioning scripts against it and within minutes it'll be ready to run your software.

The ability to easily create a new environment can also be useful outside of disaster-recovery situations. With little effort you could spin up a whole new environment using VMs, fill it with interesting dummy data to demo a new feature, and then delete the VMs after your demo is complete. The ability to create and tear down environments cheaply gives you a lot of freedom to try new things.

8.1.4 Enables tracking of configuration changes

If you manage your provisioning scripts using a version control system such as Git, and you store the logs output by the provisioning tool each time it's run, then you have a perfect record of all changes performed on your servers. You know what changes were made, who made them, why they did it (assuming they write good commit comments), and when the change was applied to each environment.

This assumes, of course, that people aren't also manually logging in and messing with configuration files and the like, but you can prevent this by locking down SSH access so that only the provisioning tool can log in.

If you don't have automated provisioning, you could try to manually maintain a record of configuration changes, perhaps using a spreadsheet. But it would be quite tedious and, because it relies on people remembering to fill it in, it would be inherently unreliable. Why not get a tool to do this work for you?

8.2   Extending automation to other environments

Taking a set of machines that have been manually provisioned for years and moving them to a system of infrastructure automation such as Ansible carries a certain risk with it. If your Ansible playbooks don't encode all the necessary steps for setting up a server, your software might not run as you intended.

Because of this, it makes sense to automate the environments one at a time, in increasing order of importance. As shown in figure 8.1, we started with the DEV environment, which we tackled in the previous chapter. We'll next automate the TEST environment, and check that everything still works, before moving on to PROD.

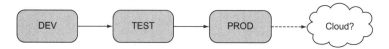

Figure 8.1   Automating environments starting with the least critical before touching PROD

At this point, you're also free to investigate moving your infrastructure into the cloud if you wish. Because you have the tooling in place to easily set up a machine from scratch, it doesn't matter whether that machine happens to be in the cloud or in your own data center. We'll talk about this more later in the chapter.

8.2.1   Refactor Ansible scripts to handle multiple environments

In the previous chapter we used Ansible in combination with Vagrant to provision the DEV environment for the UAD application. The UAD is a Java servlet application running on Resin, with dependencies on ActiveMQ, PostgreSQL, and Redis.

We want to reuse our Ansible scripts to provision TEST and PROD, but they'll need a bit of refactoring before we can do so. Specifically,

- The scripts assume that we have an OS user called `vagrant`, which will of course only be true when Ansible is run inside of Vagrant.
- In the DEV environment we want the UAD application, the PostgreSQL database, the Redis server, and the ActiveMQ broker all to run inside the same Vagrant VM, but in TEST and PROD they should be installed on separate machines.
- We want to manage multiple environments (TEST and PROD), each with a list of servers that we want to manage.

Let's tackle these problems one at a time.

INTRODUCE A USER FOR THE APPLICATION

Currently our Ansible scripts rely on an OS user called `vagrant` being present. Vagrant, of course, creates this user when we're running inside a Vagrant VM, but in a proper environment such as TEST or PROD we'll need to create a user for our application to run as. Let's add an Ansible role to create a user called `uad`.

Now is a good time to introduce Ansible's support for variables. The username is a piece of information that we'll want to refer to all over the place, so we'll make it a variable instead of hardcoding it in many different files. That way we can define the username just once, making life easier if we ever want to change its value.

The task to create a user, including a reference to the new `app_user` variable, is shown next. We'll save it as roles/user/tasks/main.yml.

```
- name: create application user
  user: name={{ app_user }} state=present
```

We should also do a quick find-and-replace on all the existing tasks, replacing any hardcoded `vagrant`s with the `{{ app_user }}` placeholder.

Of course, we also need to define the `app_user` variable, telling Ansible that it should have the value `uad`. Ansible lets us do that in a number of different ways, but we'll put it in the Playbook file, as shown next.

```
---
- hosts: all
  sudo: yes
  vars:
    - app_user: uad
  roles:
    - user
    - java
    - ant
    - resin
    - redis
    - activemq
    - postgresql
    - uad
```

Now if you run `vagrant provision` you'll see that Ansible first creates a `uad` user and then refers to that user in subsequent tasks where appropriate.

SEPARATE THE APPLICATION, DB, REDIS, AND ACTIVEMQ HOSTS

In the DEV environment we only have one machine (the Vagrant VM) and we want to perform all of our installation and configuration against that machine.

But when we set up a more complex environment, such as TEST or PROD, we'll want to provision multiple machines, doing different things based on what we'll use each machine for. For example, we don't want to install PostgreSQL on all the machines, only on the DB servers.

Luckily, Ansible has support for this. It allows you to build a so-called inventory of machines, grouping them into web servers, DB servers, and so on. Let's create an inventory file for the TEST environment with four host groups: webserver, postgres, redis, and activemq. My file looks like the following (I'm using machines in Amazon EC2) and I've saved it as provisioning/hosts-TEST.txt.

```
[webserver]
ec2-54-77-241-248.eu-west-1.compute.amazonaws.com

[postgres]
ec2-54-77-232-91.eu-west-1.compute.amazonaws.com

[redis]
ec2-54-154-1-68.eu-west-1.compute.amazonaws.com

[activemq]
ec2-54-77-235-158.eu-west-1.compute.amazonaws.com
```

Note that you can have multiple hosts per group, and any host can be a member of multiple groups. It's also possible to generate these host groups dynamically, such as by querying a cloud provider's API to get a list of hosts, rather than maintaining a static file.

Once we've defined our host groups, we can refer to them in our Playbook file. We'll update it to distribute the roles appropriately across the host groups, so it now looks like the following listing.

Listing 8.1   A playbook with roles distributed across multiple host groups

```
---
- hosts: postgres
  sudo: yes
  roles:
    - postgresql

- hosts: activemq
  sudo: yes
  vars:
    - app_user: activemq
  roles:
    - user
    - java
    - activemq

- hosts: redis
  sudo: yes
  roles:
    - redis

- hosts: webserver
  sudo: yes
  vars:
    - app_user: uad
  roles:
    - user
    - java
    - ant
    - resin
```

```
- redis
- activemq
- postgresql
- uad
```

Note how you can reuse the `user` and `java` roles for both the `webserver` and `activemq` hosts.

Unfortunately this has broken our Vagrant setup, because Vagrant doesn't know which host groups the VM should be part of. Let's create an inventory file for Vagrant, calling it hosts-DEV.txt.

```
default ansible_ssh_host=127.0.0.1 ansible_ssh_port=2222

[webserver]
default

[postgres]
default

[redis]
default

[activemq]
default
```

This tells Ansible to provision everything on the Vagrant VM.

We'll also update the Vagrantfile to tell Vagrant to use this inventory file when running Ansible:

```
config.vm.provision "ansible" do |ansible|
  ansible.playbook = "provisioning/playbook.yml"
  ansible.inventory_path = "provisioning/hosts-DEV.txt"
end
```

Finally, we'll need to refactor our Ansible roles slightly to handle the fact that the UAD application's web server and the Postgres database server are now on different machines.

We'll move the tasks for creating a database and a DB user to the `postgresql` role, adding variables along the way, and we'll update the tasks for initializing the DB schema so that they connect to the DB on the PostgreSQL server rather than `localhost`. We'll also need to make changes to the PostgreSQL server's configuration to allow the UAD application to access the database from a remote machine.

The details get a little bit fiddly so I won't go into them here. As usual, take a look at the GitHub repo to see the complete code for this chapter (https://github.com /cb372/ReengLegacySoft).

Now we're finally ready to provision our TEST environment using Ansible! Use the following command to run the Ansible playbook using the hosts-TEST.txt inventory file we prepared earlier.

```
ansible-playbook -i provisioning/hosts-TEST.txt provisioning/playbook.yml
```

You should see Ansible log in to the various servers and start running tasks, just like it did when we were using Vagrant. In just a few minutes, your TEST environment will be fully provisioned.

> **THE ANSIBLE-PLAYBOOK COMMAND**   This is the command you use to run playbooks. You haven't seen it until now because Vagrant took care of running it for us. You might need to pass some extra options to the command, such as to tell it what user to log in as and what private key to use.

ADD AN INVENTORY FILE FOR EACH ENVIRONMENT

As well as DEV and TEST, we also want to manage other environments such as PROD. We need a way to tell Ansible about our PROD hosts.

This is really easy to do. We simply create a new inventory file called hosts-PROD.txt and write our PROD hosts in there. Now we have three inventory files (hosts-DEV.txt, hosts-TEST.txt, and hosts-PROD.txt) and we pass the appropriate file to the `ansible-playbook` command depending on which environment we want to provision.

As an alternative strategy, you can keep all your hosts in one big inventory file, create host groups such as `test` and `prod`, and specify the host group when running the `ansible-playbook` command. But if you forget to specify the host group, you can accidentally run some untested provisioning scripts against all your environments at once, which could be disastrous. I prefer to keep my environments isolated in separate inventory files.

8.2.2   *Build a library of Ansible roles and playbooks*

One of the major benefits of using a provisioning tool such as Ansible, rather than provisioning manually or rolling your own solution using shell scripts, is how easy it is to reuse roles.

You saw earlier that we were able to reuse the `user` and `java` roles to create a user and install Java on both the web server and the ActiveMQ broker for the UAD application. But it would be great if we could take this farther, building up a library of generic and customizable roles and then using them to provision many different applications. This is entirely possible and quite easy to achieve, thanks to Ansible's powerful support for variables and templating.

Given that the UAD application uses PostgreSQL for its database, PostgreSQL is likely to be used by a number of Fzzle's other applications. In all cases, the basic installation steps for PostgreSQL will be pretty much the same, but the appropriate configuration will vary depending on the application. Some applications might be write-heavy while others are read-heavy, and some will produce more DB traffic than others. We could use Ansible's templating functionality to allow us to customize the PostgreSQL configuration using variables.

It's also possible to provide default values for variables. If we provide sensible default values in the `postgresql` role, it becomes very easy to set up a new PostgreSQL server: simply add a single line to your Ansible playbook to include the role. Or, if you want to tweak the PostgreSQL configuration for your particular application's work-load, you can override variables as you see fit.

So far we've been storing our Ansible scripts in a folder called `provisioning` inside the UAD application's Git repository. But if we want to start sharing these roles with other applications, the first step is to pull them out of the UAD's repository and move them to somewhere where they can be more easily shared. I would recommend having one Git repository, called `ansible-scripts` or something similar, that contains all the Ansible code for the entire organization. This makes it super easy to share roles between applications.

The folder structure inside the repository should look something like this.

```
ansible-scripts/
  common_roles/
    java/
      tasks/
        main.yml
    postgresql/
      tasks/
        main.yml
      templates/
        postgresql.conf.template
    ...                          ◄──────── Other common roles
  uad/
    roles/
      uad/
        tasks/
          main.yml
    playbook.yml
    hosts-DEV.txt
    hosts-TEST.txt
    hosts-PROD.txt
  website/
  adserver/
  data_warehouse/
  corporate_site/
  ...                            ◄──────── Other applications
```

There's a top-level folder called common_roles that contains all the roles you want to share between applications. Then there's a folder for each application that you want to provision using Ansible. Each application folder will contain a playbook.yml file that references one or more of the common roles, along with the host inventory files for each environment. You might also have application-specific roles to perform any tasks that aren't worth sharing.

After migrating to this folder structure, the UAD application's playbook.yml would look something like this:

```
---
- hosts: postgres
  sudo: yes
  vars:
    db_user: uad
```

```
    db_password: abc
    database: uad
  roles:
    - ../common_roles/postgresql
```

...   ◄────── **Other hosts**

Notice how the playbook references the common `postgresql` role. In this case we accept the role's default values for the PostgreSQL configuration, but if we wanted to override them we could do so like this:

```
- hosts: postgres
  sudo: yes
  vars:
    db_user: uad
    db_password: abc
    database: uad
  roles:
  - { role: ../common_roles/postgresql, max_connections: 10 }
```

After moving all our Ansible scripts to a common repository, one question arises: how can we use them when we want to provision a Vagrant VM? Until now the playbook and roles were inside the application's Git repository so it was easy to tell Vagrant where to find them.

This is something I haven't really found a perfect solution for, but there are a couple of options.

- Use the Git `submodules` feature to include the `ansible-scripts` repository inside each application's repository. Unfortunately this means that you need to manually update the Git submodule occasionally to get the latest Ansible scripts, and you end up with the provisioning script for a lot of unrelated applications cluttering up your repository.
- Have a convention that developers clone the `ansible-scripts` repository to a sibling directory of their working directory, and point to that in the Vagrantfile.

8.2.3 *Put Jenkins in charge*

Ansible (or more specifically the `ansible-playbook` command) needs a host machine on which to run. From that machine it will log in to the target machines via SSH and run all the appropriate commands. So where should that host machine be, and who should be running the `ansible-playbook` command?

One simple option is to let developers and ops team members run Ansible from their local machines. Because the Ansible scripts are managed in Git, everybody will have the same scripts, so it doesn't matter who happens to run the command. But this is far from ideal for a couple of reasons.

- *There is no record of the fact that Ansible was run.*   Unless the person who ran the command then emails everybody to announce that they provisioned those machines, nobody will be any the wiser. All the useful logs output by Ansible are also stuck on that person's machine, so nobody else can inspect them.

- *People might forget to run Ansible after they make changes to the provisioning scripts.* The changes get committed to Git but never get applied to the machines. Or they might apply their change to TEST but not to PROD, meaning that you'll lose that valuable cross-environment parity you're striving for.

A much better idea is to put Jenkins (or whatever CI server you use) in charge of running Ansible. You could make a build that runs the provisioning scripts against all environments periodically, or perhaps every time there's a push to the `ansible-scripts` repository. That way, you can be sure that all machines have had the latest Ansible scripts applied, and the Ansible logs are available to anybody who wants to view them.

You should also restrict `sudo` access on the target machines so that nobody apart from Jenkins (and perhaps a few ops team members) is able to run Ansible, as this would defeat the point.

Putting it all together, a provisioning workflow based on Ansible, Jenkins, and Vagrant looks like figure 8.2.

The Ansible scripts are stored in a Git repository, which is cloned both by Jenkins and by developers. Jenkins uses Ansible to provision both TEST and PROD environments, whereas developers use Ansible and Vagrant to provision a DEV environment inside a Vagrant VM running on their local machine.

> **ANSIBLE TOWER** If you start to rely heavily on Ansible for provisioning, one product worth looking at is Ansible Tower (www.ansible.com/tower). It's a graphical dashboard for Ansible that gives much better visibility than you can achieve with Jenkins. It also provides access control, so development teams are only allowed to manage and provision the servers for their own applications. Similar tools are also available for Chef and Puppet.

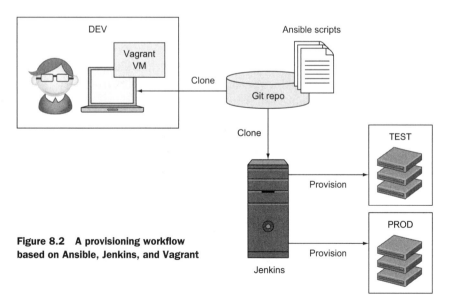

Figure 8.2   A provisioning workflow based on Ansible, Jenkins, and Vagrant

8.2.4   *Frequently asked questions*

Here are a few questions that often arise when developers and ops people start moving from a manual provisioning style towards automation using a tool such as Ansible.

WHAT'S WRONG WITH A BUNCH OF SHELL SCRIPTS?

Provisioning tools like Ansible, Chef, and Puppet can look quite intimidating at first. You need to choose a tool, learn how to use it, build up a library of scripts, and set up a provisioning infrastructure. It can be tempting to think that all this is overkill and that you could achieve the same thing by hacking together a few simple shell scripts. After all, Ansible is just SSHing into machines, copying files around, appending lines to config files, and so on.

For simple provisioning tasks, that's a perfectly reasonable conclusion. But once you reach a certain level of complexity, I find that homegrown solutions based on shell scripts become more trouble than they're worth.

First, you often end up reinventing a lot of wheels. Ansible and similar tools provide a huge number of built-in modules for performing common tasks such as copying files, creating user accounts, changing file permissions, installing packages, and so on. With a homegrown solution you have to reimplement all these things yourself. What's more, the provided Ansible modules go to great lengths to be idempotent, which can be quite tricky to get right if you implement it yourself. You also miss out on all of Ansible's great templating support. I've seen people try to implement their own templating using only bash, and it's not pretty.

Second, shell scripts are comparatively difficult to reuse. Ansible's concept of roles makes it easy to write reusable, customizable code, but shell scripts give no such support. Unless your scripts are very well written, any attempt at reuse on a large scale will descend into chaos.

HOW DO YOU TEST THIS STUFF?

OK, you got me. I don't test my Ansible scripts. I know of some people who make serious attempts to test their infrastructure automation; *Test-Driven Infrastructure with Chef* by Stephen Nelson-Smith (O'Reilly, 2011) is a great introduction to the concept. But I've never found it to be worthwhile, myself, as the benefits from testing don't justify the investment in time required to write and run the tests. (The tests involve running the playbook, and possibly even spinning up and tearing down a new VM, so they can take a very long time to run.)

I tend to rely on thorough code review of roles and playbooks rather than automated testing. And, of course, running them in the TEST environment is a great way to check that they work before unleashing them on PROD.

HOW DO YOU CLEAN UP PREVIOUSLY PROVISIONED STUFF?

If your legacy software has been running on the same servers for a number of years, you've probably noticed that these servers can become polluted over time with old versions of Java, Ruby, and so on. This software is no longer needed, but nobody bothers to delete it, so it remains on the machine, cluttering up the hard disk.

Even if you automate your provisioning, the same problem can occur. Let's say you have a task that installs the OpenJDK 7 JRE package onto a Debian machine. It probably looks something like this:

```
- name: Install Java
  apt: name=openjdk-7-jre state=present
```

One day you decide to upgrade your machines to Java 8, so you update the task, replacing the package name with `openjdk-8-jre`. You run Ansible and it installs Java 8, but Java 7 is left on the machines as well.

In my opinion, this isn't really an issue. As long as the stuff I need (as defined in my Ansible scripts) is on the machine, I don't care what else happens to be there. Hard disk is cheap!

But if this kind of laissez-faire approach bothers you, you can always ask Ansible to clean up anything that is no longer needed. For example, you could have one task to install Java 8 and another to remove Java 7:

```
- name: Install Java 8
  apt: name=openjdk-8-jre state=present

  - name: Remove Java 7
  apt: name=openjdk-7-jre state=absent
```

If you're provisioning virtual machines, there's also the option to go down the immutable infrastructure route, whereby you only ever provision a given machine once. You treat machines as if they are immutable, so once a machine has been provisioned you never alter it. If you need to make a change to the provisioning, you throw away the machine and spin up a new one. We'll discuss this in the next section when we talk about migrating your infrastructure to the cloud.

WHAT ABOUT WINDOWS?

Chef, Puppet, Ansible, and SaltStack all support managing Windows machines, but the official documentation for most of these provisioning solutions recommends using a UNIX server as the control machine. As mentioned in the previous chapter, it's possible to get Vagrant and Ansible working on Windows.

8.3   *To the cloud!*

Now that you've got automated provisioning set up for all your environments, you're in a great position to investigate whether you want to start migrating those environments to the cloud. It's not suitable for everybody, but at least now you have the option to try it out.

Cloud infrastructure provides many benefits for legacy software, which we'll go into later, but one unfortunate feature is that machines are inherently unreliable and outside your control. One of the machines running your application could disappear at any moment! (Of course, this rarely happens, but it's an eventuality you need to be aware of and be prepared for.) But with automated provisioning, this need not be a problem at all. If you lose a machine, you simply spin up another one, provision it, redeploy your application, and away you go.

8.3.1 *Immutable infrastructure*

The easy availability and disposability of machines in the cloud goes hand in hand with the concept of immutable infrastructure. This is the idea that you never provision a machine more than once. If you want to make a change to the machine's configuration, you throw the machine away and start a new one.

In a traditional data center environment, a machine would run for months or even years, with new versions of an application being deployed onto it every so often. But with immutable infrastructure you take a completely different approach. When you want to deploy your application, you spin up a brand new machine, provision it, and deploy your application onto it. Then the next time you want to deploy, you repeat the process: create a new machine and simply throw the old one away. For legacy software, deploys are unlikely to happen very often, but for a modern application this process could take place a few times a day.

Of course, if you were provisioning machines by hand, this would be completely impracticable. But with automated provisioning at your disposal, it becomes possible to get a new machine ready for action within minutes. (The other piece of the puzzle is automated deployment of your application, which we'll discuss in the next chapter.)

One benefit of thinking about infrastructure this way is that it treats deployment as a kind of controlled failure. In other words, your deployment process is exactly the same as the action you would take if a machine suddenly failed. And, of course, both these situations can be fully automated.

When you move from a process of redeploying an application onto an already running machine to an immutable infrastructure-style deployment process that involves spinning up and provisioning a new machine, you might notice that your deploys start taking significantly longer. This is a bit of a step backward, as deployment time is a key metric that you should seek to minimize. As soon as you've pushed a change to your software, whether it's a critical bug fix or an exciting new feature, you want it to be built, deployed, and available to your users as quickly as possible.

To help minimize this increase in deployment time, it's worth investigating tools like Packer (https://packer.io/) that can help you prebake a machine image. The idea is that you perform your automated provisioning (using Ansible or whatever) in advance, saving the result as a machine image. Then at deployment time you use this image to spin up a new machine, meaning you can skip the provisioning step. You could make deployments even faster by using a container architecture like Docker, which starts up much faster than a VM.

8.3.2 DevOps

Moving your legacy apps out of your data center and into the cloud means that the physical servers they were using will no longer be needed. If these machines have been recently replaced or upgraded, you could repurpose them for other apps. If they're as old as the legacy software that was running on them, you can simply throw them away and reduce the maintenance burden on your operations team.

In fact, if you move enough of your software to the cloud, you may not need an operations team at all. Moving to the cloud is a good chance to experiment with DevOps, a process whereby the team that develops a piece of software is also in charge of keeping it running smoothly in production. At the Guardian, we run virtually all of our software in AWS, with development teams performing the operations tasks needed to keep their apps running smoothly. This means that the communications overhead between development and operations teams, which is traditionally a serious bottleneck, no longer exists. After completing a gradual migration to the cloud, we disbanded our operations team completely.

If the idea of moving to a public cloud is a bit too radical, or if you've recently invested a lot of money in new hardware, you might consider converting part of your data center into a private cloud, using technology such as OpenStack. That way you get some of the benefits of DevOps, because developers can deploy and provision new machines without involvement from the ops team, and you can improve the utilization of your existing hardware.

8.4 Summary

- Disparity between TEST and PROD environments, or between individual machines within an environment, is a dangerous source of bugs.
- Automation of provisioning brings control and traceability to changes in your infrastructure, much like a version control system does for your source code.
- Although in the DEV environment we wanted to squeeze everything into one VM, we want the TEST environment to match PROD as closely as possible.
- Use the same Ansible scripts for all environments, using variables and inventory files to encode the per-environment configuration.
- Build a central library of reusable Ansible roles.
- A CI server like Jenkins is a good place to execute provisioning commands.
- Once your infrastructure is automated, you're in a good position to move into the cloud if you wish.
- Moving to the cloud goes hand in hand with immutable infrastructure and DevOps.

Modernizing the development, building, and deployment of legacy software

This chapter covers

- Migrating a legacy development and build toolchain
- Continuous integration of legacy software using Jenkins
- Automating production deployments

In the previous two chapters, we looked at provisioning—installing and configuring everything that the legacy software depends on. Now we'll switch our focus back to the software itself and see how investing some effort in updating our toolchain and workflows can make legacy software easier to maintain.

9.1 Difficulties in developing, building, and deploying legacy software

The amount of new development work on, and the frequency of releases of, a given piece of software tend to decrease over time. As the software gets older and moves into the realm of legacy, less work is done on it. This can be because it's already feature-complete and only occasional bug fixes are needed, or maybe because the codebase has rotted over the years and thus has become difficult to work on.

As a consequence of software being less actively developed and released, it becomes more difficult and error-prone to update the code and make a release on the rare occasions when you need to do so. The steps required to set up a development environment, test the software, run it locally, package it up into a library or executable, and deploy it to a production environment can become lost in the mists of time. This can lead to absurd situations like not being able to deploy the software because Bob, the only developer who knows how to do it, is away on holiday. Even worse, when Bob eventually leaves the company, his knowledge is lost completely. The next time somebody needs to deploy that software, they'll have to work everything out from scratch.

9.1.1 Lack of automation

The situation is exacerbated because developing and deploying legacy software often involves a lot of manual steps, which may not be well documented.

Sometimes developers will automate repetitive tasks but not share their solutions with others. I used to work with a lot of Java web apps that ran on Apache Tomcat. In order to run the apps locally during development, developers would build a WAR file using Ant and then run that WAR file on an instance of Tomcat installed on their development machines. But the vital step of deploying the generated WAR file to Tomcat was not automated, so I wondered how the developers in my team were doing it.

It turned out that every developer was doing it slightly differently, with differing degrees of automation. Some were using special plugins to integrate Tomcat into their IDEs, allowing automatic deployment whenever they recompiled. Others had written shell scripts or aliases to copy the generated WAR file to Tomcat's webapps directory or to make an HTTP request to Tomcat's deployment API, while a few people were actually copying the files manually, sometimes dozens of times a day!

As a consequence of this task not being automated properly, any new developer who wanted to work on the software would have to find their own way to automate it. How to deploy a WAR file to Tomcat was common knowledge for Java developers at the time, and if they didn't know, they could just ask somebody on the team, but suppose that new developer comes along a few years later, after the organization has moved away from Tomcat as a core technology. They would have to spend time and effort rediscovering how to automate a simple but important step in the development workflow.

Of course, a lot of problems related to knowledge-sharing can be solved with documentation. A few notes in the README file to describe any manual steps can be immensely useful. But the problem with documentation is that it isn't guaranteed to be up to date. In fact, a more subtle problem exists: developers tend to take documentation with a pinch of salt, because they don't trust it to be properly maintained. Even if you scrupulously maintain the instructions in your README file, anybody who reads it will assume the worst. If you put a script called deploy-to-local-tomcat.sh in your Git repository, with a pointer to it in the README, most developers are more likely to trust it. (And people can read through the script to see what it's doing, so it also does the job of documentation.)

Automation also helps to prevent errors caused by tired, distracted humans incorrectly following instructions. For example, I've seen an app whose deployment procedure included a step that involved commenting out one line in a config file, and uncommenting another, depending on whether you wanted to deploy to TEST or PROD. Luckily nobody has messed up this step so far, but it's only a matter of time before it happens.

A recent example

At work I recently inherited a legacy Python app that runs on Google App Engine (GAE). When I took over development, the section in the README on how to deploy to PROD simply said, "Use the standard Google App Engine instructions to upload the app." This turned out to involve six manual steps, including editing config files and running various commands using the GAE command-line tool. Discovering these steps took a lot of time and effort, and my first production deployment was pretty nerve-wracking.

Since inheriting the app, I've deployed it to PROD a total of six times. I've documented the manual steps involved, but I must admit I haven't yet got around to automating the process. I am, however, rapidly approaching the tipping point where the tedium of deploying manually and the fear of making a mistake in one of the steps will outweigh the effort involved in writing a script to automate the deployment process.

9.1.2 *Outdated tools*

When we developers work on software, we spend a lot of our time interacting with build tools. The build-tool landscape is constantly evolving, but at any given point there's a set of tools that enjoys mainstream popularity. The tool of choice is usually dependent on the implementation language: for Ruby it's Rake, for C# it's MSBuild, for Java it's currently a toss-up between Gradle and Maven, and so on.

A good developer becomes a master of the tools they use every day, exploiting their most powerful features to achieve amazing things. For this reason, it's a good idea to standardize your organization's build-tool choices across as many codebases as possible, including the legacy ones, so that developers can really get to know their tools and transfer those skills across all their projects. If 90% of your Java projects use Gradle, for example, and developers are used to it and are productive with it, then the context-switching costs when they start working on a legacy codebase that uses Ant can be very high. Consistently using the same build tool across all your software can also simplify things such as Jenkins configuration, and it allows for code reuse via build-tool plugins.

Of course, there's nothing inherently wrong with older tools like Ant. They're all capable of doing their intended jobs and building software, and they were probably good choices when they were introduced. The main reason for replacing them is to improve consistency between all of your organization's codebases, in order to make it easy for developers to move from one codebase to another.

To sum up, our goals in this chapter are twofold:

- *Update our legacy software's build tools to bring them in line with newer software.* This will lower the barrier to entry for developers who want to contribute, as the procedures for building the software will be similar to what they're used to. In other words, we want to break the stigma of legacy apps as "second-class citizens" that nobody wants to go near, and make it just as easy to contribute to legacy software as to a more modern codebase.
- *Increase automation at every step of the workflow, from local development to release and production deployment.* This means that anybody will be able to perform these tasks, even if they have no previous experience with the software, and it will reduce the risk of human error.

9.2 *Updating the toolchain*

Let's take a look at replacing an older build tool with a more modern one. As an example, we'll use the UAD app that you've come to know and love over the previous two chapters.

The UAD is a Java web app that currently uses Ant as its build tool. A simple Ant script (build.xml) for the UAD app might look something like the following listing.

Listing 9.1 A simple Ant build file for a Java web app

```
<project name="uad" default="compile">

  <target name="clean">
    <delete dir="dest" />
    <delete file="uad.war" />
  </target>

  <target name="compile">
    <mkdir dir="dest" />
    <javac
      debug="true"
      srcdir="src"
      destdir="dest"
      includeantruntime="false"
      includes="**/*.java">
      <classpath>
        <fileset dir="lib" includes="**/*.jar" />
```

```
      </classpath>
    </javac>
  </target>

  <target name="package" depends="clean,compile">
    <war destfile="uad.war" webxml="web.xml">
      <classes dir="dest"/>
      <lib dir="lib" excludes="servlet-api*"/>
    </war>
  </target>

</project>
```

The Ant file has targets for cleaning the project (removing any non-source files), compiling Java source files (which are stored in the src folder) into class files, and packaging those class files into a WAR file ready for deployment to an application server.

Let's assume that the organization is using Gradle as the build tool for all of its modern Java apps, so we want to replace Ant with Gradle. As a first step, we should update the directory structure to match modern conventions for Java web apps, so that Gradle can find our files where it expects them. (Alternatively we could leave the old directory structure and configure Gradle accordingly, but updating the project to use the standard structure is a little kinder to new developers.)

- Java source files should be in the src/main/java folder.
- The web.xml file should be in src/main/webapp/WEB-INF.

Once we've performed this slight rearrangement, writing a Gradle build file (build.gradle) for the UAD web app is easy. An example is shown in the next listing.

Listing 9.2 A Gradle build file for the UAD web app

```
apply plugin: 'java'
apply plugin: 'war'

repositories {
  mavenCentral()
}

dependencies {
  providedCompile "javax.servlet:servlet-api:2.5"
}
```

There, that was easy! Because we're now using a more modern build tool, we get a lot of stuff for free simply by following the appropriate directory structure conventions. We no longer need to tell Gradle how to clean, compile, and package our app like we did with Ant. We just type

```
$ gradle build
```

and it builds a WAR file for us.

In fact, there are plenty more benefits that come with upgrading to a more modern build tool. Remember how I was talking about the difficulty of deploying the WAR file to a local Tomcat instance earlier in the chapter? Well, we now have an easy solution to that. Just by adding one more line to the top of the build file, we can enable the Gradle Jetty plugin:

```
apply plugin: 'jetty'
```

This means we can start an embedded Jetty web server with our web app deployed to it, simply by typing

```
$ gradle jettyRun
```

If you really must use Tomcat even on development machines, there's also a Tomcat plugin for Gradle (https://github.com/bmuschko/gradle-tomcat-plugin), but it requires a few more lines of configuration.

> **ANT JETTY PLUGIN** In the interest of fairness, I should point out that there's also a Jetty plugin available for Ant (www.eclipse.org/jetty/documentation/current/ant-and-jetty.html). But the Gradle plugin is much easier to set up.

I've oversimplified things slightly (for example, the UAD app has a lib folder full of JARs that would have to be converted to dependencies in the Gradle file), but I think you get the idea. The effort required to replace the build tool for a project is usually quite small in comparison to the benefit of making the project more approachable to developers, so it's often worth doing.

Of course, I've used a trivially short Ant script in this example for brevity's sake. A real project will have a longer and more complex build script, so the process of moving to a modern build tool will be non-trivial. But I still think it's worth putting in the time and effort to do so. In fact, the longer and more complex the legacy script, the more value there is in converting it to something that's easier to maintain.

Developer buy-in

Replacing the build tool for a piece of software is potentially quite a disruptive operation. The developers interact with the build tool every day, so they'll need to adapt to the new tool.

Make sure that everybody who is affected by the change is on board before you start, and check that everything is working well for them after you finish. If developers aren't happy with the new build tool, they may continue to use the old one. This is a situation you want to avoid, as it means there are two build scripts to maintain and keep in sync.

You'll need to convince developers that the new tool provides enough value to make the switch worthwhile, and you might want to provide some training for people who have never used it before.

9.3   *Continuous integration and automation with Jenkins*

If you operate a CI server such as Jenkins, it should have at least the following jobs configured on it for every single codebase that you maintain:

- A standard CI job that runs the tests and builds a package every time somebody pushes to version control
- Where applicable, a job that allows one-click deployment to the TEST environment

Some projects may have extra CI jobs set up, such as to perform slow tests overnight or to perform continuous inspection (as you saw in chapter 2), but the two jobs in the preceding list are the bare minimum that people should be able to rely on.

A lot of legacy software may predate the introduction of the CI server, so their CI jobs might be missing. Just like an outdated build tool, a lack of CI jobs acts as a black mark against the legacy software, reducing developers' trust in it and setting it apart as a codebase to avoid.

Setting up the CI job to build the software and run tests on every Git push should be relatively simple, especially if you have updated the software's tool chain to bring it in line with all your other projects, so I won't go into it here. Instead let's take a brief look at how we can use our CI server to deploy software to the TEST environment. I'll be using Jenkins, but the same techniques can be used with any CI server.

Suppose we have a legacy PHP app whose deployment we want to automate. We have a folder full of .php files on a server in the TEST environment, which are interpreted by Apache using mod_php5. To deploy a new version of the software we have a few options.

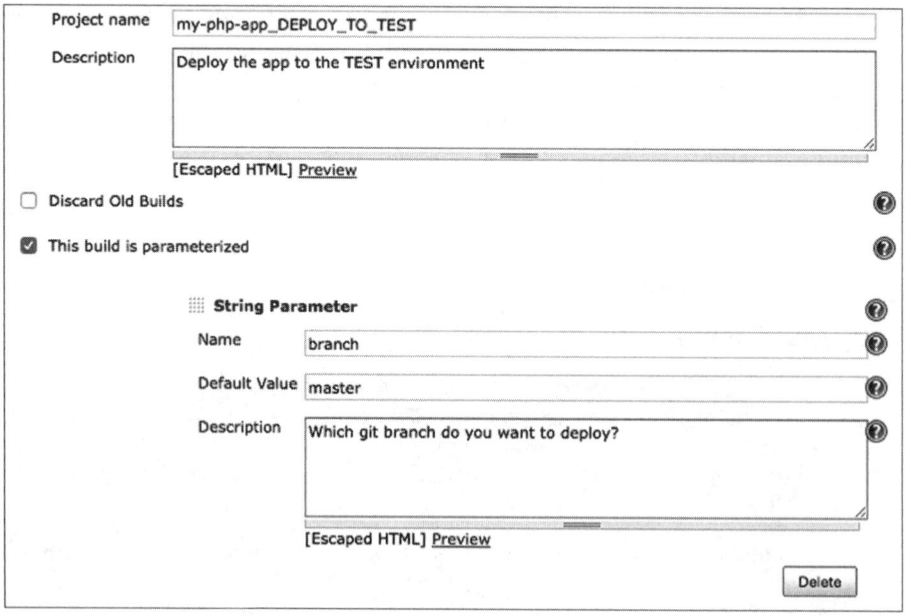

Figure 9.1   Some of the Jenkins config for the PHP app deployment job

We could get Jenkins to bundle the .php files into a tarball or zip file, copy it to the TEST server, and then log in via SSH and extract it into the appropriate folder. Or, if we have the application's Git repository cloned on the TEST server, Jenkins could SSH into the machine and simply `git checkout` the appropriate revision. It doesn't really matter which deployment strategy we use. Let's go with the `git checkout` one, just because it requires slightly less code.

I've created a new Jenkins job and started configuring it. As you can see in figure 9.1, I've added a build parameter so people can choose which Git branch they want to deploy.

Figure 9.2 shows the other interesting parts of the job configuration. I have a build step that runs a shell script to perform the deployment, which we'll implement in a second, and I'm also using the Email Extension plugin to send an email to all developers so that everybody is kept informed about deployments. (Of course, if email is a bit too 20th century for your tastes, you could send a notification to Slack, HipChat, or whatever.)

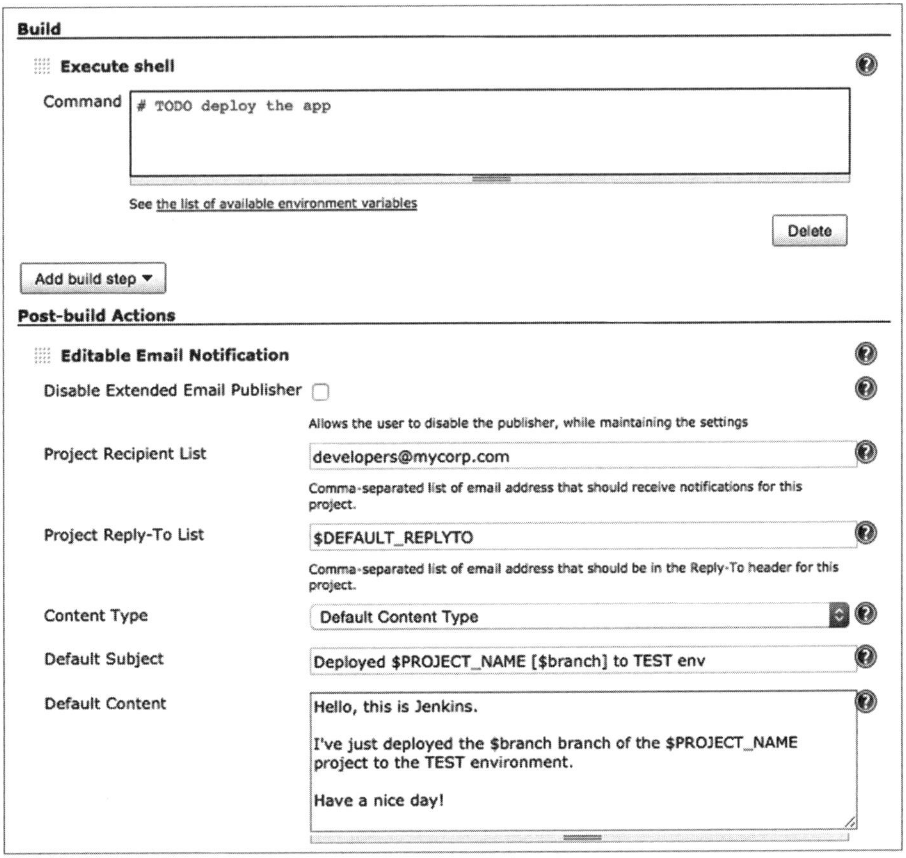

Figure 9.2   More Jenkins config for the PHP app deployment job

All that remains is to implement the meat of the Jenkins job: the shell script that deploys the application. Assuming that the application's code has already been cloned on the TEST server, and that Jenkins has SSH access, we could write something like this:

```
host=server-123.test.mycorp.com
cmd="cd /apps/my-php-app && git fetch && git checkout origin/$branch"

ssh jenkins@$host "$cmd"
```

As you can see, there's no rocket science going on here, but this is an important piece of automation. Now that we have this Jenkins job in place, everybody will know how to deploy our legacy application to TEST, not only now but in a few years' time, after we've moved on to greener pastures and somebody else has to start maintaining the application.

This has also been a useful stepping stone to prepare us for the remainder of the chapter. In the next section we'll achieve the holy grail: one-click deployment of our legacy application to PROD using Jenkins.

9.4   *Automated release and deployment*

The scariest things to do after inheriting a piece of legacy software are the first release and the first deployment. People sometimes misuse or conflate these terms, so before we continue let's make sure our terminology is clear.

- *Release*—Making a release means building one or more artifacts and labeling them with a version number of some kind. Usually a tag is also created in the version control system to mark the snapshot of the codebase that was used to create the release. The first rule of release management is that releases are immutable: once you've released a given version of the software, you can't make changes and then re-release it. If you need to make any changes, you must release a new version. Releasing often includes a publication step, whereby the released artifacts are uploaded somewhere to make them available for people to download and use.

- *Deployment*—Deployment means installing a released artifact onto a machine and running it. Depending on the type of software, this could involve anything from installing a Windows desktop application to extracting a tarball on a web server, and it might be performed by either you or your users.

DEPLOYMENT DOESN'T NECESSARILY IMPLY RELEASE   You need to build an artifact before you can do a deployment, but that doesn't necessarily mean you need to make a release. At the Guardian, where I work, we practice continuous deployment for many of our web applications. As soon as a branch is merged into the master, our CI server builds an artifact. Then our deployment server, RiffRaff (https://github.com/guardian/deploy), automatically deploys that artifact to production. There is no formal "release" step in this process, and we don't use any version numbers.

So why are release and deployment of inherited software scary? Simply because you've never done it before, so you have no way of knowing whether you're doing it right. If you get the procedure wrong, you might release and publish a completely broken artifact to the world at large, or deploy an artifact incorrectly and make the application unavailable to end users.

Luckily, both of these processes are inherently amenable to automation, which means that they can survive the transition from one generation of developers to another. For release, if you already have a job on your CI server to build artifacts and run tests, then it's trivial to extend that job to perform release tasks such as creating Git tags as well.

Automation of production deployment is a little more interesting. We looked at deploying a PHP app to TEST in the previous section, but when we deploy to PROD we need to be more careful. We have to take extra steps to make sure that deployments are completely invisible to end users of the site.

In production, the site is running on multiple Apache web servers, fronted by a load balancer, so we want to do a rolling deployment, gracefully restarting one server at a time.

The deployment strategy looks like this for each server:

1 Detach the server from the load balancer, so it doesn't receive any requests while we're updating it.
2 Stop Apache.
3 Do a Git checkout like we did in TEST, but this time we'll check out a tag rather than a branch.
4 Start Apache.
5 Call a healthcheck endpoint to make sure everything is working normally.
6 Reattach the server to the load balancer and move on to the next server.

Healthcheck endpoint

We're assuming that the application has a healthcheck endpoint. Any web application that you run in production should have one of these. It should be a trivial endpoint that simply returns OK. Using this endpoint, a monitoring tool can tell that the physical machine is alive, the correct ports are open, the web server is running normally, and so on.

You may also want to provide a "good to go" endpoint that checks whether the application is able to usefully service user requests (ensuring it can access its DB, its cache servers, other services' APIs, and any other external dependencies).

We could do all of this using shell script in Jenkins, but it would become quite unwieldy. Instead I'm going to use a handy Python tool designed specifically for deploying software, called Fabric (www.fabfile.org/). Fabric makes it easy to run commands on multiple remote hosts using SSH, which is exactly what we want to do.

Fabric is configured using a *fabfile*, which is just a normal Python script that calls functions in Fabric's API. A code sample is worth a thousand words, so let's get started. The following listing shows a skeleton for our fabfile. We'll fill out the tasks one by one.

Listing 9.3   **The beginnings of a fabfile for deploying our PHP app**

```
from fabric.api import *
env.hosts = [
    'ubuntu@ec2-54-247-42-167.eu-west-1.compute.amazonaws.com',
    'ubuntu@ec2-54-195-178-142.eu-west-1.compute.amazonaws.com',
    'ubuntu@ec2-54-246-60-34.eu-west-1.compute.amazonaws.com'
]

def detach_from_lb():
    puts("TODO detach from load balancer")

def attach_to_lb():
    puts("TODO attach to Load Balancer")

def stop_apache():
    puts("TODO stop Apache")

def start_apache():
    puts("TODO start Apache")

def git_checkout(tag):
    puts("TODO checkout tag")

def healthcheck():
    puts("TODO call the healthcheck endpoint")

def deploy_to_prod(tag):
    detach_from_lb()
    stop_apache()
    git_checkout(tag)
    start_apache()
    healthcheck()
    attach_to_lb()
```

The hosts we want to deploy to. You can pass these as command line args if you prefer.

Makes a separate Python function for every step of the deployment process. We'll implement them soon.

The entry point to the script. It will run each of the deployment steps in turn by calling the corresponding Python functions.

As you can see in the listing, we've defined a Python function for each task that we want to perform. We've also defined a `deploy_to_prod` task that will act as our entry point. The function takes a Git tag name as an argument, which we can pass in from the command line.

If you run Fabric, you can see that it runs all of our tasks against each remote host in turn.

```
$ fab deploy_to_prod:tag=v5
[ubuntu@ec2-54-247-42-167...] Executing task 'deploy_to_prod'
[ubuntu@ec2-54-247-42-167...] TODO detach from load balancer
[ubuntu@ec2-54-247-42-167...] TODO stop Apache
[ubuntu@ec2-54-247-42-167...] TODO checkout tag
[ubuntu@ec2-54-247-42-167...] TODO start Apache
[ubuntu@ec2-54-247-42-167...] TODO call the healthcheck endpoint
```

```
[ubuntu@ec2-54-247-42-167...] TODO attach to Load Balancer
[ubuntu@ec2-54-195-178-142...] Executing task 'deploy_to_prod'
[ubuntu@ec2-54-195-178-142...] TODO detach from load balancer
[ubuntu@ec2-54-195-178-142...] TODO stop Apache
[ubuntu@ec2-54-195-178-142...] TODO checkout tag
[ubuntu@ec2-54-195-178-142...] TODO start Apache
[ubuntu@ec2-54-195-178-142...] TODO call the healthcheck endpoint
[ubuntu@ec2-54-195-178-142...] TODO attach to Load Balancer
[ubuntu@ec2-54-246-60-34...] Executing task 'deploy_to_prod'
[ubuntu@ec2-54-246-60-34...] TODO detach from load balancer
[ubuntu@ec2-54-246-60-34...] TODO stop Apache
[ubuntu@ec2-54-246-60-34...] TODO checkout tag
[ubuntu@ec2-54-246-60-34...] TODO start Apache
[ubuntu@ec2-54-246-60-34...] TODO call the healthcheck endpoint
[ubuntu@ec2-54-246-60-34...] TODO attach to Load Balancer

Done.
```

Now we need to go through the fabfile, implementing the functions. Let's start with some very simple tasks and stop the Apache web server:

```
def stop_apache():
    sudo("service httpd stop")

def start_apache():
    sudo("service httpd start")
```

> **FABRIC OPERATIONS** The run and sudo functions execute commands on the remote machine, whereas the local function executes on the local host. Detailed descriptions of these and other operations can be found on the Fabric documentation site (http://docs.fabfile.org/en/latest/api/core/operations .html).

The commands to check out the specified Git tag are also pretty simple:

```
def git_checkout(tag):
    with cd('/var/www/htdocs/my-php-app'):
        run('git fetch --tags')
        run("git checkout %s" % tag)
```

Now we'll implement the code to call the PHP application's healthcheck endpoint and check the result. It calls the healthcheck repeatedly until it returns OK, giving up after 10 attempts. This code is a little more interesting than the previous tasks, as it shows how you can write logic that depends on the output of a remote command:

```
def healthcheck():
    attempts = 10
    while "OK" not in run('curl localhost/my-php-app/healthcheck.php'):
        attempts -= 1
        if attempts == 0:
            abort("Healthcheck failed for 10 seconds")
        time.sleep(1)
```

Finally, we need to write the Fabric code to detach instances from the load balancer and re-attach them later. In my case I'm using Amazon EC2 instances and an Elastic Load Balancer (ELB), so I'll use the AWS command-line tool to attach and detach instances, as shown in listing 9.4. If you're using a load balancer inside your own data center, it will probably have an HTTP API that you can call from your script. Don't worry too much about the details of this listing, as it's quite AWS-specific. How you attach and detach instances will depend on your particular load balancer.

Listing 9.4   Fabric tasks to attach and detach instances from an Amazon ELB

```
elb_name = 'elb'
instance_ids = {
    'ec2-54-247-42-167.eu-west-1.compute.amazonaws.com': 'i-d1f52a7c',
    'ec2-54-195-178-142.eu-west-1.compute.amazonaws.com': 'i-d8ee3175',
    'ec2-54-246-60-34.eu-west-1.compute.amazonaws.com': 'i-dbee3176'
}
```

Removes the instance from the load balancer, then waits a few seconds for it to finish handling connections

```
def detach_from_lb():
    local("aws elb deregister-instances-from-load-balancer \
        --load-balancer-name %s \
        --instances %s" % (elb_name, instance_ids[env.host]))

    puts("Waiting for connection draining to complete")
    time.sleep(10)
```

Adds the instance to the load balancer, then waits until the load balancer reports 3 healthy instances

```
def attach_to_lb():
    local("aws elb register-instances-with-load-balancer \
        --load-balancer-name %s \
        --instances %s" % (elb_name, instance_ids[env.host]))

    while "3" not in local(
        "aws elb describe-load-balancers --load-balancer-names elb \
        | jq '.LoadBalancerDescriptions[0].Instances | length'",
        capture=True):
        puts("Waiting for 3 instances")
        time.sleep(1)
```

Uses jq to extract and count certain fields from the JSON output of the aws command

```
    while "OutOfService" in local(
        "aws elb describe-instance-health --load-balancer-name elb",
        capture=True):
        puts("Waiting for all instances to be healthy")
        time.sleep(1)
```

USING JQ   jq is an insanely useful tool for processing JSON on the command line. If you work with JSON a lot, I highly recommend installing it and learning how to use it.

And with that, our Fabric script is complete. Sample output from running the script against three servers in EC2 is shown in listing 9.5. (Note that some output has been abbreviated and line breaks have been added for formatting purposes.)

Listing 9.5 Sample output from running the Fabric script against 3 EC2 machines

```
[ubuntu@ec2-176-34-78-4...] Executing task 'deploy_to_prod'
[localhost] local: aws elb deregister-instances-from-load-balancer \
    --load-balancer-name elb --instances i-158ed9b8
{
    "Instances": [
        {
            "InstanceId": "i-168ed9bb"
        },
        {
            "InstanceId": "i-178ed9ba"
        }
    ]
}
[ubuntu@ec2-176-34-78-4...] Waiting for connection draining to complete
[ubuntu@ec2-176-34-78-4...] sudo: /opt/bitnami/ctlscript.sh stop apache
[ubuntu@ec2-176-34-78-4...] out: /.../scripts/ctl.sh : httpd stopped
[ubuntu@ec2-176-34-78-4...] out:

[ubuntu@ec2-176-34-78-4...] run: git fetch --tags
[ubuntu@ec2-176-34-78-4...] run: git checkout v5
[ubuntu@ec2-176-34-78-4...] out: ...
[ubuntu@ec2-176-34-78-4...] out: HEAD is now at 6a968c1... Version 5
[ubuntu@ec2-176-34-78-4...] out:

[ubuntu@ec2-176-34-78-4...] sudo: /opt/bitnami/ctlscript.sh start apache
[ubuntu@ec2-176-34-78-4...] out: /.../ctl.sh : httpd started at port 80
[ubuntu@ec2-176-34-78-4...] out:

[ubuntu@ec2-176-34-78-4...] run: \
    curl http://localhost/my-php-app/healthcheck.php
[ubuntu@ec2-176-34-78-4...] out: OK
[ubuntu@ec2-176-34-78-4...] out:

[localhost] local: aws elb register-instances-with-load-balancer
    --load-balancer-name elb --instances i-158ed9b8
{
    "Instances": [
        {
            "InstanceId": "i-168ed9bb"
        },
        {
            "InstanceId": "i-158ed9b8"
        },
        {
            "InstanceId": "i-178ed9ba"
        }
    ]
}
[localhost] local: aws elb describe-load-balancers \
    --load-balancer-names elb | \
    jq '.LoadBalancerDescriptions[0].Instances | length'
[localhost] local: aws elb describe-instance-health --load-balancer-name elb
[ubuntu@ec2-176-34-78-4...] Waiting for all instances to be healthy
[localhost] local: aws elb describe-instance-health --load-balancer-name elb
```

```
[ubuntu@ec2-54-195-18-54...] Executing task 'deploy_to_prod'
[localhost] local: aws elb deregister-instances-from-load-balancer \
    --load-balancer-name elb --instances i-178ed9ba
{
    "Instances": [
        {
            "InstanceId": "i-168ed9bb"
        },
        {
            "InstanceId": "i-158ed9b8"
        }
    ]
}
[ubuntu@ec2-54-195-18-54...] Waiting for connection draining to complete
[ubuntu@ec2-54-195-18-54...] sudo: /opt/bitnami/ctlscript.sh stop apache
[ubuntu@ec2-54-195-18-54...] out: /.../scripts/ctl.sh : httpd stopped
[ubuntu@ec2-54-195-18-54...] out:

[ubuntu@ec2-54-195-18-54...] run: git fetch --tags
[ubuntu@ec2-54-195-18-54...] run: git checkout v5
[ubuntu@ec2-54-195-18-54...] out: ...
[ubuntu@ec2-54-195-18-54...] out: HEAD is now at 6a968c1... Version 5
[ubuntu@ec2-54-195-18-54...] out:

[ubuntu@ec2-54-195-18-54...] sudo: /opt/bitnami/ctlscript.sh start apache
[ubuntu@ec2-54-195-18-54...] out: /.../ctl.sh : httpd started at port 80
[ubuntu@ec2-54-195-18-54...] out:

[ubuntu@ec2-54-195-18-54...] run: \
    curl http://localhost/my-php-app/healthcheck.php
[ubuntu@ec2-54-195-18-54...] out: OK
[ubuntu@ec2-54-195-18-54...] out:

[localhost] local: aws elb register-instances-with-load-balancer \
    --load-balancer-name elb --instances i-178ed9ba
{
    "Instances": [
        {
            "InstanceId": "i-168ed9bb"
        },
        {
            "InstanceId": "i-158ed9b8"
        },
        {
            "InstanceId": "i-178ed9ba"
        }
    ]
}
[localhost] local: aws elb describe-load-balancers \
    --load-balancer-names elb | \
    jq '.LoadBalancerDescriptions[0].Instances | length'
[localhost] local: aws elb describe-instance-health --load-balancer-name elb
[ubuntu@ec2-54-195-18-54...] Waiting for all instances to be healthy
[localhost] local: aws elb describe-instance-health --load-balancer-name elb
[ubuntu@ec2-54-195-12-215...] Executing task 'deploy_to_prod'
[localhost] local: aws elb deregister-instances-from-load-balancer \
    --load-balancer-name elb --instances i-168ed9bb
```

```
{
    "Instances": [
        {
            "InstanceId": "i-158ed9b8"
        },
        {
            "InstanceId": "i-178ed9ba"
        }
    ]
}
[ubuntu@ec2-54-195-12-215...] Waiting for connection draining to complete
[ubuntu@ec2-54-195-12-215...] sudo: /opt/bitnami/ctlscript.sh stop apache
[ubuntu@ec2-54-195-12-215...] out: /.../scripts/ctl.sh : httpd stopped
[ubuntu@ec2-54-195-12-215...] out:

[ubuntu@ec2-54-195-12-215...] run: git fetch --tags
[ubuntu@ec2-54-195-12-215...] run: git checkout v5
[ubuntu@ec2-54-195-12-215...] out: ...
[ubuntu@ec2-54-195-12-215...] out: HEAD is now at 6a968c1... Version 5
[ubuntu@ec2-54-195-12-215...] out:

[ubuntu@ec2-54-195-12-215...] sudo: /opt/bitnami/ctlscript.sh start apache
[ubuntu@ec2-54-195-12-215...] out: /.../ctl.sh : httpd started at port 80
[ubuntu@ec2-54-195-12-215...] out:

[ubuntu@ec2-54-195-12-215...] run: \
    curl http://localhost/my-php-app/healthcheck.php
[ubuntu@ec2-54-195-12-215...] out: OK
[ubuntu@ec2-54-195-12-215...] out:

[localhost] local: aws elb register-instances-with-load-balancer \
    --load-balancer-name elb --instances i-168ed9bb
{
    "Instances": [
        {
            "InstanceId": "i-168ed9bb"
        },
        {
            "InstanceId": "i-158ed9b8"
        },
        {
            "InstanceId": "i-178ed9ba"
        }
    ]
}
[localhost] local: aws elb describe-load-balancers \
    --load-balancer-names elb | \
    jq '.LoadBalancerDescriptions[0].Instances | length'
[localhost] local: aws elb describe-instance-health --load-balancer-name elb
[ubuntu@ec2-54-195-12-215...] Waiting for all instances to be healthy
[localhost] local: aws elb describe-instance-health --load-balancer-name elb
[ubuntu@ec2-54-195-12-215...] Waiting for all instances to be healthy
[localhost] local: aws elb describe-instance-health --load-balancer-name elb

Done.
Disconnecting from ec2-176-34-78-4...... done.
Disconnecting from ec2-54-195-18-54...... done.
Disconnecting from ec2-54-195-12-215...... done.
```

All that remains is to wrap it in a Jenkins job that runs Fabric, passing it the appropriate Git tag name. This can be done using a parameterized build that does the following:

- Takes a single parameter called `tag` (in the same way that we passed the branch name in figure 9.1).
- Checks out the repository containing the Fabric script.
- Runs Fabric, passing it the tag that was specified in the parameter, such as `fab deploy_to_prod:tag=$tag`.

With this in place, we've reached nirvana! Any developer or ops team member can now deploy our legacy app to production with one click. What's more, we've future-proofed the deployment process using automation. No matter who joins or leaves the team in the future, the app will remain deployable. Of course, the deployment process for your real-world applications may be more complex than this example, involving database migrations and so on, but the principle remains the same. In general, it's possible to automate virtually any deployment process.

On the other hand, it's worth remembering that infrastructure code (like this Fabric script) is code, and is therefore potential legacy code. If nobody deploys the PHP app for a year, it's quite probable that the Fabric script will stop working for one reason or another. The best way to prevent this kind of bit-rot is to exercise the code regularly. You could set up a scheduled job on Jenkins to deploy the PHP app once a week, even if there have been no changes to the application code.

The complete Fabric script is available in the GitHub repo: https://github.com /cb372/ReengLegacySoft/blob/master/09/php-app-fabfile/fabfile.py.

9.5   *Summary*

- A few small changes such as replacing an outdated build tool can remove barriers to entry and motivate new developers to contribute to a legacy codebase.
- A manual deployment process is knowledge that can easily be lost over time. Automating the process reduces the risk of an application becoming undeployable in the future.
- A CI server such as Jenkins can be used to deploy applications.
- Tools such as Fabric can be used to automate complex deployment tasks. The corresponding scripts also act as documentation, showing the various steps in the process.

Stop writing legacy code!

This chapter covers

- Applying the techniques you've learned to new code as well as legacy code
- Writing disposable code

By now you should have a good idea of how to start tackling any neglected legacy code that you inherit and nurse it back to health. We've looked at rewriting, refactoring, continuous inspection, toolchain updates, automation, and a whole lot more. But you probably spend at least some of your time writing new code as well. You may be wondering whether all code is doomed to become legacy, or if there's anything you can do to prevent the code you're writing right now from becoming somebody else's nightmare in a few years' time.

We've covered an enormous range of material over the last nine chapters, but a few key themes kept appearing throughout the book, either explicitly mentioned or implicitly assumed. We've been discussing these ideas in the context of legacy code until now, but a lot of them are equally applicable to greenfield projects. These themes, which I'll recap in this final chapter, are as follows:

- The source code is not the whole story.
- Information doesn't want to be free.

- Our work is never done.
- Automate everything.
- Small is beautiful.

Let's look at them each in turn.

10.1 *The source code is not the whole story*

From a programmer's point of view, the source code is often the most important part of a software project, so you may have been surprised and even disappointed to find that less than half of this book deals directly with the code.

The reasons for this are twofold. First, much of the work you do on legacy code will be refactoring, but there are already plenty of good books about refactoring available, and I don't have much to say that hasn't already been said. I also believe that refactoring is an art that can't be learned from a book—you need to try it yourself, build up experience, and get a feel for it. A great way to become better at refactoring is to pair with an experienced developer and learn from them.

Second, and more importantly, I wanted to use this book to stress the idea that the source code is not the whole story. There are many factors that contribute to a successful software project, and high-quality source code is only one of them.

The most important thing, far more important than anything we can say about the code, is to build software that provides value to its users. If you're building the wrong thing, nobody will care what the code looks like. How to make sure your software provides value is outside the scope of this book, so let's assume for now that we have a great product manager to take care of that for us.

Apart from that, there are plenty of other factors that affect the success of a software project. (I haven't defined the notion of success, but it generally includes things like development speed, the quality of the resulting product, and how easy it is to maintain the code over time.) We've looked at a lot of these factors, some technical and others organizational.

Technical factors include selecting and maintaining a good development toolchain, automating provisioning, using tools such as Jenkins to perform CI and continuous inspection, and streamlining the release and deployment process as much as possible. *Organizational factors* include having good documentation, maximizing communication within and between development teams, making it easy for people outside of the team to contribute to the software, and fostering a culture of software quality throughout the organization so that developers are free to spend time on maintaining quality without facing pressure from other parts of the business.

This is all relevant to new projects as well as legacy ones. In fact, if you can get this stuff built into the project early on, it'll be much easier than trying to retrofit it onto a legacy codebase.

10.2 *Information doesn't want to be free*

The sarcastic title of this section is, of course, a play on Stewart Brand's famous declaration that "information wants to be free." More accurately, I should say that information (about a piece of software) may want to be free, but developers won't put much effort into helping it on its way.

Ask any developer if it's a good idea to share knowledge with their colleagues about the software that they work on, and of course they'll agree that it is. But when it comes down to the nitty-gritty of sharing information, most developers are pretty bad at doing so. They don't enjoy writing and maintaining documentation, and they rarely share information with colleagues through other means unless they're prompted to do so.

Unless we actively promote communication between developers and foster an environment in which information flows freely, we'll end up with certain developers becoming silos of knowledge. When these developers move away from the team, a huge amount of valuable information can be lost.

So what can we do to prevent this from happening?

10.2.1 *Documentation*

Technical documents can be an excellent way to pass information from developers both to contemporaneous colleagues and to future generations of maintainers. But documentation is only valuable if it is

- Informative (that is, it doesn't merely state what the code is doing; it tells you how and why it's doing it)
- Easy to write
- Easy to find
- Easy to read
- Trustworthy

As mentioned earlier, making documentation concise and putting it as close as possible to the source code (specifically, inside the same Git repository, if not embedded in the source code file itself) helps with all of these. Putting it inside the Git repository makes it easy to write and update, because developers can commit it alongside any changes they make to the code. This is much easier than, say, finding and updating a Word document on a network share. It also makes it easy for other developers to review the documents, just like they review changes to source code, which helps to keep them trustworthy.

For the reader, the documents are easy to find if they're in the same place as the source code, and they're easy to read if they are concise.

You should periodically review your documentation and delete any document that's not up to date. If it hasn't been well maintained by developers, that means it's probably not a useful document. It's better to delete the dead weight than to try and salvage it, as it will only fall into neglect again in the future. I call this the Darwinian approach to documentation—survival of the fittest!

10.2.2 *Foster communication*

The other piece of the puzzle, namely encouraging developers to share information through means other than documentation, is more challenging. There are plenty of things you can try, but every team is unique. You'll need to keep experimenting until you find tools that are a good fit for you and your team. Here are just a few ideas.

- *Code reviews*—This is a no-brainer in this day and age: all changes to the code should be reviewed by at least one other developer. Not only can you check for any mistakes in the code and discuss stylistic issues, but you can also learn more about what other developers are working on. It's worth taking the time to find a code review system that works well for your team, which might involve huddling around somebody's IDE or using an online service such as GitHub.

- *Pair programming*—This can be quite controversial amongst developers. Some people love it and some really don't.[1] I suggest giving it a try for a few weeks (long enough to let developers get over the initial weirdness of it) and then leaving people to decide whether and how they want to continue with it. The ideal to strive for is a situation whereby developers start pairing without being asked to.

- *Tech talks*—A couple of companies that I've worked for have had tech talks on Friday afternoons. They're often the highlight of my week. They give the presenter a chance to show off their skills or something they've built, and everybody else gets to learn about what other people are up to. Putting tech talks on a Friday afternoon, of course, means they often lead to developers going for a beer together afterward, which can't be a bad thing.

- *Present your projects to other teams*—Setting up a semi-regular session where each development team presents a technical overview of one of their products (legacy or otherwise) can be really valuable. It's surprising to discover how little developers know about what other teams are working on. Once they find out, they often spot ways to share knowledge or reduce duplication of effort between teams.

- *Hack days*—This is a chance for developers to work with people from different teams, play with new technologies, and build cool stuff, preferably outside of the office environment. I wrote a blog post about a hack day I attended, "Hack day report: Using Amazon Machine Learning to predict trolling" (https://www.theguardian.com/info/developer-blog/2015/jul/17/hack-day-report-using-amazon-machine-learning-to-predict-trolling), which will give you a hint of what to expect.

---

[1] For an example of loving it, see "Why Pair Programming Is The Best Development Practice?" from the SAPM Course Blog (https://blog.inf.ed.ac.uk/sapm/2014/02/17/why-pair-programming/). For a less enthusiastic opinion, see "Where Pair Programming Fails for Me" by Will Sargent (https://tersesystems.com/2010/12/29/where-pair-programming-fails-for-me/).

10.3 *Our work is never done*

Maintaining the quality of a codebase is a never-ending mission. You need to be constantly vigilant and tackle quality issues as they arise. Otherwise they'll quickly pile up and get out of control, and before you know it you'll have an unmaintainable mess of spaghetti code. Just like the old adage "a stitch in time saves nine," the sooner you fix a piece of technical debt, the easier it will be.

It's difficult to do this work alone, so you also need to encourage a culture in which the team takes collective responsibility for the quality of the code.

10.3.1 *Periodic code reviews*

Every change to the code should be reviewed as part of the standard day-to-day development procedure. But if you only review at the level of individual changes, it's easy to miss overarching problems with the software's design, large-scale improvements that could be made to the structure of the codebase, or issues in parts of the code that nobody touches very often.

For this reason I find it useful to schedule regular reviews of the codebase as a whole. A few simple rules can make the process run smoothly.

- Ask everybody to take an hour or so to look through the code beforehand and take notes. This means people can spend the review discussing things, rather than just staring at the code in silence.
- Ask one person who is knowledgeable about the code to lead the review. They'll spend a few minutes introducing the codebase and then go around the room asking people for their comments.
- The review should take about one hour. If that's not enough to cover the whole codebase, have multiple sessions over a number of weeks.
- Write up a list of the review's conclusions, divided into concrete actions and non-specific ideas or things to investigate. Share the document with the team and ask them to update it when they complete any of the actions. Check on progress a few weeks later.

There's an example of a writeup from a review I performed recently on GitHub (http://mng.bz/gX84).

10.3.2 *Fix one window*

In *The Pragmatic Programmer* (Addison-Wesley Professional, 1999), Hunt and Thomas use the famous one broken window theory of criminology as a metaphor for software entropy. The idea is that if an empty inner city building is in good condition, people are likely to leave it alone. But as soon as it falls into disrepair, with a broken window here and there, people's attitudes toward the building change. Vandals start to smash more windows and the disorder rapidly escalates.

The analogy with software is, of course, that you need to keep on top of your codebase and keep it neat and tidy. Leave too many hacks and pain points unfixed, and the quality of the code will rapidly deteriorate. Developers will lose their respect for the code and start to get sloppy.

But this idea can work both ways. Just like seeing a broken window can provoke people to break more windows, watching somebody repair a broken window can inspire them to lend a hand. For a developer, seeing somebody put in the effort to clean up a piece of technical debt on a codebase can remind them that it's everybody's responsibility to maintain quality and prevent the code from falling into disarray.

Try making it a personal objective to fix one "broken window" in your codebase every couple of weeks, and make sure that these efforts are visible to other developers. Code review is a good tool for spreading the word.

10.4 *Automate everything*

Throughout the book, I've touched on automation of various kinds, including using automated tests, automating builds, deployments, and other tasks with Jenkins, and using tools like Ansible and Vagrant to automate provisioning. These are merely examples, and your situation may call for a different set of tools and techniques, but the key point is that you should always be on the lookout for parts of your development workflow that can be automated further. You don't need to automate everything at once, but every time you manage to automate something that previously depended on a human typing the right sequence of commands, or clicking a button, or holding some specialist knowledge inside their head, it's a step in the right direction.

Automating manual tasks is useful for two reasons:

- *It makes life easier for you*—Not only does it mean you don't have to waste time performing the same tasks over and over again, it also means you have to write and maintain less documentation, and you don't get people coming over to your desk and asking you to explain how to do stuff. And of course it reduces the risk of your making a mistake and having to clean up after yourself.
- *It makes life easier for your successor*—Automation makes it easier to pass a piece of software from one generation of developers to the next without losing any information.

10.4.1 *Write automated tests*

It goes without saying that any modern software should have some automated tests, but it's worth pointing out that tests are particularly useful in the context of preventing legacification (let's pretend that's a real word) of new code.

First, a suite of high-level tests (functional/integration/acceptance tests rather than unit tests) can act as a living specification document for the software. Specification documents are often written at the start of a project and are rarely kept up to date as the software evolves, but automated tests are more likely to be in sync with how the software behaves. The reason is, of course, that if you change the behavior of the code without updating the tests to match, the tests will start to fail and your CI server will complain.

This means that when a new developer inherits the software years later, they can look through the test suite and quickly grasp how the software behaves. They can also see what parts of the behavior are specified (meaning there's a test to assert that the software behaves in this way) and what parts are not.

Second, code with automated tests is easier to maintain and therefore less likely to rot. A test suite gives developers the confidence to refactor code to keep it in shape and keep entropy at bay.

> **Unit tests**
>
> In terms of sharing information about the behavior of existing code, I find functional tests and those higher up the testing hierarchy to be more useful than unit tests. Unit tests are too detailed and don't help much in understanding the codebase as a whole.
>
> Unit tests are useful when writing new code, as they let you exercise that code against a number of different input patterns with a very fast feedback cycle.
>
> Once your new unit of code is written and working, the unit tests have served their main purpose. After that point, if you find that they're hindering development, I say it's okay to delete them, as long as you have higher-level tests to protect against regressions. If, for example, you can't refactor a piece of code without having to fix or rewrite dozens of tests, that may be a sign that your unit tests are becoming more trouble than they're worth.

10.5   *Small is beautiful*

The larger a codebase gets, the more difficult it becomes to work with. There's a larger volume of code for developers to comprehend, there are more moving parts, and it's more difficult to understand how a change to one part can affect others. This makes it more difficult to refactor the code, meaning its quality will decrease over time.

A large codebase is also difficult to rewrite. There's a large psychological barrier that prevents us from throwing away a large amount of code in one go, no matter how horrible that code might be. And, as we discussed in chapter 6, rewriting a large application is a very risky undertaking. For a start, it's very difficult to estimate how long it will take.

The key to keeping your codebase lithe and nimble and preventing it from becoming somebody's Big Rewrite a few years down the line is simple: keep it small. Software should be designed to be disposable: make it so small that it can be thrown away and rewritten in a matter of weeks, if not days or even hours. This means that if your successor doesn't happen to like the code they inherit, they can simply discard it and write a new one from scratch, with very little risk. Of course, it's a little depressing for a developer to think that their lovingly crafted code will be dead and gone in a few years' time, but it's more sensible than keeping geriatric code on life support indefinitely just because it's too big and important to die.

To clarify, I'm not suggesting that you should only produce tiny pieces of software with a minimal set of features, or that you should argue against adding a useful feature because you fear it will bloat the code. The key point is that modularization—building a large piece of software out of many small, decoupled components—should be your top priority when designing software. Because the code is disposable at the component level, the software as a whole will enjoy robustness and therefore longevity.

The idea of writing disposable code goes hand in hand with the recent fashion for microservices, but it doesn't necessarily mean you need to split your code into separate tiny services. You could achieve the same goal by building a monolithic application out of dozens of tiny, isolated, and replaceable components.

Chad Fowler has lots of interesting things to say on the topic of building disposable software. In particular, I recommend his keynote from Scala Days 2014 (www.parleys .com/tutorial/legacy). In it he makes a nice analogy with automobiles: the reason that a Ford Model T can still run today, many decades after it was built, is that it is made up of hundreds of small components. Each component has a different lifetime, will fail independently from the others, and can be replaced individually. If you build your software in a similar way, you can replace each component when it reaches the end of its useful life, but the system as a whole can live on indefinitely. Given enough time you might end up replacing all the components at least once, at which point you might start to wonder about Theseus' paradox, but I'll leave that for you to ponder.

THESEUS' PARADOX   The paradox of the ship of Theseus was first documented by the ancient Greek historian Plutarch. He reports on how the ship in which Theseus sailed home from Crete after defeating the Minotaur was preserved for posterity. It was maintained for several centuries, with craftsmen replacing planks of wood as they rotted. Plutarch questioned what would happen if every plank in the ship were replaced. Would it still be the same ship? Does the ship have an identity that transcends the individual parts from which it is made?

10.5.1 *Example: the Guardian Content API*

The back end that powers the Guardian website and mobile apps is known as the Content API. It's a good example of a system built out of disposable components, in this case microservices. A high-level view of the architecture is shown in figure 10.1.

The system has two services in charge of receiving new content. One polls a database for changes, while the other consumes data from the content management system (CMS) and various other systems via queues. Both services send this content, via a queue, to another service whose sole job is to read it from the queue and write it to the datastore. Finally, another service sits in front of the datastore, handling requests from clients.

Although the system as a whole is complex (it actually includes a number of other services and applications not pictured in this simplified diagram), each component is small, simple, and, most importantly, disposable.

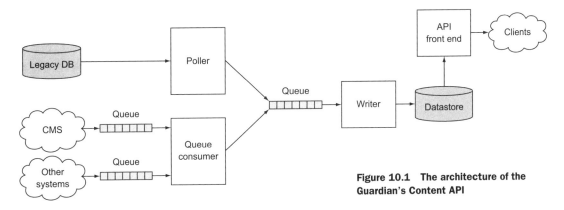

Figure 10.1   The architecture of the Guardian's Content API

We recently wrote a new Content API component in Clojure, simply because one of the developers wanted to try the language. It's a small piece of code that polls a couple of APIs, transforms the responses, and writes them to a queue. It's been running fine for a few months, with no need for maintenance. But recently we received a feature request that involves adding more code to the component, and we've decided this will be easier if we rewrite the whole component in Scala (a language that the team is more familiar with). We estimate that it will only take a day or two to rewrite, so there's very little risk in doing so.

This ability to throw away a part of your software and start again without any risk is the true value of disposable software.

10.6   *Summary*

- If you want to keep your project healthy, don't focus only on the source code. Documentation, toolchain, infrastructure, automation, and the culture of the team are all important.
- Information about your software will gradually leak away into the ether, unless you constantly guard against it.
- Good technical documentation is worth its weight in gold. And a team that communicates so well it doesn't need documentation is even better. You need documentation to prevent knowledge being lost as team members leave, but if developers prefer asking each other questions rather than referring to the documentation, that's a sign of a healthy team.
- Build large software out of components small enough to be discarded and rewritten without risk.

And so we reach the end of our journey through the landscape of legacy software. This book was ambitious in scope, so I've only been able to touch briefly on an enormous range of topics, but I hope I've inspired you to love your code, legacy or otherwise. If you wrote it, take pride in it. If somebody else wrote it and passed it on to you, give it the respect it deserves and nurture it, for the sake of those who came before you and those who will follow you.

Throughout the book I've been treating "legacy" like it's a dirty word, but it doesn't have to be. We'll all leave a legacy to the next generation of developers, whether we want to or not, so let's do our best to make it a legacy to be proud of.

Good luck!

index